ONE DAY
I'LL WORK
FOR
MYSELF

The Land of Enterprise:
A Business History of the United States

Lobbying America:
The Politics of Business from Nixon to NAFTA

ONE DAY
I'LL WORK
FOR
MYSELF

The Dream and Delusion
That Conquered America

BENJAMIN C. WATERHOUSE

W. W. NORTON & COMPANY

Independent Publishers Since 1923

For information about permission to reproduce selections from this book, write to Permissions,
W. W. Norton & Company, Inc., 500 Fifth Avenue, New York, NY 10110

For information about special discounts for bulk purchases, please contact
W. W. Norton Special Sales at specialsales@wwnorton.com or 800-233-4830

Manufacturing by Lake Book Manufacturing
Book design by Chris Welch
Production manager: Louise Mattarelliano

ISBN 978-0-393-86821-0

W. W. Norton & Company, Inc.
500 Fifth Avenue, New York, N.Y. 10110
www.wwnorton.com

W. W. Norton & Company Ltd.
15 Carlisle Street, London W1D 3BS

1 2 3 4 5 6 7 8 9 0

Para Daniela,
minha empresária favorita, pela vida

In practice, nobody cares whether work is useful or useless, productive or parasitic; the sole thing demanded is that it shall be profitable. In all the modern talk about energy, efficiency, social service and the rest of it, what meaning is there except "Get money, get it legally, and get a lot of it"? Money has become the grand test of virtue.

George Orwell, *Down and Out in Paris and London* (1933)

If you ever get annoyed, look at me, I'm self-employed. I love to work at nothing all day.

Bachman-Turner Overdrive, "Takin' Care of Business" (1973)

Contents

Introduction:
On Our Own

Modern culture whispers in your ears. If you listen closely, you can hear it everywhere. In ads on the Internet. From parents and coaches. From professors, politicians, and preachers. *Be an entrepreneur. Start your own business. Work for yourself.*

What these whispers are telling you is that you're on your own. When it comes to getting ahead in the world today, you can't simply go work for someone else. Real success comes to people who break the mold, seize their own destiny, and do it themselves. If you want a shot at material success, they say, you must be your own boss.

Going it alone looks different, of course, depending on where you are on the economic spectrum. At the high end, it means getting into the start-up game. Launch a new enterprise, preferably with somebody else's money, and then sell it for a mint. Further down the ladder? You are *still* in charge of your own economic future. You cannot—and should not—count on a stable job with good pay and benefits. "I am a millionaire in the making," the megachurches tell you to say, but those riches can only come through entrepreneurship, through creating something new. Like Jay-Z says, you have to be a business, man.

The whispers might sound innocuous. But underneath the bland inspiration lies a dark and alarming set of justifications. Are you underpaid? Work more. Unemployed? Try gig work. Run a side hustle. Take on debt to "invest in yourself." Still struggling? That's on you.

This fixation on going it alone—the cult of the hustle, the gig economy—has become so pervasive that we can overlook just how thoroughly it has saturated our entire culture. If you step onto a college campus like UNC–Chapel Hill, where I teach, you'll see its influence in all the buzz around business start-ups. To be sure, many of the students who take college entrepreneurship courses want to learn how to get rich. But what is striking is the convictions of the socially conscious ones, the altruistic folks who want to do good for the world. They, too, have been swayed by those whispers. For them, fixing social problems doesn't involve political activism, legal reform, or movement building. Rather, the cure is always a new business venture.

Reality, of course, is far messier than mythology. *Sometimes* working for yourself turns out great, but many, many businesses fail. Some people discover a certain freedom in hustling from gig to gig, but many others get screwed, working for less than minimum wage, going into hock, or falling victim to get-rich-quick scams that prey on the appeal of "being your own boss."

Of course, we can't blame the kids. Today's college students have grown up in a culture that is as obsessed with entrepreneurship as it is disillusioned with traditional political action. They have been told from birth that individual initiative breeds innovation, even as social problems—from poverty and inequality to environmental disaster and war—appear insurmountable. Their natural takeaway is that focusing on political organizing and reform efforts is naïve, doomed to failure. What's more, all but the most elite and privileged confront a world of work where jobs are less stable, real wage growth is worse, and benefits more paltry than when their parents or grandparents entered adulthood. Little wonder that so many are lured by those whispering voices, the ones that tell them that individual initiative, start-ups, and for-profit businesses are the keys to changing the world and getting paid in the process.

———

This book is about those cultural whispers—where they came from, how they became so pervasive, and how they shaped not only personal decisions but also our politics and public life. It asks how our conception of work became so individualized and how so many people became convinced that the path to success lay in working for themselves.

There are more than 33 million businesses in the United States today. Only about 4,000 are publicly traded corporations (that is, owned by stockholders), and only another 16,000 are "large" by the government's definition (more than 500 employees). More than 99.9 percent of all companies, in other words, are "small." And the overwhelming majority—81 percent, or 27 million—have no employees. The only people who work for them are the owners. All told, the U.S. government estimates that about 1 in 9 people in the workforce can be described as "working for themselves" today. The puzzle of this book is how that vast and unorganized community of business owners came to embody a cultural ideal, and how that ideal came to dominate our national conversation about economic life.

At first glance, we might assume that this is nothing new at all. Our history books, after all, are chock full of paeons to self-made men (and, once in a while, self-made women). As far back as the 1780s, Thomas Jefferson famously praised independent yeoman farmers as bastions of democratic virtue, since they controlled their own livelihoods. "Rugged individualism" has been a central part of America's national mythology since before the advent of the term itself, which is linked in our collective memory to the mythos of Teddy Roosevelt at the turn of the twentieth century. For many people, and for centuries, "independence" has literally meant that you don't *depend* on anyone else—a government, a family, a master, or even an employer.

Yet despite those deep roots, America's individualistic culture has not always translated into a call to work for yourself. Although self-interest and individual responsibility are central to capitalism, nothing about the capitalist ethic is incompatible with working for someone else. To the contrary, throughout the history of capitalism, that was the whole point—laborers, managers, and executives alike all traded their time and energy for wages and salaries.

In the United States, the ideal of working for someone else reigned supreme as recently as the mid-twentieth century, buttressed by a very different economy from the one we know today. In the quarter century after World War II, economic growth was rapid and, relatively speaking, evenly shared. Average incomes went up across the board. The gap between rich and poor got smaller. Rising numbers of people ascended into the middle class, with its amenities like affordable homes and cars, as well as family vacations and college for the kids. And the central vehicle for that growth was reliable, well-paid work—typically at a large company—for the (generally male) family breadwinner. For the people who were included, this was the dream. For those who were kept out, including especially people of color, women, and the very poor, it became the thing to mobilize and fight for. Success and opportunity were *not* defined by going it alone in the postwar years but rather by steady employment. By working for somebody else.

So, what changed? Americans in the 1950s and 1960s were every bit the ideological descendants of Thomas Jefferson and Teddy Roosevelt that we are today. Why does this individualistic ethic now push us toward self-employment, business start-ups, gigging, and so on, when it didn't back then?

If it's tempting to think that our go-it-alone culture has always existed, it's perhaps equally tempting, however paradoxically, to conclude that it has emerged just in the past few years with the advent of new tech and recent economic hard times. In the first quarter of the twenty-first century, new communications technologies—from smartphone apps and social media to GPS and Zoom—have upended modern life. When you can manage your workforce, optimize your logistics, and microtarget your marketing all on your phone from the comfort of your living room, working for yourself seems easier today than ever before. Add in the long-term deterioration of the traditional job market since the Great Recession, compounded by the Covid-19 pandemic and its aftermath, and it would seem that the cocktail for the do-it-yourself economy is complete.

But while it's certainly true that new tech and economic fragility are vital parts of the story, they don't answer the question by themselves. Despite what we always hear—that such-and-such a device or app "changes everything" or that economics is destiny—neither technology nor economic circumstance operate in a vacuum. Neither can change society all by itself. To really understand how history happens, to figure out where those cultural whispers come from, we have to find the people who propagate them. The story of how the dream of working for yourself became so overpowering in the United States, in other words, is fundamentally a story about people—people with interests, agendas, ideas, and often businesses themselves. I am a historian of American business, economic culture, and politics, and I have spent decades writing about the places where those things intersect. Those kinds of people are exactly the ones I've been trained to study. So I set out to find them.

What I discovered was a disparate but influential cadre of individuals and organizations who, between the 1970s and the early 2000s, promoted a new vision of work. Some of them are well known: politicians, business theorists, and national lobbying associations. Others are more anonymous, from the creator of a women's home-based business network to consultants, how-to authors, and journalists. What united them, though, was their common project: to repurpose long-held tropes about self-sufficiency and success into a public case that individual business ownership was the cure for long-term economic decline. Their activism—which was nearly always aligned with their own business interests—created a new set of values about work, opportunity, and what it meant to get ahead. Ultimately, they redefined what millions of people meant by the words "American Dream."

So while the economic crises and technological changes of the last fifteen years have nurtured our culture of independent work, they didn't create it. Instead, today's cultural whispers trace back less to Jefferson in the eighteenth century and more to the social turmoil and economic upheavals that began in the early 1970s. Those were the years when a series of recessions and persistently high inflation battered the country, bringing an abrupt end to the postwar "growth economy." Since then, even in good times, economic growth rates have never matched what people had gotten used to in the previous several decades. And that disjuncture, that gap between old expectations and new realities, has had major social and political consequences.

In terms of jobs, the American economy since the 1970s has come to center more on services than on manufacturing. Rising global trade and foreign competition put new limits on America's once-dominant factories, which moved production from high-wage to low-wage regions, and eventually out of the country entirely. By the 1980s, plant closings, unemployment, and poverty—both in cities and in rural communities— dominated the headlines. That process only accelerated by the late 1990s and early 2000s. The "Steel Belt" became the "Rust Belt."

At the same time, the service sector—from banking and professional services at the high end of the pay scale to retail, hospitality, and caregiving at the low end—became the primary source of jobs. But since labor unions had traditionally been much stronger at big industrial corporations, that shift meant that labor was increasingly on its back heels, organizationally as well as politically. In a historic reverse, inequality in the United States, which has been shrinking since the 1930s, started rising again after 1980. In economic terms, the "returns to capital" (that is, investing) outpaced "returns to labor" (that is, working). Rich people, who had more to invest (and lower taxes than before) got richer. Corporate consolidation, new tax policies, and old-fashioned greed all combined to jack compensation at the high end, even as workers' wages stagnated and benefits dwindled at large and small companies alike. The nation suffered no financial crises between the 1930s and 1970s, but in the decades since, the economy lurched onto a roller-coaster ride of boom-and-bust cycles that were reminiscent of the nineteenth century. Weaker regulations led to speculative bubbles, prompting observers to declare that the United States had become a "casino economy." An elite few struck it rich through big bets, while most people went home empty-handed.

As the widely shared prosperity of the postwar period became a memory for so many people, American culture turned inward. Faced with political and foreign-policy scandals and disasters, as well as with economic malaise, people lost faith in the government, organized labor, and large corporations alike. In the same years, though, public faith in the *individual* was on the upswing. From politics to popular culture to personal finance, a long-subdued fixation on *self-reliance* bubbled to the surface. Individual retirement accounts replaced pensions for millions. Personal identity, for many people, became as linked to being a "consumer" and "owner" as to being a member of a class. Not that everyone started to do it—the self-employment rate ticked up only slightly, and the start-up rate for new businesses actually declined consistently from the late 1970s onward. But the *fascination* took over. The dream of working for yourself came to dominate our culture and politics like never before.

This book sets out to connect the dots between the changing economic landscape since the 1970s and the widespread belief that working for yourself is the key to economic success. In an era of massive global corporations, ever-expanding big-box stores, and high-flying finance, how did we decide that self-employment was the dream? How did we become convinced to go it alone?

The people you'll meet in this book are the keys to piecing that story together. From policy activists and b-school professors to small-town shopkeepers and tech start-up founders, they mobilized around a range of interconnected but distinct ways of "working for yourself." Some were boosters for "small business"—an amorphous concept that eludes easy definition and that really exists more as a cultural touch-stone than a clear economic category. Others focused more on a company's *newness* than its size, affirming the virtues of entrepreneurship and innovation. Still others trained their fire on individual choices, encouraging everyday people to abandon the corporate rat race. Work from home, they said, or open a new business or franchise. Become an independent contractor or multilevel marketing distributor. Join the app-based gig economy.

In the hands of this community, individual initiative and personal responsibility became powerful buzzwords that shaped public debate over a host of issues. Business-friendly regulatory reforms, weaker labor rights and worker protections, the decline of the inflation-adjusted minimum wage, tax policies that rewarded speculation rather than work, the drastic underfunding of infrastructure, social welfare, and education—all of these were justified by what they would bring to busi-ness owners, investors, and entrepreneurs. The ideal of business own-ership has both emerged from and fed upon a political culture that frames policy decisions as a sharp choice between "the government" and "the individual" (or, even more abstractly, "the market").

This book is not a knock on business ownership itself. To invoke a tacky cliché, some of my best friends are business owners. My wife, my father, my wife's father, his sons, my uncle on my dad's side—they all own or used to own their own businesses. I myself am a part-owner of my wife's company. I have no problem whatsoever with people who work for themselves in any capacity. What I do have a problem with is hype: the blind faith in fanciful promises, the unquestioned assumptions about the magic of entrepreneurship, the idea that business start-ups will somehow solve our economic problems *and* help someone get rich in the process. I take issue with a political culture that puts the burden of economic survival squarely on the individual, ignoring the root causes of economic injustice and rejecting policies like public interest regulation, worker protections, and a higher minimum wage because they are "bad for business owners." Finally, I disagree with the notion, so common among people who fetishize entrepreneurship and private initiative, that the big, public institutions that played such a key role during the growth years of the mid-twentieth century, from universities to government agencies like NASA, are relics that should be confined to the dustbin of history.

Putting all our faith in the promise of individual business ownership is both overly simplistic and a political smokescreen than blocks alternative visions to addressing social problems. A political culture that trips over itself to appease business owners risks forgetting about society's most vulnerable—people who are underpaid, who work without benefits, who cannot pay their bills or their loans or their caregiving expenses. I worry that, when the dominant cultural whispers tell those people to go it alone, they become convinced that they have no other options. That they should seek instant wealth online as social media influencers or freelance content creators. Or buy into the false promises of the gig economy. Or lose hope in any society-wide efforts to make things better. And I worry that the rest of us will decide that's OK.

I started down the road of deciphering the rise of this work-for-yourself ethos in the wake of the Great Recession. By the time I was writing this book, the Covid-19 pandemic had hit, throwing an already fragile national economy into acute turmoil. Both cataclysms laid bare the economic schisms that define modern life in the United States, casting a harsh light on a system where too many people have no safety net, no steady job, no benefits. Where some 30 million Americans earn income through online gig-economy platforms that do not offer benefits or the minimum wage, and a third of them consider that work their main job. As we make our way through the post-pandemic world, Americans face a reckoning over how, where, and why we work, over what we can and should ask of our employers, and over whether we should listen to those cultural whispers in our ears.

Our ability to answer those challenges depends on understanding why we think about work the way we do. Ultimately, our modern vision of employment—atomized, individualized, precarious—did not emerge automatically, driven by the inexorable logic of the market, or the self-evident power of entrepreneurship, or the magical technology of our fancy phones. Instead, it was the product of people, of their intellectual and cultural movements, and of their political decisions.

This book asks how that happened. I am less concerned with judging anyone's decision to work for themselves than I am in understanding why that ideal became so pervasive, so unquestioned, and so easily exploited by today's gig-economy companies. By tracing today's cult of the hustle to economic failure—bad jobs, stagnant wages, inequality—this book asks why and how Americans embraced business ownership as the last best defense against the ravages of capitalism. It does so through the stories of the shopkeepers, consultants, writers, and politicians who all became evangelists for entrepreneurship. My hope is that by understanding their history, we can figure out how our blinkered way of looking at work has hampered our ability to tackle the economic challenges of our lifetimes.

ONE DAY
I'LL WORK
FOR
MYSELF

1

THE WAY WE WORKED

You are an old man who thinks in terms of nations and peoples. There are no nations. There are no peoples. . . . There is only one holistic system of systems. One vast and immane, interwoven, interacting, multivariate, multinational dominion of dollars. . . . That is the natural order of things today.

There is no America. There is no democracy. There is only IBM and ITT and AT&T and DuPont, Dow, Union Carbide, and Exxon. Those are the nations of the world today.

The world is a college of corporations, inexorably determined by the immutable laws of business.

didn't write that. That comes from the famous speech that earned actor Ned Beatty an Oscar nomination, in the 1976 film *Network*. In the movie, Beatty portrays the chairman of a giant media conglomerate who is berating a TV news personality—the film's hero, Howard Beale—for daring to use his celebrity to interfere with an international business deal.

When I teach college students about the 1970s, I use *Network*—and the Ned Beatty speech in particular—to make a point about just how large the specter of corporate dominance loomed over the popular imagination in those years. Beatty's speech was designed to terrify the audience, to violate their sense of justice and tradition. They were supposed to sympathize with Beale, an otherwise bizarre and unlikable man, and see him as the oppressed voice of the individual. Their hackles were to go up as he cowers in horror while the evil, all-powerful CEO tells him that he has no country. That the world is ruled by a collection of unfathomably large and complex corporate goliaths. That the individual is nothing. As viewers, we root for Beale to rise up and fight back, and then we collapse in despair when he doesn't. Instead, he capitulates, agreeing to change his message to support the business deal. In the end, the corporation wins.[1]

The Ned Beatty scene in *Network* is so riveting, and such a good teaching tool, because it captures a vital aspect of American culture that was rooted in a very real economic phenomenon. Not only in the 1970s but throughout the post–World War II period, Americans confronted an ever-more vast, global, and unknowable economic order. At the center of that economy sat what the Beatty character called a "college of corporations" that presided over the "multivariate, multinational dominion of dollars." Those mammoth economic institutions—and the political institutions that supported them, from the Federal Reserve to the World Bank—shaped every aspect of modern life. What foods and medicines we put in our bodies. How we moved from place to place. The way we worked.

In a world in which more and more people depended on big companies for their livelihoods, the whole system seemed impersonal, cold, domineering, and frightening. At the peak of the post–World War II economic boom, most economists agreed with historian Thomas Cochran, who, in the early 1940s, had declared that the "age of individual enterprise, its fables, folklore and mythology, was finished."[2]

But that cultural critique contained a major irony. The economic order that put corporations at the center, that employed millions of people, and that seemed to dominate the world was also singularly responsible for the tremendous economic prosperity Americans enjoyed in the postwar years. As scary as that might have seemed in the abstract, it brought real, tangible benefits to a lot of people.

Historian Richard Hofstadter put it succinctly in 1964: "The public is hardly unaware that the steepest rise in mass standards of living has occurred during the period in which the economy has been dominated by the big corporation."[3]

Rising living standards, the widespread availability of consumer goods, new technological innovations—all these came about through the efficiencies and scale of large companies. The people who were privileged enough to work for them had better salaries, better benefits, better security, and better prospects than their parents or grandparents had had. And those who were *excluded* from that bounty—women, African Americans, the rural poor, the old—wanted nothing more than access to it. Their struggles for civil rights and inclusion were, to a great extent, rooted in a demand for the right to work at those types of companies.

The clash between those competing visions of large employers became a central feature of American life, particularly by the late 1960s and early 1970s. At its heart was a fundamental question: What did a good job actually look like? Was it corporate, impersonal, and steady? Was it independent and self-sufficient? On the one hand, many people bristled at the corporate workaday life. On the other, many aspired to it. The roots of this divide ran deep into the nation's history, but the postwar period brought it to the fore in a pronounced way. By the early 1970s, that division had come to define the culture of work itself.

———

"It is a comparatively simple matter to . . . amass a modest fortune, a $25,000 home, and a circle of friends with the same determination," journalist Curt Gerling wrote about Rochester, New York, in 1957. "Some believe the formula is as unburdensome as getting a job at Kodak and learning to pat the proper posteriors."[4]

That was a slight exaggeration, as Gerling conceded, "but not enough to detract from the basic premise." And he was right. The basic premise—the availability and desirability of well-paying, stable jobs at large corporate employers—was the cornerstone of the postwar economy. The point was not lost on those who were left out.

In the early 1940s, in the very early years of the Black Freedom Struggle, African American union leader A. Philip Randolph organized the "March on Washington Movement" against racial discrimination. Randolph's idea was to hold a massive mobilization in the nation's capital to pressure President Franklin Roosevelt to deny government war contracts to companies that refused to hire Black workers. Roosevelt, who very much wanted to avoid such a march, offered a compromise: an executive order calling on government agencies and defense contractors to end racial discrimination. Two decades later, as the movement for civil rights became more powerful and widespread, organizers continued the pursuit of racial justice in the workplace. Fulfilling Randolph's original vision, civil rights leaders in 1963 mobilized the famous March on Washington . . . for Jobs and Freedom. Including "jobs" in the name of the event sent a clear message: freedom for African Americans meant freedom to *work*.[5]

Full access to the world of work was also a central goal of the women's movement, which self-consciously built on the gains of the civil rights struggle. In 1964, feminist activists had successfully incorporated the word "sex" into the list of protections in Title VII of the Civil Rights Act, the part that explicitly barred discrimination in hiring. But steep sexist barriers remained. As the founding Statement of Purpose of the National Organization for Women (NOW) put it in 1966: "Working women are becoming increasingly—not less—concentrated on the bottom of the job ladder." Women workers in the mid-1960s earned 60 percent, on average, as much as their male counterparts, and they were routinely relegated to worse-paying jobs.[6] (The gender pay gap shrunk to 83 percent by the 2010s, although there are signs it is growing again; Latina and Black women currently make only 58 cents and 63 cents, respectively, for every dollar a white man makes.)[7] For NOW and other feminist organizations in the 1960s and 1970s, the real measure of equality would only come when women broke those glass ceilings and worked on par with men.

These activist movements focused on employment for precisely the reasons that Curt Gerling had glibly noted: jobs in the booming postwar economy, for those who were included, were safer, better paid, and more stable than they had ever been. And that was true up and down the income ladder, for white- and blue-collar workers alike. The modern economy seemed to have cracked the code on how to make good jobs.

That in itself was a major historical departure. For most of human history, all but the elite few had worked in drudgery. Most people labored constantly, accumulating very little wealth and embracing precious little leisure time. Industrial capitalism began to change that, albeit slowly. In the second half of the nineteenth century, large corporations began mass producing industrial goods at a pace never seen before. Within a few decades, they expanded into consumer goods—cars, refrigerators, radios—and launched a mass-consumption society. At the same time, working people mobilized and fought for safer conditions, shorter days, weekends, vacations, and higher wages. Their successes came slowly and were far from complete, but in the darkest depths of the Great Depression, the American labor movement won its greatest victories, guaranteeing a seat at the bargaining table and cementing its political power.

Starting in the late 1940s, on the heels of fifteen years of depression and war, the American economy entered a quarter century of remarkable growth. Average household incomes doubled, even accounting for inflation. The poverty rate fell from approximately 33 percent in the late 1940s to 11 percent in the early 1970s, and the distribution of income and wealth between the richest and the poorest got smaller. Across the board, America became more equal. Yes, society still creaked under the weight of nuclear anxieties, racial oppression, sexism, and war. But economically speaking, all signs pointed up. Recessions had been tamed by good fiscal management. Wages, profits, and productivity all rose.

In the early 1960s, John F. Kennedy popularized the aphorism that "a rising tide lifts all boats."[8]

At the center of this new order were the big corporations. The mid-twentieth century was the highwater mark of what business theorists refer to as "managerial capitalism"—an economic order centered on large, vertically integrated, and bureaucratically managed firms, especially in manufacturing and extractive sectors.* Behemoths like the ones Ned Beatty invoked—AT&T, Exxon, and DuPont—stretched from coast to coast, employing thousands of workers, dominating their industries, and sending their products around the world.[9]

For better or worse, parts of society that had once been the purview of the autonomous individual—like creativity and the pursuit of progress—were now taken over by big companies. As early as 1950, *Nation's Business* magazine (the print arm of the U.S. Chamber of Commerce, the country's biggest business lobbying group) summed up the prevailing view: "In the past century," it explained, "the private inventor was our public glory." But in the modern world, "most big-time inventions are produced by corporations and their staffs of trained engineers." The old image of the solitary inventor alone in a workshop had been replaced by corporate research and development offices, all bringing you the miracles of modern life. "Television is the work of several

---

* This type of corporate structure is often referred to as the "Berle and Means corporation," taking its name from a 1932 book, *The Modern Corporation and Private Property*, by future-New Deal lawyer Adolf Berle and economist Gardiner Means. In corporate bureaucracies, Berle and Means argued, day-to-day control was vested in the faceless class of professional managers, rather than the stockholders who owned the companies. That separation of ownership from control, they worried, potentially made corporations—whose economic power rivaled the political power of governments—difficult to regulate in the public interest. But it also had a stabilizing effect, encouraging corporations to look to the long term rather than try to maximize short-term gains for a quick cash-out.

corporations, all highly capitalized. Talking pictures were developed by research teams at Warner Brothers," the magazine concluded.[10]

Perhaps no mainstream economist captured public enthusiasm for the new world of big companies as famously as liberal Harvard professor John Kenneth Galbraith. "No one seriously argues," Galbraith wrote in 1964, "that the small firm is ordinarily more efficient, more progressive, more responsible, more enlightened, that it pays better wages, or that it sells at lower cost than the large corporation." Yes, corporations wielded massive economic power, Galbraith conceded, but that could be offset by large government regulatory agencies and strong labor unions. This theory of "countervailing power," which Galbraith began to popularize in the 1950s, promised a way for modern societies to have a robust, capitalist economy without surrendering democratic governance. A properly regulated and balanced capitalist system, in other words, could reap the benefits of economic bigness without losing its soul or handing over control of society to unaccountable corporations.[11]

For all that big companies did to boost consumer society in the postwar years, their most significant role by far was to recalibrate popular expectations around work. Hard-won victories by organized labor led to what historians have called a "new social contract" between big businesses and their employees. Under this new regime, large employers (their hands forced by union contracts) provided not only wages but also a range of social and personal benefits, from skills training to health insurance to family assistance.[12] Moreover, as many of the most arduous tasks of the industrial era became automated, workers came to expect that jobs would be easier and faster, leaving more time for leisure. The excitement was palpable: In 1950, the Twentieth Century Club, a liberal think tank, made the heady prediction that the standard workweek would decrease from 40 to 37.5 hours by 1960, a decline of more than 6 percent. It didn't, but the prediction typified the widespread faith in the promise of the new economy.[13]

Vitally, these rising expectations about work in the postwar period were tied to the ideal of *working for someone else*. Between the Great Depression and the 1970s, the percentage of Americans who worked for themselves fell consistently year over year, continuing a decades-long trend.[14]

This pattern makes good sense. As economists tell us, self-employment tends to correlate negatively to a country's wealth—that is, more people work for themselves in poor countries than in rich countries. If you travel through the developing world, you will see this phenomenon clearly: The poorer a community is, the more you will see hardworking people scraping together odd jobs and running independent operations, both licit and illicit, to make ends meet. In the United States, self-employment declined consistently starting with the advent of the industrial economy in the mid-nineteenth century. As wage employment became more common and more regularized, and as employers got larger, fewer people worked for themselves.[15]

We don't have very precise measures of how many Americans considered themselves self-employed before the Bureau of Labor Statistics started conducting surveys in the late 1940s. What is clear, though, is that the decline in self-employment proceeded steadily throughout the postwar boom economy. The numbers of shopkeepers, restaurant owners, and small factories declined as big corporations and national brands spread. In 1948, about 18.5 percent of American workers worked for themselves; by the late 1960s, the figure was below 10 percent. Much of that decline was due to the rapidly falling number of people who were self-employed in the agricultural fields. If you only count non-agricultural workers, the rate of self-employment fell from 12 percent in 1948 to bottom out at approximately 7.3 percent in the late 1960s. It ticked up in the 1970s and 1980s and has remained somewhat constant at around 10 percent ever since. Although all those figures need to be taken with a grain of salt because of discrepancies in how the government does the counting, the basic trend is clear: working for

Self-Employment in the Mid-20th Century

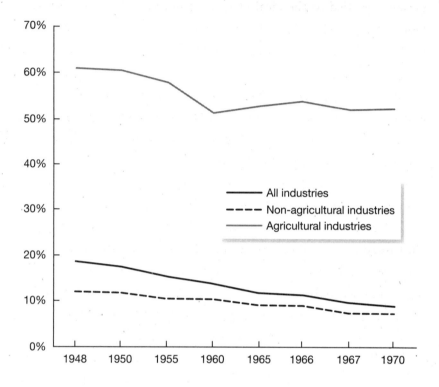

The percentage of Americans who worked for themselves fell markedly in the years after World War II. *Source: Steven Hipple, "Self-Employment in the United States: An Update,"* Monthly Labor Review, *July 2004, p. 14.*

yourself became a less and less popular choice during the peak of the postwar boom.[16]

The post–World War II American economy had a lot to recommend it, in the view of its defenders. Economies of scale meant greater productivity and a general prosperity that could unlock new frontiers of freedom and human potential. The "social contract" between big unions and big corporations led to rising wages and steady, protected jobs with good benefits. Little wonder the trend was *away* from self-employment and toward around unlimited work at established firms, and that such employment remained the aspiration for those Americans still excluded from it.

Yet discontent bubbled under the surface.

———

Even at the heights of the postwar economic boom, a rising chorus of voices charged that the modern economy's central ethic ran counter to cherished American ideals. Hierarchical and profit-driven corporations, the critique went, hoarded and abused their power and ran roughshod over democracy. On a more personal level, they subordinated the individual to the collective, reducing workers to mere cogs in a vast and impersonal machine.

Dissent came from many corners. Traditionalists waxed nostalgic for quaint notions of a wholesome Main Street full of mom-and-pop stores. Theirs was a moral as well as an economic argument, rooted in concern for what had happened to localism, individuality, and self-reliance.

At the same time, radicals mocked the bourgeois conformity of middle management and cookie-cutter suburbs while social justice activists attacked corporations' political power. Both damned their complicity in war and oppression.

Modern corporate capitalism, critics averred, created a stultified and conformist society, an insult to the scrappy spirit of independence so many Americans valued. After all, personal economic independence has been a bedrock American ideal since the early days of the Republic. In the 1780s, Thomas Jefferson argued in his *Notes on the State of Virginia* that material self-sufficiency was essential for true political liberty. "Dependence," he wrote, "begets subservience and venality, suffocates the germ of virtue, and prepares fit tools for the designs of ambition." Ideally, Jefferson claimed, everyone would till their own land, since people "who labour in the earth are the chosen people of God" and were "his peculiar deposit for substantial and genuine virtue." Jefferson envisioned a world of free, landholding farmers, beholden to no one.[17]

Jefferson himself, of course, depended on the forced labor of hundreds of enslaved people for his worldly wealth. But cosmic hypocrisies aside, the notion that self-sufficient work was the thing that made citizens free became entrenched in American thought. By the nineteenth century, as industrialization spread, the Jeffersonian ideal expanded beyond farming to encompass manufacturing and other types of business activities as well. What remained constant was a cultural fixation on personal independence.

Consider how Abraham Lincoln contrasted "independent" people from those who worked for somebody else in his first address to Congress in 1861: "Many independent men everywhere in these States a few years back in their lives were hired laborers." But the goal in America, he continued, was that the "prudent, penniless beginner in the world labors for wages awhile, saves a surplus" and eventually "hires another new beginner to help him." Lincoln's interpretation of the dream—the "just and generous and prosperous system which opens the way to all, gives hope to all"—affirmed Jefferson's vision even as he updated it for a manufacturing age.[18]

A century later, by which time large corporations had become the central features of the economic landscape, those old nostrums about independence and self-reliance formed the backbone of academic and popular critiques of modern employment. Sociologists like C. Wright Mills and David Riesman led the way, dissecting the effects of massive organizations, especially corporations, on American society. Riesman's bestselling *The Lonely Crowd*, released in 1950, argued that corporate work tended to select for a certain personality type—the "other-directed" person who was flexible and willing to accommodate other people to gain approval. Mills's 1952 book *White Collar* warned that well-to-do corporate employees and middle managers had sacrificed all their independence and become merely "the cog and the beltline of the bureaucratic machinery."[19]

Perhaps no book captured the intellectual critique of the large corporation, and by extension all of postwar American culture, better than *The Organization Man*. Published in 1956 by *Fortune* magazine journalist William H. Whyte, the book decried the demise of individuality and initiative in public life. The era's best and brightest young people—all prosperous white men, in Whyte's eyes—had become "a generation of bureaucrats," mired in the conformity of corporate employment. Their sense of individuality, of independence, and of making a difference in the world had all been subordinated to the needs of the "organization."

Although Whyte maintained that corporate employment was "the most conspicuous example" of the decline of individualism, he believed it was a society-wide phenomenon. "The collectivization so visible in the corporation has affected almost every field of work," he wrote. "Blood brother to the business trainee off to join DuPont is the seminary student who will end up in the church hierarchy, the doctor headed for the corporate clinic, [or] the physics Ph.D. in a government laboratory." Conformity and hierarchy were everywhere in the world of employment.

Most important, Whyte observed, the types of talented young people who were being sucked into the "organization" (however you defined it) lacked any spirit of individual initiative. They cared about the minor points of technical problems that they solved in order to help the system function better, but they were "comparatively uninterested in the problems themselves." Instead, the "organization man" was content to be merely "a technician, a collaborator" who wanted, above all, "to work for someone else."

This dearth of entrepreneurial ambition was central to Whyte's critique. "Paradoxically," he wrote, "the old dream of independence through a business of one's own is held almost exclusively by factory workers—the one group, as a number of sociologists have reported, least able to fulfill it." Among privileged and highly educated young people (Whyte surveyed seniors at Yale), "less than 5 per cent express any desire to be an entrepreneur." In fact, most looked disparagingly on the very concept. Instead, they thought of the independent business owner as "a selfish type motivated by greed" who was "furthermore, unhappy."[20]

The critique of corporate employment spread throughout American society. As social protest movements in the 1960s mobilized to combat racism, the war in Vietnam, and environmental degradation, among other social woes, they focused on the pernicious role of large corporations in perpetuating injustice. Most tellingly, widespread condemnation of the "military-industrial complex"—a concept first articulated by President Dwight Eisenhower in his 1961 farewell address—brought public attention to the way corporate interests profited from war, racism, sexism, and entrenched poverty, and how they corrupted democratic government to do so.

Even when social activists were fighting for other causes, their language contained a sharp rebuke of the world of corporate employment. Consider the famous oration by Berkeley student and free-speech activist Mario Savio in 1964. Condemning University of California president Clark Kerr for siding with the school's Board of Regents rather than students (over the question of distributing political pamphlets on campus), Savio assailed Kerr as nothing more than a "manager" beholden to his "board of directors." The feckless faculty, in this analogy, were "a bunch of employees!" For Savio, nothing was quite so damning as being compared to a corporate worker.[21]

The same contempt for materialist society also dripped from popular music. One example is the song "Little Boxes," written by folk songwriter Malvina Reynolds in 1962 and made into a hit by her friend Pete Seeger the next year. Lampooning the insipid sameness of suburban housing developments and the faceless, white middle-class professionals who lived there, Reynolds managed to both deride cultural conformity and highlight its gross inequities at the same time. As she made clear, "ticky-tacky" conformity was a privilege not enjoyed by all, but mostly by the white and male. "And the boys go into business and marry and raise a family, in boxes made of ticky tacky and they all look just the same," went the final verse.[22]

By the late 1960s, the critique of corporate employment formed a central pillar of what became known as the "counterculture"—a movement that rejected prevailing cultural norms entirely and sought to escape them. According to Theodore Roszak, the historian and novelist typically credited with coining the term, the "counterculture" was at heart a repudiation of corporations' grip on American society. What William Whyte saw as an affliction of well-to-do professionals who were bludgeoned into conformity, Roszak condemned as a system-wide assault. The "capitalist enterprise," he wrote in 1968, "now enters the stage at which large-scale social integration and control become paramount interests in and of themselves: the corporations begin to behave like public authorities concerned with rationalizing the total economy."[23]

Finally, the notion that the modern economy sucked the individuality out of its participants also permeated the attitudes of working-class Americans, especially (though not exclusively) young people. In the late 1960s and early 1970s, in the wake of years of general prosperity and labor strength (at least compared to what came before and after), a sense of existential frustration spread among many workers. In addition to pushing for better material conditions like pay and hours, many came to reject the central bargain of the dead-end job itself and to demand something more fulfilling.

The crowning moment came during a three-week strike at the Lordstown, Ohio, General Motors plant in 1972. Unafraid of being fired, and inspired by a decade of protest culture, the mostly young strikers of Lordstown declared that they wanted more than just a steady job for thirty years. To be sure, the strikers did have concrete demands: specifically, that GM scale back a recently announced acceleration of the assembly line to an industry-leading pace of 101 cars per minute, which forced individual workers to complete their tasks in less than 36 seconds. But over and above that, they also gave voice to a desire for less tangible, even existential, goals. Their real aim, they said, was quality of life, and even an escape from the ennui of factory work itself.[24] Ultimately, the strike was partially successful—the speed-up plan was canceled, and the plant returned to its old process. But more important, it marked a cultural turn that extended far beyond the event itself. The "Lordstown syndrome," as observers branded the new mindset, signaled workers' new willingness to push back against the conformity and drudgery of work and to reject what a later commentator called the "boredom and petty tyranny of factory life."[25]

The Lordstown syndrome spread beyond the factory floors to a range of work environments. In his 1974 book *Working*, the great chronicler of American experience Studs Terkel captured the pervasiveness of dissent and disillusion throughout the world of employment. His interview with one young office worker typified the increasingly common indifference to authority. "I'm not afraid of the boss," the man told Terkel. "I think he's sort of afraid of me. He's afraid of the younger people at work because they're not committed to the job." While an older employee might have "his whole life wrapped in the organization," younger workers felt the sort of freedom that came from not being invested in the institution itself. As a result, "the boss doesn't have that power over us, really. The tables are sort of reversed. We have power over him, because he doesn't know how to persuade us."[26]

These critiques of the stultifying conformity of modern work— whether from intellectuals, songwriters, or workers themselves— reflected not only the general privilege of an affluent society but also a powerful faith in personal initiative, in the limitless rewards that could come from striking out on one's own. During the growth economy of the mid-twentieth century, they coexisted in awkward equilibrium with a competing set of values, one that promised success by participating in the established system. When the promises of that established system faltered, the equilibrium began to crack.

Inflation and Unemployment

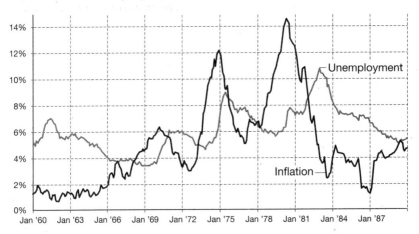

The unemployment rate and the inflation rate usually move in opposite directions;
prices tend to fall during recessions when joblessness is up. At several points in the
1970s, however, the lines moved in the same direction, creating the miserable phenomenon of "stagflation"—economic growth declined but the cost of living rose.
Source: Federal Reserve Bank of St. Louis.

By the dawn of the 1970s, the debate over what made a good job had
been marinating for decades in an economic culture largely defined by
prosperity. The deprivations of the Great Depression were decades in
the past. An entire generation of Americans, the largest demographic
bubble in history, had begun to enter adulthood knowing little but Kennedy's rising tide that seemed to lift all boats. Whatever position one
took on the question of corporate capitalism, the economy appeared to
have reached a permanently high plateau.

It didn't stay that way.

Between 1969 and 1981, the U.S. economy slipped into recession
four times.* Three of those four recessions lasted longer than anything

* The private and nonprofit National Bureau for Economic Research declares a
recession when the U.S. economy declines across a range of metrics for a significant
period of time; the common shorthand for the criteria, which is usually but not always
accurate, is "two consecutive quarters of negative GDP growth."

the country had seen since the 1930s, and even the short one (in 1980) was followed by only a one-year recovery before another downturn hit. Unemployment peaked at 9 percent in 1975 and then at 10.8 percent in 1982, never dropping below 4.6 percent for the entire decade.[27] And compounding the perils of joblessness was the persistent and pernicious rising cost of everyday goods.

After hovering below 2 percent for the first half of the 1960s, the rate of inflation more than tripled between 1965 and 1970. But it didn't stop there. Annual inflation rates peaked at 12 and 14 percent following supply shocks in the energy sector in 1973 and 1979, the result of events involving Middle Eastern petroleum producers. (The first was caused by an embargo by Arab members of OPEC in protest of U.S. support for Israel during the Yom Kippur War; the second followed the Iranian Revolution.) Only extremely tight monetary policy by the Federal Reserve Board—the so-called Volcker Shock, named after Fed Chair Paul Volcker, which set off recessions in 1980 and again from 1981 to 1982—ended the Great Inflation.[28]

The acute economic crisis of the 1970s and the long-term realignment that followed marked the end of the postwar "growth economy." Spiking consumer prices at a time of layoffs and business failures fostered cynicism and disillusion that permeated American society. Rather than boundless opportunity, modern economic life now came with a clear set of limits.

And it was amid that tumult that the long-simmering clash over what it meant to have a "good job" came in for a major reappraisal. Big, clunky bureaucratic institutions—from corporations and labor unions to universities and government agencies—were no longer delivering on their promises. But if the bureaucratic economy had failed, perhaps the old Jeffersonian vision, nurtured but often latent in the postwar period, was worth another look. Perhaps the individualized economy, where people of talent and skill could go it alone and make their own way in the world of work, could pick up the slack.

This reassessment of the virtues of individualism, and particularly the renewed attention to individual business ownership, did not come about easily, quickly, or automatically. It depended on the ideas and actions of an expanding cohort of boosters and supporters who believed that, from the rubble of the 1970s economy, something new and liberating could arise.

And their first order of business was to affirm the importance of small companies.

2

AMERICA REDISCOVERS SMALL BUSINESS

Just after 8:30 p.m. on a cold, clear January evening in 1980, President Jimmy Carter took the stage at the International Ballroom of the Washington Hilton. He was there to offer welcoming remarks to a first-of-its-kind gathering: the White House Conference on Small Business. In the ballroom sat several thousand delegates from across the country who had assembled for five days of activism and political hobnobbing designed to bolster the voice of America's small business community.

"I know firsthand how important this must be. I'm one of the few businessmen ever to serve in the White House," Carter told the crowd, nodding to his experience managing his family's peanut farm in Georgia. What's more, he continued, he still lived the small business life: "As you know, I live right next to the store where I work."

Bad jokes aside, Carter affirmed the solemn importance of a mass mobilization of small business owners in the nation's capital. The White House conference, he insisted, "fulfills a long-time ambition of mine to have the voice of small business heard loud and clear in Washington."[1]

Getting that voice heard was more critical than ever before, Carter believed. As the 1980s began, the country was in dire shape. Sky-high prices on everything from food to energy, along with business failures, unemployment, and foreign-policy mishaps, had all combined to sap public morale and breed disillusion, cynicism, and malaise. America needed economic as well as spiritual uplift. Reviving the political voice of those men and women (though far more commonly men) who owned their own businesses, who took charge of their own fortunes, might just revive the country's flagging mood.

The 1980 White House Conference on Small Business was no spur-of-the-moment gathering. The result of years of lobbying and cajoling by politicians and business owners, it marked a coming-of-age moment for a movement. Starting in the early 1970s, during the waning years of the midcentury growth economy, a bipartisan community had come together to bemoan the decline of small business owners as central figures in American life. In a political world of sprawling government bureaucracies and a business landscape marked by multinational conglomerates, the folks who owned small-time enterprises, independent of national chains and megabrands, seemed to be getting the squeeze.

Arthur Levitt, the Wall Street CEO whom Carter tapped to head the 1980 White House conference, put the point bluntly: "For years all over America, small businessmen and women have felt disenfranchised, frustrated, voiceless and powerless," he said. The country, he concluded, had lost its small business tradition.[2]

Resurrecting that tradition, Levitt believed, meant putting greater political power in the hands of the people who owned their own companies. Indeed, when politicians and other boosters praised "small business" in the abstract, what they were really doing was hailing the virtue of business *owners*—the millions of individuals who ran independent companies, as opposed to the people who worked *for* them or did business *with* them. And the inverse was true as well: to praise business *ownership* was to praise the owners of *small* companies (even if the definition of "small" was quite capacious). After all, it made little sense to talk about the "owners" of large, publicly traded companies whose stocks were held by faceless investors. As cultural touchstones, the "business owner" and "small business" effectively fused into the same thing. And as they did, the campaign to resurrect their political voice took on a strikingly bipartisan tone, even if those on the right and the left interpreted the politics of small business differently.

For conservatives, the plight of business owners was a clear consequence of bloated modern government. *Wall Street Journal* columnist Irving Kristol, the so-called godfather of neoconservatism, for example, opined that small business owners suffered from a political economy biased toward unions and big government agencies. The small business owner had become "the new forgotten man," Kristol declared, riffing on Franklin Roosevelt's description of the working class.* "No one is leading a crusade against him," Kristol explained, "and no one really wants to. He is merely being chided, harassed, ruined and bankrupted by a political process that takes him for granted and is utterly indifferent to his problematic condition."[3]

Liberals also worried that small business owners had been left behind by the modern economy, but they were more inclined than conservatives to pin the blame on big business and its political clout. As Wisconsin senator Gaylord Nelson, most often remembered as the driving force behind the first Earth Day celebration in 1970, put it: "Despite outstanding contributions of small business to the American economy

---

* The term "forgotten man" was coined by social thinker William Graham Sumner in the late nineteenth century to describe the burden he believed confronted middle-income Americans who were not so poor that they received charity nor so rich that they didn't have to worry about money. Instead, they found themselves pinched by well-meaning laws (passed by much wealthier people than they) that imposed a tax burden on the middle to benefit the poorest. During the Great Depression, Franklin Roosevelt coopted the phrase, applying it to people "at the bottom of the economic pyramid"—those who were overlooked, impoverished, and degraded by the ravages of capitalism and industrialism. In popular usage, Roosevelt's definition effectively supplanted Sumner's.

and society, decades of neglect had left the small business community in this country on the critical list by the mid-1970s."[4] Sen. Hubert Humphrey of Minnesota, the longtime civil rights champion, former vice president, and failed Democratic presidential nominee in 1968, shuddered to think what would happen "if the decline of economic power of small business in the last 25 years will continue unabated." Given "the increasing economic concentration of large multinational conglomerates," he wrote in a letter to the editor of the *Washington Post* in 1976, preserving small firms was "fundamental to our competitive enterprise system and the bedrock of the thousands of small towns that tie the nation together."[5]

To be sure, affection for the bootstrapping little guy remained as alive in popular culture and political rhetoric as it had been in the days of Thomas Jefferson and his odes to the yeoman farmer. In terms of sheer numbers, small businesses remained far and away the most common type of company: if we use the Small Business Administration's standard definition—fewer than 500 employees—about 99 percent of all U.S. firms were "small" in the early 1970s. (That figure, incidentally, hasn't changed since then.)[6] Seen that way, small business wasn't exactly "lost."

But in the economic culture of midcentury corporate capitalism, it wasn't crazy to observe that small businesses frequently seemed like an atavistic afterthought. And economic turmoil only exacerbated matters. The handwringing over the "forgotten man" echoed the populist distrust of all things *big*—from corporate conglomerates to government agencies—at a time when the major institutions of the midcentury economy looked to be failing.

But the push to rediscover America's small business tradition was more than a nostalgic effort to recover an idealized past. What made its boosters so influential was their ability to update their ideas to suit modern problems. Earlier generations had venerated local shops and individual proprietors as guardians of free competition, hard work, thrift, and community. For the boosters of the 1970s, however, small businesses also became something else: economic saviors. As sources of innovation, job creation, and dynamism itself, business owners were charged with nothing less than the revival of a moribund economy.

———

Prior to the late nineteenth century, *all* business was small. The pre-industrial American economy was a system of thousands of single-unit firms with simple organizational structures that manufactured and distributed goods, grew and sold crops, and provided services. Yes, some companies were fantastically wealthy, particularly slave plantations, banks, and trading ventures that moved goods, people, and credit in complex networks around the world. But even those rich enterprises were limited to a handful of investors and employed a relatively small number of managers and workers. Before the Civil War, nearly all manufacturers and retailers were family owned and generally did little business beyond their immediate surroundings. And none were specifically defined by mass production, mass employment, or economies of scale, which the big corporations of the late nineteenth century would be.[7]

The first true "big businesses," which emerged in the 1860s and 1870s, changed all that. Railroads got the party started and were quickly joined by steel, petroleum, chemicals, tobacco, and other industries. What made these corporations historically distinctive was their scale and scope. Using complex bureaucratic structures and multidivisional hierarchies, they ably brought together many different business functions into a single organization. The result was a network of middle managers, superintendents, and division heads who bore collective responsibility for day-to-day operations. That diffuse complexity was what made them "big," and different from what had existed before.

What all this meant was that the idea of "small business" as a distinct type of enterprise took on real meaning only in contrast to the "big business" that emerged in the 1870s. In short order, however, moral as well as economic distinctions between the two types became clear. In the 1880s, public outrage arose against corporate monopolies like John Rockefeller's Standard Oil Trust, which dominated its market largely by undercutting smaller petroleum refiners on price until it ran them out of business or absorbed them. Pro-monopolists argued that concentrating business in a handful of colossal corporations allowed them to produce goods at lower cost, bringing down prices for everyone. Their opponents disagreed, and Ohio congressman John Sherman (brother of the famous Civil War general William Tecumseh Sherman) authored the Sherman Anti-Trust Act of 1890, inaugurating America's antitrust legal tradition. Arguing for Sherman's bill, anti-monopolists rightly pointed out that Standard Oil regularly jacked its prices back up once it monopolized a market. But more to the point, low prices weren't the only thing that mattered. "I do not believe that the great object in life is to make everything cheap," Republican senator Henry Teller of Colorado argued before Congress. Preserving the "industrial liberty" of smaller operators, in other words, was as worthy a goal as low prices.[8]

The Sherman Act remained mostly on ice for more than a decade, but the Department of Justice eventually brought suit against the most egregious monopolies between 1904 and 1911. Yet despite that famed "trustbusting," including the forced breakup of Standard Oil and other behemoths, large corporations remained politically and economically dominant. No return to the status quo ante of small shops and quaint factories was in the offing. Small companies did receive some legal protections and large corporations faced greater regulation, to be sure, but entities with names like General Electric, U.S. Steel, Ford Motor Company, and American Telephone and Telegraph (AT&T) became the face of early twentieth-century corporate society.[9]

That's not to say that little companies vanished. To the contrary, many thrived. Specialty tool producers, jewelers, and furniture makers, for example, focused on flexible production for niche markets that the big producers did not fill. Smaller enterprises also remained vital players in sectors like retail and personal services, particularly when the efficiencies of size were less substantial.[10]

In an economic world that often seemed starkly divided between the owners of capital and the masses who toiled for them, small-scale manufacturers and shopkeepers crafted a new and clear class identity, straddling traditional lines. Unlike the working-class proletariat, they controlled the means of production and owned the fruits of their labor. So long as their businesses remained afloat, they could hope to enjoy a middle-class existence and social status comparable to those of professionals like corporate managers, lawyers, or accountants. Yet unlike the titans of industry—or their wealthy stockholders—small business owners could not count on financial stability, and they typically did not have the leisure time to pursue philanthropic, cultural, or artistic concerns. Running a small business, then as now, took herculean effort and long hours, and there was often little left over once the bills were paid. The class that Marxists call the "petite bourgeoisie" thus occupied a unique place in the social order: they owned like capitalists, but they worked like labor.[11]

———

In the early decades of the twentieth century, that small business identity ran headlong into the buzzsaw of the national chain-store movement.

It all started with the emergence of department stores and then regional and national chains, which successfully applied the organizational techniques of industrial corporations to retailing. In short order, these new models took the country by storm, challenging and often replacing traditional stores and shops. Chain retailing grew from 4 percent to 20 percent of national sales during the 1920s, and the total number of chain-store units topped 100,000 in 1930.[12] By combining sophisticated management, efficient logistics, and deep pockets, these national chain stores offered low prices and a rationalized, predictable shopping experience for consumers. But the small shop-keepers with whom they competed saw things differently. There were real social costs to those low prices, small proprietors argued, and they were too high to bear. "Absentee owners" siphoned money away from local communities. "Itinerant" managers did not care about local people or issues. National retailers weren't a sign of progress—they were the "Chain Store Menace."

"Efficiency can be carried too far," argued a lobbyist for the (not disinterested) National Wholesale Grocers Association in 1930. "Sooner or later it comes into conflict with humanity."[13]

As chain stores grew, a powerful political movement emerged in opposition, crystallizing a popular set of values and beliefs about small businesses. Unlike big, impersonal (and implicitly corrupt) national companies, small firms were locally embedded and their owners were public leaders. They cared about their communities and local affairs. They kept their wealth in town, investing in hospitals, parks, and youth sports. They took care of their workers as well as their customers. In short, they embodied classical masculine and paternalistic virtues: reliability, strength, hard work, and civic-mindedness.

In the late 1920s, chain-store politics kickstarted the career of Texas Democrat Wright Patman, who would become small business owners' greatest advocate in Washington over the coming decades. The son of poor tenant farmers in rural west Texas, Patman was first elected to Congress in 1928 at the age of thirty-five. He quickly established himself as a latter-day prairie populist in the tradition of William Jennings Bryan. As his campaign platform declared, he was: "Against monopolies, trusts, branch banking and excessive and discriminative freight rates." Like nearly all Southern Democrats of the era, he also supported white supremacy and opposed anti-segregation, anti-lynching, and civil rights legislation. In Patman's view, however, his contributions to the oppression of African Americans were simply the means to an end, necessary to stay in power to fight the good fight. The real focus of his long legislative career—which stretched into the 1970s—was the predations of organized capital, or as he said, the "money barons of the East."[14]

In the 1930s, Patman became the most outspoken congressional defender of small stores against the nefarious specter of distant capital. The heart of the problem, he charged, was that large stores arranged preferential discounts from their suppliers, which they then passed along in the form of lower consumer prices. Smaller stores, which could not strike the same deals, were thus undercut on price. In 1935, Patman proposed legislation, written and backed by grocery wholesalers, to severely limit those discounts and thus level the playing field between large and small retailers. "When all independent merchants can receive the same prices from manufacturers that the banker-controlled retailers receive, competition will be preserved and the consumer protected," he argued.[15]

The ensuing debate over Patman's proposal exposed the fraught politics of small business, particularly considering the power of gender roles and the "separate spheres" of men and women over questions of business. Like many rural populists before him, Patman deployed the rhetoric of *producerism*, which identified (implicitly and often explicitly) male producers as the cornerstones of a society. National consumer groups and the League of Women Voters looked at the issue from the other side—that of the consumer (often depicted as the discerning housewife). They argued that blocking large stores from cutting deals with suppliers would raise prices, and so they came out against Patman's proposal.

What's more, even many of Patman's fellow Democrats questioned whether any law could really defend small businesses when large corporations boasted so many economic advantages. "There is no way by legislation to afford protection to the less fortunate or the less efficient merchant," explained Democratic senator Marvel Logan of Kentucky. "We cannot prevent efficiency; we cannot stop progress."[16] President

Franklin Roosevelt himself could not reconcile the conflict between economic efficiency and the desire to protect small business owners, and the White House largely sat out the issue.

Despite opposition from the chain-store industry and consumer groups, not to mention the lukewarm support he got from fellow Democrats, Patman managed to get his bill passed. What ultimately carried the day was his ability to manage a grassroots lobbying campaign fueled by the persistent power of anti-elitist politics. In the lead-up to the vote, anti-chain-store activists flooded Congress with petitions and held a 1,500-person "March of the Little Men" (a not-so-subtle affirmation of who the "producers" in "producerism" were) in Washington. The political optics of protecting small operators were too strong to be denied, particularly during the Great Depression. President Roosevelt, overcoming his reticence, signed the "Robinson–Patman Act" into law in 1936. (Senate Majority Leader Joseph Robinson, a Democrat from Arkansas, was co-sponsor.)[17]

The Robinson–Patman Act, its supporters hoped, would signal the start of a new civic commitment to small business. What soon became clear, however, was that it really marked the beginning of the end for Patman's populist quest to confront the pernicious power of economic concentration.

First, large companies quickly found ways to render the law toothless. Big retailers used complex accounting to convince the Federal Trade Commission (FTC), which enforced the law, that they were entitled to special discounts under the language of the law. The FTC, for its part, put a higher premium on large stores' ability to reduce costs and thus prices.[18]

Moreover, the triumph of efficiency over tradition only accelerated as the Great Depression gave way to World War II. Wartime mobilization made clear the tremendous power of mass production and the advantages of large, modern, bureaucratic operations, from the assembly lines at munitions factories to the U.S. military itself. And when the end of the war brought a renewed focus on domesticity and the comforts of inexpensive consumer products, the populist fervor that had animated Patman's Depression-era campaigns faded into the background.[19]

By the postwar period, the battle between small and large business appeared to have been won. Big corporations, boasting big research grants from big government agencies and in collaboration with big universities, begat modern life—from pharmaceuticals to aerospace, from communications to computers. Well-heeled advertising executives, public-relations experts, and management consultants deployed en masse into Fortune 500 companies (*Fortune* magazine started its famous list in 1955) to craft strategy and public image. Corporate lobbyists and business associations promoted the interests of those big corporations within the growing apparatus of the federal government. Issues like local commerce and small-town values certainly retained their rhetorical and sentimental power, but serious structural reforms largely disappeared from the nation's political menu.[20]

What's more, major business institutions wanted little to do with small companies. The U.S. Chamber of Commerce, the country's premier business lobbying association, typified the culture. At a sales and recruiting meeting in Chicago in the 1950s, a division manager pointed out that the Chamber's flagship publication *Nation's Business* focused almost exclusively on national economic policy and the country's biggest corporations. "We are selling *Nation's Business* to an awful lot of small-business men and women," the division manager explained to an editor. "Couldn't we have one article a month addressing small-business problems?"

"Over my dead body," the editor replied.[21]

———

In the era of bigness that followed the Second World War, the political movement to nurture independent business ownership was largely sidelined, but it was not completely extinguished. In addition to political hymns to the virtues of local shops, a handful of policy initiatives did seek to encourage Americans to strike out on their own and build their own businesses.* In spite of themselves, however, those limited policy advances only reaffirmed the notion that "small business" held second-class status. Two cases—the founding of the Small Business Administration in the 1950s and the Nixon administration's initiative on *Black capitalism* in the late 1960s and early 1970s—typified the trend: even when policymakers encouraged people to go into business, they mostly focused on marginalized constituencies, implicitly confirming the superiority of big business over small.

The Small Business Administration (SBA) was established in 1953. Institutionally and philosophically, it was the descendent of a government agency known as the Reconstruction Finance Corporation (RFC), which Congress had created in 1932, the final year of the Hoover administration. First designed to float government-backed loans to businesses and state and local governments struggling through the Great Depression, the RFC had limped on into the postwar period. But its continued existence provided a model and an opportunity for community activists who worried that small manufacturers and other companies risked being outcompeted in the postwar economy. In the 1950s, small business owners and their lobbyists convinced President Dwight Eisenhower that if he didn't take a stand in their defense, he would look like a shill for big business, and that would be bad politics. Just as Roosevelt had signed the Robinson–Patman Act of 1936 as a matter of political expediency, so, too, did Eisenhower get on board with this new plan. With his backing, Congress abolished the RFC as an independent

---

* In political rhetoric, the distinction between "starting a business" and "owning a small business" was usually quite muddled, even though they are two quite different things from an economic point of view. Nearly every start-up is small by definition, but plenty of small companies endure for generations and are thus not especially new, innovative, or entrepreneurial. You can be a small business owner who didn't start the business. More on this in chapter 4.

agency and transferred many of its functions—including preferential loans and training programs for small companies—to the new Small Business Administration.[22]

From the outset, the SBA exercised little real power and was far from central to American economic policy. Only a small fraction of the country's millions of enterprises ever took out an SBA loan, despite its grandiose charge in the enabling legislation to "aid, counsel, assist, and protect insofar as is possible the interests of small-business concerns."[23] Nothing in the agency's charter or early political history suggested any real interest in redressing the imbalances between large and small companies in the way activists like Wright Patman demanded.

In addition, it was far from clear what exactly defined the "small businesses" the SBA was supposed to serve. According to Congress, a "small business" was "independently owned and operated and . . . is not dominant in its field"—a definition so vague as to be mostly meaningless. Effectively, the SBA decided on its own who did and did not qualify for a loan. While employment size (fewer than 500 workers) was the most common metric, there was a time in the 1960s when the agency used *market share*, in certain industries, to decide who counted. For example, according to a rule that applied to the automobile and tire industries, companies with less than 5 percent of total sales among their competitors were considered "small" and thus eligible for preferential loans. That definition led to the somewhat comical scenario whereby the American Motors Company (AMC), the struggling number-four seed in the auto industry, qualified for SBA help. The Detroit-based carmaker, whose past CEO was the Republican governor of Michigan, George Romney, boasted only 3 percent market share, but it also employed 30,000 people and sold a billion dollars' worth of vehicles every year. Such confusion of purpose led many people to conclude that the SBA was just for show, not a viable means to promote business ownership.[24]

In the late 1960s, a policy initiative by the Nixon administration likewise demonstrated that, while policymakers appreciated the

rhetorical appeal of small business ownership, they were far from prepared to devote serious energy to it.

For President Richard Nixon, pandering to the tradition of independent business involved a myopic, if not outright cynical, approach
to the burning problems of civil rights and racial injustice. The Black
Freedom movement had many causes, including the persistence of
racial segregation and discrimination in hiring, education, and access
to public space and services, not to mention suppressed wages for Black
workers, disenfranchisement, police violence, and systemic poverty. Yet
the cure to these ills, Nixon argued, lay not in social reform of white
society but in Black communities themselves—through personal and
individual uplift.

"What most of the militants are asking for is not for separation, but to
be included in—not as supplicants, but as owners, as entrepreneurs—to
have a share of the wealth and piece of the action," he proclaimed from
the campaign trail in 1968.[25]

As president, Nixon sought not only to create a politically conservative and "pro-business" approach to civil rights but also, quite deliberately, to appeal to Black voters through his vision of "Black capitalism."
The centerpiece of that program was the Office of Minority Business
Enterprise, established by executive order in 1969. Today known as
the Minority Business Development Agency, the office created special
funding sources for small minority-owned companies, much like the
SBA did. Critics attacked the program as simultaneously, and paradoxically, both underfunded and wasteful, even as some African American leaders heralded the opportunities it created in a racially exclusive
business world.[26]

What was significant about Nixon's initiative was that it explicitly
avoided the challenge of integrating Black Americans into the mainstream of economic life. Instead, by encouraging small-scale business
ownership, from local stores to franchises, it endeavored—theoretically,

at least—to create an environment for Black entrepreneurs to make it on their own.

Policy overtures like the SBA and "Black capitalism" acted as rehearsals for what was to come in the 1970s, when the national economy began to sputter. In a time of malaise, the political class began to take more seriously the old nostrums that it had given lip service to for years. The time had come to rethink the virtues of small business ownership.

Those shifting political winds were on clear display in 1976 when Congress created a public-relations department for the SBA known as the "Office of Advocacy." No longer was the SBA just about loans. Now Congress explicitly charged the agency with defending and publicizing small firms' contributions to, basically, all aspects of the national economy. According to the updated law, its job now included: "improving competition, encouraging economic and social mobility, restraining inflation, spurring production, expanding employment opportunities, increasing productivity, promoting exports, stimulating innovation and entrepreneurship, and providing an avenue through which new and untested products and services can be brought to the marketplace."[27]

Even the U.S. Chamber of Commerce, which in the 1950s had so contemptuously dismissed the idea of catering to small business concerns, changed its tune. In the 1970s, the venerable old business association dramatically increased its lobbying as well as its membership. Central to that newly expansive mission was a promise to represent *all* types of businesses. Wright Patman had believed that small and big companies were inherently at odds, but the Chamber blurred any distinctions based on size.

"There is a growing sense across the entire business spectrum," the group claimed, "of the need for a common agenda for all business and for a common action plan to put that agenda into effect."[28]

On Labor Day, 1976, *Washington Post* writer Colman McCarthy penned a paean to the work performed by small business owners. On one level, his nostalgic portrait could have come straight out of the chain-store debates of the 1920s and 1930s. The men (he only mentioned men) who owned local groceries and convenience stores were "personally identified with, and accountable for, what they sell." They didn't report to out-of-town boards or investors. They had "affectionate feelings for the neighborhood." Because they catered to the needs of specific local communities, they could provide "the kind of service and products that the oversized and depersonalized chain stores can't care about."

But because it was Labor Day, and because the national economy in the mid-1970s was mired in a depressing slump, the writer added an important twist. Local shopkeepers, he explained, "have character and heart because they delight in their work." They provide a clear lesson to children that "a man's labor need not be his drudgery." At a time when growing numbers of Americans reported deep dissatisfaction with their jobs, he hailed individual business owners who "escaped the monotony of modern labor and had a say in their own working conditions."[29] This ode to the small shopkeeper, read gleefully into the *Congressional Record* by Senator Hubert Humphrey, captured the urgency of resurrecting sustained attention to small business and stressed its economically liberating potential. Business ownership, in other words, could be both economically and personally fulfilling.

The tide was shifting. Wright Patman had died earlier that year, his lifelong quest to stick it to the East Coast elites, the Wall Street banks, and the national chains largely unfulfilled. Antitrust law had entered a new phase, concerned less with corporate size than with the question of "consumer welfare."[30] A wave of mergers in the 1960s had created a sea of faceless corporate conglomerates that seemed only to reinforce the existential despair. But while bigness was still everywhere, calls to reconsider the role of small companies grew louder as the strong postwar economic growth stalled out. Patman's quest to bring attention to the plight of small enterprise began to experience a revival.

The terms of the debate, however, had changed, and the politics of small business in the 1970s departed in vital ways from Patman's politics. Small business ownership would no longer be an *antidote* to the disruptive and rough-and-tumble modern economy; it would be the *cornerstone* of that economy. The stagflationary funk of the 1970s meant no more talk of a trade-off between the virtues of small companies and the mass efficiencies and growth to be gained from big ones. Instead, small business would be seen as the engine of growth itself.

The result was a paradox—even as business dynamism declined and the economic power of small companies waned, the notion that new, scrappy, innovative companies represented the cure for malaise would become more and more entrenched.

————

The campaign to raise the flag of individual business ownership—of working for oneself, of running a small business—made two vital and interconnected arguments in the 1970s. First, it stressed the traditional virtues of small size and localism: small business ownership was *good for you*. Second, and as important: small businesses were *more* efficient and *more* innovative than big businesses. Critically, in an era of high unemployment and disgruntled workers, they created more jobs.

Except they didn't, and they never had. Once you adjust for fluctuations in the business cycle and keep track of all the businesses that fail, rather than just those that succeed, there is no economic evidence that a firm's size has much to do with its economic success or its ability to create jobs. Nonetheless, the notion that small business was the key to innovation and job creation—and thus that encouraging people to become small business owners was an important policy objective—became one of the most persistent myths of the late twentieth century.

And no single person was more responsible for drilling that idea into the American political consciousness than a policy analyst named David L. Birch.

Trained first as an engineer and computer programmer at Harvard in the 1950s, Birch earned a PhD in economics in 1966 from the Harvard Business School, where his dissertation examined the economics of the U.S. space program. In 1974, he took a position as the director of the MIT Program on Jobs, Enterprises, and Markets, studying American cities and urban design. That work prompted his interest in job creation and ultimately his highly influential report, *The Job Generation Process*, written for the U.S. Department of Commerce in 1979.[31]

Birch's study examined the credit reports of many American companies pulled together by the Dun & Bradstreet credit rating agency. Using those figures, Birch performed one of the first (if not the very first) systematic and longitudinal count of employment figures, firm creation, and firm deaths at individual business establishments.[32] His analysis led him to a striking conclusion: Between 1969 and 1976, he reported with authority, firms with fewer than one hundred employees accounted for 80 percent of new private-sector jobs.[33] Eight years after his first study, in 1987, he published a widely cited follow-up book, *Job Creation in America*, that raised the stakes even higher. Between 1981 and 1985, Birch now claimed, companies with fewer than twenty employees created 88 percent of all new jobs.[34]

These shocking statistics became gospel, and they thoroughly permeated political discourse. The "eight out of ten" claim was repeated verbatim and unquestioningly by world leaders like Jimmy Carter and Margaret Thatcher, the international economic research group OECD, and lobbyists at the Chamber of Commerce, as well as popular writers like the conservative George Gilder.[35] The figure's popularity isn't hard to understand, of course. After years of stagflation, slow recovery, industrial layoffs, and corporate downsizing, Birch's conclusions confirmed exactly what people wanted to hear: small businesses created jobs.

The trouble was that the claim was wrong. Critics were quick to point out major methodological flaws in Birch's analysis that rendered his conclusion quite overstated. His definition of "small," for example, varied among his reports, books, and popular articles. Sometimes it meant companies with fewer than 20 employees but sometimes the cut-off was 50, 100, or the SBA's figure, 500.[36] What's more, follow-up studies failed to replicate Birch's findings. Other analysts, in fact, found that the share of jobs created by small firms was closer to 55 percent, or approximately the same as their total share of employment. Employment size, they concluded, had no particular bearing on whether a company created jobs or not.[37] Moreover, the share of employment in companies with fewer than 500 employees had drifted downward through the 1960s and 1970s before rising modestly in the early 1980s, without any clear correlation to the national economy.[38]

Birch himself eventually backed off the "eight out of ten" claim. It was, he conceded to reporters from the *Wall Street Journal* in 1988, a "silly number" that was "misleading and uninteresting" by itself. The ability of small businesses to be net job creators (that is, for the number of people they hired to exceed the number they laid off due to going out of business or weathering an economic slowdown) fluctuated with the overall economy. In any given year, small business's share of job growth, Birch added, "depends almost entirely on the experience of large business." When big businesses shed jobs, as in a recession, many of those newly unemployed people find work at small companies, so when the economy picks back up again, it looks like it is because of all that hiring by small companies. But when the economy is doing well, the reverse happens.[39]

Nonetheless, Birch remained adamant that small-scale employers were important for qualitative reasons. Large firms employed lots of people when times were good, he argued, but they also let many go, and quickly, when the economy turned. Employment at smaller companies was stickier; they didn't fire workers as readily or in as large numbers,

Birch believed. So while individual small firms might fail at high rates, small business as a sector was a relatively steady net job creator.*

By the late 1980s, Birch expressed some frustration with the way his work was being used, especially in political circles. As he told the *Wall Street Journal*, "it bothers me a great deal" when lobbyists and advocates for small companies used his data to argue that being small, in and of itself, made a company a good job creator. Instead, he explained, the key variable wasn't size but age. Most companies "reach their initial size in the first year or so and remain more or less at that size for their lifetime." Younger firms have the most room to grow, and thus account for the most rapid rates of hiring.[40]

Birch's personal backtracking was relatively muted compared to the public splash his studies had made and came far too late to put the genie back in the bottle. In political rhetoric, few people showed much interest in technical questions about how to measure job creation. What mattered was the key takeaway, the snappy headlines, and the memorable soundbites.

So whether Birch was right or wrong about job creation ultimately didn't matter. What mattered was the way he satisfied the public's longing for a David and Goliath story, reinforcing longstanding cultural ideas about the virtue of the little guy. With an expert's stamp of authority, he affirmed the link between owning your own business and being economically important—being an entrepreneur, an innovator, or what we would later come to call an "influencer." In that light, small business was no longer a quaint relic of Main Street, USA, but rather a hub for progress and growth.

---

* A recent study of "Main Street" businesses during the Covid-19 pandemic provided anecdotal evidence of this tendency among small companies to go to great lengths to avoid laying off employees, given the closer personal and community ties between owners and workers and perhaps a greater sense of paternalistic responsibility among employers. See Gary Rivlin, *Saving Main Street: Small Business in the Time of Covid-19* (HarperCollins, 2022).

A practical problem remained, though: What did it mean to stick up for small business owners? What policies, programs, rules, or agencies could nurture individual initiative and spur innovation, while still protecting less competitive small players from large entities that threatened their livelihoods?

Jimmy Carter's White House Conference on Small Business ultimately crumbled on those thorny questions. The conference had been the brainchild of liberal senator Gaylord Nelson of Wisconsin, who pitched it to Carter during the 1976 campaign. It was a political no-brainer, Nelson insisted: Bring together thousands of delegates from all over the country to "study the problems that beset the small business community" and come up with solutions. What could be better, he argued, than "a workshop for greater participation by small business people in the task of formulating economic policy" that would, not inconsequentially, "highlight the importance of this area to the general public"?[41]

The conference did generate a policy agenda, primarily around well-worn business complaints: the high cost of credit (a function of interest rates and inflation), intrusive workplace and environmental regulations, and high taxes. All that was standard fare, even for liberals like Nelson and Carter.[42] Where the conference had far less success, however, was in articulating a clear sense of community or common purpose among participants, or convincing many people that Jimmy Carter, entering what would ultimately be his final year in office, was as entrepreneurial as his peanut-farmer pedigree would suggest.

One participant—Lois Jenkins, of Pasadena, California—noted that, while she appreciated the chance for "individuals to vent their frustrations," she found the event to be full of platitudes but short on specifics. In particular, she chastised a childish animated film clip that extolled the virtues of small business in the style of a Hanna-Barbera cartoon, calling it "truly an insult to the intelligence of those attending." It all made her wonder whether, rather than a grassroots movement, the whole affair was really just "a very well orchestrated public relations program to further the image of Jimmy Carter."[43]

Other conference-goers took issue with Carter's obvious efforts at racial and gender inclusivity. As a reporter for *Inc.* magazine put it: "Although the typical small businessman is neither female nor of minority extraction, the conference organizers were committed to seeing—through appointment, if necessary—that those groups were sufficiently represented."[44] The effort to push back against small business's prevailing (and accurate) image as overwhelmingly male and white was not lost on the attendees. One participant from West Virginia complained to Carter that five of the ten delegates selected from his region were Black, even though only ten to fifteen of the several hundred people at the planning meeting were. If such over-representation were common, he concluded, "then the whole Program has become a farce, and small business has lost, not gained."[45]

The "rediscovery" of small business was a complex affair that involved competing interests, ideological warfare, and vitriolic politics, all of which made the move from slogans to policy action difficult. Raising public attention to the historical struggles of independent businesses was one thing; overcoming the weight of parochialism, cynicism, and real policy disagreements was another. It would take a new kind of organizational effort, one led by small and independent business owners themselves, to move beyond the hifalutin political rhetoric and academic scribblings and complete the journey of putting business ownership squarely on the nation's cultural agenda.

3

BUSINESS OWNERS
OF THE WORLD,
UNITE

While political elites and academics were "rediscovering" the virtues of small and independent companies, business owners saw an opportunity to take political action. Throughout the 1970s, a movement began to coalesce from the bottom up, or at least from the middle out, around a wide range of policy issues. Through associations, support groups, political action committees, and direct lobbying, this community made its voice heard at the highest levels.

"Small-business people are beginning to understand their own collective importance," observed Arthur Levitt in 1981. The head of the American Stock Exchange (now known as NYSE American) who had helped organize Jimmy Carter's conference the year before, Levitt was excited by the real promise of independent companies—those not stuck in the ruts of the big corporations—to influence economic and social policy. "They are getting organized in important ways," he noted, "and developing a sense of unity that I believe will soon make them one of the most potent influences in the economic history of the United States."[1] Time would prove him right.

The political mobilization of small and independent business owners unfolded in the wake of an extended period of social movement activism in the 1960s and 1970s, and it took many cues from its forebears. In those years, Americans of all political stripes parlayed group identity and ideological conviction into political power. Pathbreaking social movements like the Black Freedom Struggle and opposition to the Vietnam War inspired activists across a range of issues, from environmentalism to feminism and gay rights. Social traditionalists also mobilized, uniting in opposition to abortion rights and the Equal Rights Amendment and often drawing on the tactics of progressive movements. At the same time, big businesses also became more politically organized. Associations like the U.S. Chamber of Commerce adopted some of the techniques of social movements—network building, community activities, ideologically straightforward sloganeering—to buttress their direct lobbying against the power of organized labor, environmental regulation, and consumer-protection laws.[2]

The small and independent business community fit uneasily into that political world. "Small business" is as difficult to define politically as it is economically—it is a capacious category that encompasses a wide range of political views, goals, ideologies, and policy preferences. In the 1970s, many social activists believed that independent businesses offered a path to progress and equality, a viable alternative to capitalist oppression, ecological degradation, racism, and sexism. Many were inspired by the proliferation of feminist bookstores, Black-owned record shops, and natural-food cooperatives in major cities.[3] Some counterculturalists, particularly those tuned in to the new possibilities of cybernetics and computer technology, likewise saw the potential of business ownership. The famous *Whole Earth Catalog*, published by Stewart Brand, included resources not only for going "back to the land" but also for using new technologies to create sustainable, entrepreneurial companies.[4]

Yet in the main, the business owners that achieved the biggest platforms, and who did the most to promote a policy vision centered on small and independent companies, were not radicals seeking to undermine capitalism. Rather, they were committed to expanding its bounty, if not to society at large then at least to their constituent members. How exactly they proposed to do so, however, varied considerably.

Two of the most prominent and influential organizations to blossom during the 1970s, the National Federation of Independent Business (NFIB) and the National Association of Women Business Owners (NAWBO), typified both the variety as well as the common commitments within this movement. At first glance, they appear starkly different in their political identity, goals, and activism. The NFIB, which had its origins in the 1940s, pushed traditional "small business" policy positions on regulation and tax reform as it exploded in size and reach. NAWBO, on the other hand, was created in the 1970s. A direct product of the women's movement, it embodied the corporate side of modern feminist politics.

Yet despite their different origins and policy focus, each was founded in response to frustrations business owners felt with the political, economic, legal, and social worlds in which they operated. Each was dedicated to a clearly defined membership—"mom-and-pop" companies in the case of the NFIB; woman-owned firms for NAWBO—and drew on the grassroots enthusiasm of those constituencies to fuel their activism. And vitally, each ultimately embraced an economic vision that saw private initiative through business ownership as the key to America's future, in stark opposition to the social welfare state and government regulation. Their success in building community, a sense of common purpose, and a favorable political atmosphere established an enduring legacy that continues to encourage individual business ownership today.

———

The way Wilson Harder described it, the vision came to him as a sort of epiphany. It was 1942, and Harder—then in his early forties—was staring out the window of his office building above the port of San Francisco. Below him, young American soldiers embarked for battle in World War II. *What will become of them when the war finally ends?* he wondered.

When he returned home that night, he shared his worries with his wife, Dode. "I don't want to see those boys have to come back and sell apples on the streetcorners as they did after World War I," he told her.

As the war raged in Asia and Europe, Harder, like many Americans, worried that the hard times of the 1930s would come rushing back when the fighting ceased. Echoing the fears that animated Wright Patman's fight in Congress against chain stores and corporate monopolies, Harder believed that the most severe domestic threat to the nation lay in the seemingly inexorable trend toward economic consolidation. And for him, the risk was bigger than corporations. *All* oversized institutions, from New Deal government agencies to labor unions and even the war mobilization itself, created a dangerously concentrated economy. When everyone depended on a handful of massive entities, one slip-up—like the 1929 stock-market crash—could cause a tidal wave of catastrophe.

The solution, he believed, was an economy rooted in self-sufficient, independent businesses, where economic power was diffuse. While he appreciated the top-down anti-monopoly approach of politicians like Patman, Harder had another strategy in mind—mobilizing business owners themselves to push for state and federal policies that would strengthen the companies that could provide an antidote to economic concentration: small ones.

Wilson Harder came from the world of independent business. Born at the turn of the twentieth century, he grew up in a family of commercial fishers in Michigan. As a young man, he worked in the automobile industry and eventually bought his own Dodge dealership. Early in the Great Depression, he sold that business and went to work for the U.S. Chamber of Commerce. But he grew frustrated that the higher-ups at the Chamber did not deem small business worthy of their attention.

That afternoon, watching soldiers on the San Francisco waterfront, something finally clicked.

He quit his job in January 1943. In May, he officially incorporated a new business, the National Federation of Small Business, with his wife, Dode Harder, as the only other stock owner. (Harder lovingly called his organization "the Fed," but there is little evidence that the nickname went further than the founder.) In 1949, the Harders restructured as a nonprofit and replaced "small business" with "independent business" in the organization's name. That move, ostensibly done to avoid confusion with another trade association, in fact better reflected Harder's ideological commitment. What really mattered to him was not a firm's *size*, per se, but the economic and social *independence* of its owners. Independent business owners, in his view, were beholden to no one and thus could truly bring stability and prosperity to the country.[5]

In legal form and tax status, the NFIB looked like a small business version of national lobbying groups like the Chamber of Commerce and the National Association of Manufacturers (NAM). Those groups were the big guns of the business community, alongside Washington-centered policy organizations like the Business Council and the Committee for Economic Development, and they all focused on macroeconomic policy and tended to privilege big firms. But in terms of its actual operational model, the NFIB had much more in common with a small private start-up, and that feature distinguished it among business associations.

Like a typical trade organization, the NFIB was funded by dues-paying members. But unlike the other groups, Harder offered his members more than a nebulous promise of political support or "voice." Instead, the NFIB's "product" was information—specifically, the collected and collated views of independent business owners about legislation currently up for debate in Congress. After paying their dues (initially set at $8.50, they quickly rose), NFIB members would reply to survey questions about various policy issues. Harder would then synthesize their responses into a publication called *The Mandate*, which he mailed back to his member-clients. In addition, he sent *The Mandate* to members of Congress, insisting that it represented the unfettered views of the entire small business community. His client base and the bulk of his labor force, in other words, were effectively the same: his members.

At first, the Harders ran their micro-operation from home. As membership increased, they quickly expanded, appointing trusted member-clients as divisional chairmen and assigning them the task of tabulating survey responses from their respective regions. Just like a small start-up outgrowing its founders, the organization also hired permanent staff members to compile and write *The Mandate*, which grew from a single-page flyer to a four-page newsletter that included not only survey questions and answers but editorial comments on pending or upcoming legislation. In 1958, the NFIB added a state-level member survey to its poll on federal policies, and it expanded its contact list to include governors and state legislators as well as Congress.

In the very early years, Harder clearly divided the sales side of his operation from the lobbying side. His full-time lobbyist, a fellow independent business owner named George Burger, had run a tire dealership and garnered twenty years of experience representing himself and other tire dealers in Washington. Leaving Burger the job of talking to Congress, Harder stayed in California, generating revenue by building and managing what he called his "field force"—the men who sold subscriptions to *The Mandate*. By the 1960s, the NFIB had hundreds of thousands of members.

Despite its growth, the NFIB remained a relatively minor player in national affairs for twenty-five years. In a political environment that favored large corporations, the group struggled to gain much traction. Not helping matters was the prickly character of its boss, who—like many founders—oversaw the operation closely and at times autocratically. Wilson Harder was a conservative Republican who, in the words of one staffer, "hated Democrats."[6] Perhaps due to his rigid partisanship, the survey questions he mailed to members tended to be doctrinaire and strident, good for political advertisements but less useful as instruments of policymaking. Typically, members were simply asked whether they were "for" or "against" complex questions about taxes, economic concentration, social welfare, and regulation. And often the phrasing suggested that Harder had a particular answer in mind. For example, a question about a bill to "grade restaurants in the District of Columbia," presumably in the interest of consumer welfare, included the following editorial note from Harder: "This is more regulation of private business and could work many hardships on small business." Little wonder that the survey results typically came back lopsided, often split 75-25 or more.[7]

Everything about the NFIB in its first quarter century embodied the stereotypes of a scrappy start-up—tight control by a committed and rigid founder, a barebones operation built on personal relationships, and even a succession crisis. When Wilson Harder died in 1968, the NFIB's board of directors made his son John the company president. Yet within six months, the younger Harder proved a less capable boss than the old man, and he lost the job. From then on, the NFIB looked and acted a lot less like a small business and more like a sophisticated, integrated, and hierarchically structured corporate machine.

A new president, Wilson Johnson, took over, sharing not only the founder's first name (by coincidence) but also his commitment to nurturing political influence. Treating the NFIB like the major operation he hoped it would become, Johnson created an employee pension program, computerized its membership and survey data, and expanded the ranks of management. During the 1970s, he doubled the group's membership and bolstered its political operations. In 1972, the NFIB launched a parallel publication to *The Mandate* called *How Congress Voted*, through which it explained important legislative issues and detailed specific stances taken by members of Congress. In the same years, Johnson also expanded the NFIB's lobbying presence in both Washington, D.C., and the states. By the mid-1980s, he had a lobbyist or contractor in every statehouse in the country.

Like many businesspeople in the 1970s, NFIB leaders protested long and loud that too many Americans fundamentally did not comprehend what they called the "free enterprise system." In their view, people just did not understand "the way the world works," and their ignorance led to misguided tax, labor, and regulatory politics.* Indeed, the complaint went back decades. During the 1930s, the anti-Roosevelt American Liberty League, funded largely by the DuPont company, had blamed the popularity of New Deal regulatory policies on the public's ignorance of the benefits of capitalism. In 1945, the Foundation for Economic Education began producing pamphlets and record albums about the virtues of unfettered markets, and the U.S. Chamber of Commerce created cartoons for kids starting in the 1950s. In 1972, the NFIB joined the tradition, creating an education department that targeted the country's elementary schools, high schools, and colleges.[8]

In the 1970s, as the economy groaned under stagflation and public disillusion with liberalism grew, the NFIB followed the trend among business groups to create political action committees (PACs) that solicited and doled out campaign contributions. (Business-oriented PACs had been relatively rare until the mid-1970s, when the Federal Election Campaign Act and subsequent Supreme Court decisions clarified the legality of the system.)[9] Formed in 1977, the NFIB's PAC cast itself as strictly nonpartisan by applying a simple but rigid test to determine which candidates it would support. Known internally as the "70/40 rule," the policy insisted that an incumbent had to vote according to

---

* Jude Wanniski, the conservative economics editor at the *Wall Street Journal*, published a book with that title in 1978, laying out many of the anti-regulatory, anti-tax arguments associated with Reaganomics in the 1980s. Wanniski would go on to become a prominent Reagan advisor.

NFIB positions 70 percent of the time to be eligible for support. If the incumbent voted with the NFIB less than 40 percent of the time, the challenger would get the group's money instead.[10]

By the late 1970s, the NFIB had distinguished itself as the definitive mouthpiece of independent business owners. With hundreds of thousands of members receiving and responding to its surveys—and gaining an insider's view into how their representatives voted—the organization successfully created the appearance of widespread political support for its favored policies. And its star was clearly rising. Bestowing the blessing of fiscal conservatism on the small business agenda, economist Milton Friedman proclaimed: "Of the various business organizations, the only one I have found that is almost always on the right side is the National Federation of Independent Business."[11]

In 1983, Wilson Johnson retired and turned the reins over to John Sloan, the CEO of First Tennessee Bank. A former member of the Small Business Administration's National Advisory Council and the U.S. Chamber of Commerce's Small Business Council, Sloan brought an even higher degree of professionalism to the now-mature lobbying group.[12] Under his leadership, the NFIB firmly established itself on the national scene. By the late 1980s, one journalist commented, "no one on Capitol Hill thinks of small business as weak and unorganized." Instead, Sloan commented in 1989, "We have reached a maturity level that makes it easier for us to hold their feet to the fire."[13] When it came to amplifying the voice of Main Street in the halls of Congress, the NFIB led the way.

———

As Wilson Johnson worked to bolster the NFIB's political clout from his headquarters in California in the 1970s, another group of business owners was getting organized in the nation's capital with a very different conception of the problems their companies confronted. A corporate offshoot of the broad-based movement known as second-wave feminism, the National Association of Women Business Owners (NAWBO) took shape amid the same tense political and economic environment that underlaid the NFIB's expansion. Yet for its founders, the central challenge they faced was not merely the size of their firms but the gender of their owners.

As with many entrepreneurial origin stories, often embellished over years of retelling, NAWBO's began with an "aha!" moment.[14]

In the early 1970s, Denise Cavanaugh and Dottie Gandy owned a consulting firm in Washington, D.C., that specialized in employee training. Like many independent business operators, they found that their expertise and "market edge" did not always extend to all the nitty-gritty aspects of running their company. In their case, the problem was the paper they needed to print brochures.

"The printer kept showing us all this paper stock, and I know nothing about paper stock," Cavanaugh recalled. "We said, 'We'll come back later. Who do we know who knows about paper?'"

But that was the rub. If Gandy and Cavanaugh had been members of the local Rotary Club or the United States Junior Chamber (the Jaycees), they would have had an obvious network of contacts to mine for referrals, suggestions, and advice. But business groups like that did not admit women members. (The Jaycees, formed in 1915, offered to make Gandy and Cavanaugh "honorary wives." The organization officially admitted women in 1984.)[15] At the time, the women's movement was only in the early stages of its campaign against sex discrimination in public spaces, including business associations and other professional clubs. And even as some of the old walls of discrimination, including prohibitions on married women taking out loans in their own names, began to crumble, the old-boy networks persisted. Institutions that built "social capital" among business owners, middle managers on the rise, and executives in the high-rise offices were largely out of reach for women.[16]

Facing those roadblocks, Gandy and Cavanaugh decided they needed to create their own networks—an "old-girls" system, as they called it. Through regular meetings in the back of their D.C. office, they brought together a community of women business owners. First six, then eight, then a dozen attended, sharing ideas, experiences, and professional advice. "In the beginning we certainly did not have the vision of starting a national organization," Gandy reflected years later. The real purpose was mutual support and creating a network of references: "I'll market your business, if you market mine," she explained.[17]

NAWBO emerged in a period marked by tremendous social change. Years of protest, lobbying, and litigation by women activists changed the landscape for women in public life and in employment. Feminist political organizing led to state and federal restrictions on sex discrimination, opening up new business opportunities. Especially important was the Equal Credit Opportunity Act of 1974. Its first incarnation banned bankers from discriminating against would-be borrowers on the basis of sex or marital status; it was later expanded to prohibit discrimination based on race, age, religion, and national origin as well.[18]

In response to these achievements, the ranks of women business owners began to expand significantly. Women owned only 4.2 percent of all companies in 1972 and just 7 percent in 1977, but by the late 1980s, that figure had risen to 30 percent. What's more, the rate of business creation among women, particularly sole-proprietor (one-owner) firms, doubled that of men throughout those decades.[19] In response to the rapid growth in women-owned firms, the Small Business Administration created an "Office of Women's Business Ownership" in 1979. Its inaugural director, Sally Bender, marveled at the rapid pace of the transformation. "The massive change is that women are considering this now. Owning their own business."[20]

As the number of women-owned businesses grew, the need for an organization like NAWBO became more pressing. In 1975, the group incorporated as the Association of Women Business Owners under the leadership of founding president Susan Hager, one of three women owners of the Hager, Sharp, Klass consultancy. The next year, they added the word "National" to their title, symbolically embarking on a countrywide mission to provide contacts, networks, and advocacy for women business owners. The mission, as Hager put it, was plain: "Get a seat at the table, or build your own table, and make sure to include other women."[21]

NAWBO's founders retained a profound sense of being a part of a movement. Among their first objectives was the relatively straightforward task of raising the visibility of woman-owned firms, pushing back against the old-boy networks that stymied people like Denise Cavanaugh and Dottie Gandy.

"There are many people who would like to patronize women's businesses—especially women," explained NAWBO member Jody Johns of Baltimore. "Women would like to do business with each other."[22]

In 1976, the group secured a $20,000 grant from the Equitable Life Assurance Society of New York, one of the country's largest insurance companies, to compile a first-of-its-kind directory of approximately 1,000 woman-owned and -operated companies in the Baltimore/Washington area.[23] Over the next several years, it continued to identify and promote member companies as it established a network of regional chapters in major metropolitan areas like Chicago and Boston, and eventually nationwide. To this day, NAWBO shares lists of its members to help support their businesses.

The group's early efforts sparked criticism as well as praise, however. Predictably, some radical feminists charged that women business owners were essentially shills for corporate capitalism and patriarchy.[24] More conservative critics, on the other hand, attacked NAWBO for unfairly seeking special treatment for women business owners, in essence discriminating against men. Marianne M. Doctor of Baltimore, in a letter to the editor of *The Sun*, wondered why "we, the women, are supposed to favor women-owned businesses" at all. "Why don't women just set up their businesses and compete with men on an equal basis?" she asked.[25]

In response, Jody Johns argued that NAWBO's fundamental aim *was* to create an equal basis between men- and women-owned businesses. But doing so required recognizing the structural barriers women faced that might appear invisible to outside observers. "Frequently people think of business owners as owners of a retail store competing for the trade of the general public," she explained. Such stores competed on things like price, location, and quality, and perhaps the gender of the owner did not matter much. But, Johns continued, what the general consuming public did not always see were the "business to business" transactions: companies that "sell services and products to organizations—other businesses, public and private agencies, institutions." In those interactions, "women entrepreneurs experience pervasive discrimination"—including stereotypes about their abilities and "deeply imbedded feelings about 'women's place.'" By actively publicizing women-owned businesses through directories, NAWBO hoped to interrupt those patterns and create a level playing field where none existed. In addition, Johns explained, directories would also "enable women business owners who are tired of dealing with sexist male suppliers to do business with women who will treat them as people" and "dispel some ignorance about the kinds of businesses owned and managed by women."[26]

NAWBO's commitment to combating systemic sexism through community- and network-building gave a corporate gloss to strategies deployed by the women's movement more broadly. Indeed, many of the group's founders played prominent roles in the struggle against patriarchal notions of "separate spheres" and "women's work" as active members of the women's movement. Among the most prominent was Mary E. King, part of the initial cohort of NAWBO founders. A civil rights activist and organizer with the Student Nonviolent Coordinating Committee (SNCC), King rose to national prominence in 1965 as coauthor—with Casey Hayden—of a widely circulated essay "Sex and Caste: A Kind of Memo." King and Hayden drew attention to the discrimination, exploitation, and obstacles that women in the civil rights movement encountered and formed an essential part of an emerging feminist consciousness within activist circles.[27]

In 1968, King moved from social activism to government, spending four years at the Office of Economic Opportunity. There, she helped implement legislation that mandated the creation of neighborhood health services facilities aimed at the nation's rural and urban poor. In 1972, she entered the private sector, launching a consultancy in Washington, D.C. (Consulting was a common avenue for independent business ownership among professional women, perhaps because of the relative ease of entry and the direct control they maintained over how to profit from their expertise.) She participated in Gandy and Cavanaugh's early back-office meetings and served as NAWBO's second president, from 1975 to 1976, when she stepped down to join Jimmy Carter's presidential campaign.[28] On the campaign trail, she led Carter's women's affairs committee and his health-policy task force. In 1977, she became the new president's "special advisor on women," a position from which she challenged the tendency she observed for many in the administration to "feel that women are just another special-interest group that won't go away."[29]

King's frustration with White House politics reflected the challenge NAWBO faced: confronting the real impediments to women business ownership without seeing their work marginalized by stereotypes about "women's issues." As the group expanded its networks and local chapters in the late 1970s, it also mobilized politically. To put the problems of women-owned businesses on the national radar, NAWBO leaders paid personal visits to President Carter and testified before Congress.[30] In response to their advocacy, Carter appointed an Interagency Task Force on Women Business Owners in 1977 "to encourage women to become business owners, to mitigate conditions and practices that place women at a competitive disadvantage, and to enhance Federal assistance to women entrepreneurs."[31]

NAWBO's advocacy played a key part in raising the public profile of women-owned businesses, as well as the structural challenges they faced. Carter's task force released the first national study of women business owners in 1979, shortly after which the SBA created its Office of Women's Business Ownership. In the 1980s, NAWBO's role in national affairs grew, ensuring that its members were elected as delegates from every state to the 1986 White House Conference on Small Business (the Reagan administration's follow-up to the conference Jimmy Carter hosted in 1980). In 1988, it helped push through the Women's Business Ownership Act, which expanded government set-aside programs and provided SBA funding for woman-run start-ups.[32] From its backroom origins, the group had grown into a national powerhouse.

Like the NFIB, NAWBO combined its ideological commitment to its constituency with savvy political organizing to get its voice heard. The divergent histories of those two organizations illustrate how widespread and diverse the growing political power of independent businesses was. Yet in their own ways, each also typified a growing consensus within the community of small business owners that increasingly dovetailed with the agenda of large corporations. When it came to the pressing question of what role government should play in private enterprise, business owners of all stripes tended to converge. While NAWBO devoted most of its early energies to *using* the power of the state to address discrimination and level the playing field, by the 1980s it largely adopted the policy positions of traditional economic conservatives. As a result, it took on a much more anti-government tone.

———

Amid the economic turmoil of the 1970s, popular grievances were widespread, and the federal government came in for especially harsh judgment. The prevailing sentiment was neatly captured in a story that *Nation's Business* magazine ran in 1977.

What was the biggest problem independent business faced? a reporter asked William Alton Carter III, owner of an Amoco gas station and family-run farm products enterprise in rural Georgia. His answer: government.

"No question about it, government at all levels," he elaborated, "but especially at the federal level."

Of course, businesspeople had always complained about the government and its rules and regulations. NFIB founder Wilson Harder had built his whole organization on that principle, after all. What's more, since the mid-1960s, a wave of consumer, environmental, and workplace safety and protection laws had dramatically increased the complexity and cost of regulatory compliance, further revving up the critique. So this particular denunciation of government overreach from a Southern business owner was in many ways unremarkable.

What made it especially damning, though, was that it came from the younger brother of the man who, a few months earlier, had moved into the White House.

Billy Carter, it turned out, was more than a gas-station owner. Fifteen years younger than his famous brother, Jimmy, he was also one of seven joint owners of Carter Farms, Inc., which grew peanuts on a 3,000-acre plot outside the town of Plains, Georgia, and manager of Carter Warehouse. Throughout his brother's presidency, Billy developed a national reputation, as *Nation's Business* put it, as "a hell-raising, hard-drinking, irreverent yokel." A prolific beer drinker, he licensed his name to the makers of "Billy Beer," which created a pop-culture sensation as a collector's item, although not a sustainable business model. (Apparently quite unpalatable, the product was discontinued after a year.) His business aspirations also created embarrassing headaches for the president: Billy's attempt to buy out his brother's stake in the warehouse business, which Jimmy had put into a blind trust managed by longtime associate Charles Kirbo, led Kirbo to force him out of the business in September 1977. Even more seriously, Billy used his famous name to successfully solicit business loans from the Libyan government, spawning a Senate investigation.[33]

Although Billy Carter became something of a political punch line, his condemnation of the government's intrusion into the workings of small businesses was anything but crude. In his own folksy way, he embodied a persistent and ever-more-vocal critique within the politics of business ownership. At the heart of it was the accusation that a vast array of government policies—from workplace safety rules and environmental protection to labor laws and the minimum wage—conspired against salt-of-the-earth entrepreneurs like him.

What made workplace regulations especially insidious to small operators, Billy Carter explained, was the costs of taking precautions that seemed like unnecessary overkill. "We had to spend $400 for some guardrails up there," he told the *Nation's Business* reporter, pointing to the top of a grain elevator at the Carter Warehouse, even though "one man might go up there once a year." All told, Carter claimed, his family spent $1.2 million on warehouse improvements to comply with government regulations.

Big government also drove up the cost of labor, Billy Carter argued. Everything from federal support for labor unions to workplace safety measures made it more expensive to employ people. The minimum wage came in for special critique. First enshrined in law in the Fair Labor Standards Act of 1938, the real (inflation-adjusted) minimum wage peaked in 1968 and then declined during the inflationary recessions of the 1970s. (In nominal terms, the minimum wage was $1.60/hour in the late 1960s; that would be around $14 in 2023.) Increases in the statutory minimum in 1974, 1975, and 1976 clawed back some of those losses, but the trend toward a lower real minimum wage continued.[34]

Even though the real minimum wage was falling, those nominal increases were too much for independent business owners like Billy Carter. "Every time the minimum wage goes up," he said, "we have to lay off a few more people." And economics aside, Carter noted, he simply disagreed with the principle of the thing, even if saying as much was politically inconvenient for his brother. "You know, I shouldn't be talking like this. . . . But I'm going to say it again. A lot of people simply aren't worth the minimum wage," he confided.[35]

Billy Carter's story resonated with the small and independent business community precisely because it reflected the central arguments that were fast becoming mainstays of the "business lobby" rhetoric in Washington. As the NFIB expanded its lobbying prowess in the 1980s, it joined forces with the major mouthpieces of large firms—the U.S. Chamber of Commerce, the Fortune 100-centered Business Roundtable, and the National Association of Manufacturers, in particular—in a full-court press against regulations and worker protections. "Congress needs to revise [the Occupational Safety and Health Administration's] basic philosophy from one of punishing businesses, often capriciously, to one of *encouraging and assisting businesses to improve workplace safety*," the NFIB argued in 1981 (emphasis added).[36] Don't make us do it, they argued. Make us *want* to do it.

NAWBO, for its part, navigated the political scene somewhat differently. Rather than situate itself within traditionally libertarian circles and align against liberal government regulatory and labor policies, the organization instead found itself squaring off against other interest groups. Yet even so, it ultimately wound up on the conservative side of many policy debates. Despite the close institutional links between the women's business movement and the civil rights struggle—through the experiences of women like Mary King—tense conflicts emerged. If the NFIB saw itself as part of a war on government itself, NAWBO clashed over whom the government should support and how.

NAWBO faced particular challenges when the politics of gender intersected with the politics of race. As the organization expanded its influence, a number of vocal Black leaders argued that it was too focused on gender-based discrimination against white women business owners and insufficiently attuned to the challenges that women business owners of color faced. Black businesses in general had suffered disproportionately during the recessions of the 1970s, and Black women were particularly underrepresented among business owners.[37] In the wake of President Carter's announcement of a task force on women business owners, Inez Kaiser—president of the National Association of Minority Women in Business—argued that NAWBO was too white. And as a result, she argued, women's business activism paid too much attention to sex discrimination at the expense of awareness of racial discrimination. Such a course would only perpetuate the neglect and marginalization of minority businesswomen.

"The time has come for us to be heard and we as minority female business owners are given the same consideration as our counterparts," Kaiser said. "As tax payers in this country of ours, we are financing programs that non-minority women business owners are receiving the most benefits from."[38]

A particularly fierce conflict unfolded over the minority-owned business set-aside initiatives at the Small Business Administration known as "Section 8(a)" programs. Under the original Small Business Act, the SBA was permitted to enter specific contracts with "any small business concerns." In the wake of protests and violence in the mid-1960s, the Johnson and Nixon administrations informally used the language in Section 8(a) of the law to provide "special encouragement" (in the words of the 1967 *Kerner Report*, written by the presidential commission created to study the country's race problems) to Black-owned companies. In 1978, Congress amended the Small Business Act to explicitly empower the SBA to subcontract with "socially and economically disadvantaged small business concerns."[39]

Would that category include women? NAWBO leaders believed that it should. National president Dona O'Bannon (who succeeded Mary King in 1977) argued that the quantity of federal contracts available far outstripped the number of minority-owned businesses able to fill them. Sharing some of that federal bounty with companies owned by white women would provide a boon without hurting anyone else, she maintained.

But minority business owners and their political advocates disagreed. "If white women get into 8(a), we can forget it," proclaimed Sidney Daniels of the National Association of Black Manufacturers. "If procurement agencies ever have to make a choice between dealing with a white firm and dealing with a minority firm, the white firm is going to get the contract, female or not. Cut and dried. We've made a lot of progress in this country, but not that much," Daniels concluded.[40]

Ultimately, the 8(a) program did not expand its purview to consider women as a "socially and economically disadvantaged group" for contracting purposes. It does, however, offer some special opportunities for women. The SBA's Women-Owned Small Business Federal Contract Program sets a goal of awarding 5 percent of its contracting and subcontracting budget to women-owned small companies. Nonetheless, the central tensions that emerged in the 1970s and 1980s were never resolved, and the debate persisted for decades to come.

————

Once upon a time, a journalist summarized in the late 1970s, independent business owners "whispered complaints that sounded much like Rodney Dangerfield's punchline, 'I don't get no respect.' But lately they've been griping loudly, and politicians and candidates are returning their phone calls, answering their surveys, inviting them for consultations on issues such as inflation, overregulation and paperwork, and addressing their groups' meetings."[41] Emerging from the wreckage of the 1970s economy, the community of business owners had found a way to get organized.

The NFIB firmly ensconced itself within national politics and policymaking during the 1980s. Its staff members kept close tabs on a wide array of policy issues that affected the costs small companies bore, from workplace and environmental regulations to employee benefits and healthcare, as well as fiscal policy. Its success in computerizing data and targeting messages to specific business owners turned its 600,000 members into a grassroots lobbying force. "My problem now is to keep them all happy and working," said the group's chief lobbyist, John Motley, in 1990.[42]

NAWBO likewise achieved a level of influence beyond the dreams of its founders, helping make women into the new face of business ownership in the United States. Research groups, some independent and some linked to universities, formed to collect data and conduct studies to support political advocacy. Those groups included NAWBO's research and leadership development arm, the National Foundation for Women Business Owners (NFWBO), as well as the National Education Center for Women in Business (NECWB).[43] During the George H. W. Bush administration, Republican politician Susan Engeleiter—the first woman to head the Small Business Administration—boasted of the substantial increase in women-owned businesses. Counting both employer and non-employer firms, women owned about one-third of all American companies. There was, Engeleiter boasted, "great potential for women to add even more vitality to the national economy."[44]

The political mobilization of independent business owners marked a powerful turn in national life, and the political class was paying attention. On Capitol Hill, as a reporter for the *Washington Post* noted, politicos no longer thought "of small business as weak and unorganized. Members on both sides of the aisle recognize that small-business owners are numerous, well-organized and very combative."[45]

By the 1980s, years of mobilizing by organizations like the NFIB and NAWBO had successfully redefined the nation's political agenda and drawn strength from an evolving culture rooted in individual initiative. While both the NFIB and NAWBO have persisted to the present, their most significant contributions to national political culture came in those early years, when they successfully cultivated a sense of community and common purpose among the owners and operators of independent companies. In a political environment so often remembered for President Ronald Reagan's folksy hostility to big-government liberalism, the movement of business owners fit in perfectly.

Their organizational efforts laid vital groundwork for a cultural change in how people thought about business ownership in general and business *start-ups* in particular. In Reagan's America, as the economy finally emerged from its prolonged collapse and began, haltingly and unequally, to improve, a new public fascination with entrepreneurship began to take hold. More and more, being a business owner became synonymous with being an entrepreneur, and being an entrepreneur meant being at the center of economic growth. If you could jump on that train, you could live the dream of working for yourself. Running a sleek and sophisticated new company would put you on the imagined path to a prosperous future.

4

WHITE-COLLAR GROWTH MACHINE

n the first half of 1980, the owner of a specialty steel mill in Philadelphia saw orders dry up and his business fall off by 20 to 30 percent.
"We are going through a catastrophic era, the worst business conditions since the 1930s," he reported.

A third-generation owner of a department store in Provo, Utah, also
faced ruin. In the wake of inflation and recession, consumer spending
was cratering. "Ironic, isn't it?" the store owner observed. "My grandfather broke away from J.C. Penney's to start his own business at the
height of the Depression in 1936." The grandfather had made it, but in
1980, his grandson didn't. He couldn't compete with the lower prices at
the national-name stores at the mall, and he couldn't afford to borrow
the money it would take to transition into a niche boutique—not with
interest rates at 20 percent.

"So we decided to go out in style," he explained. "We had a
grand closing."[1]

It's perhaps too easy to overlook how sharp the economic contraction
that began in the 1970s was, and how long its effects lingered. The third
recession of the post-postwar economy began in early 1980 after new
Federal Reserve Chair Paul Volcker committed to wringing out inflation, which had hit an annual rate of 14 percent, with a rigidly tight
monetary policy. He succeeded eventually, but only by thrusting the
economy into a nosedive. Officially, a "recovery" began that July, but it

The "Unfavorable Economic Indicators"

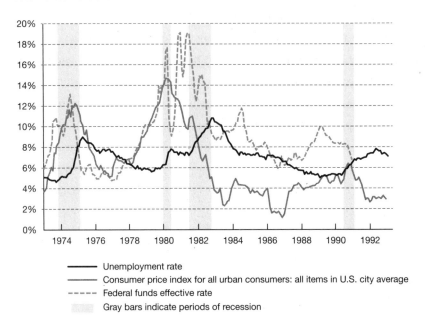

- ——— Unemployment rate
- ——— Consumer price index for all urban consumers: all items in U.S. city average
- - - - - Federal funds effective rate
- ▭ Gray bars indicate periods of recession

High interest rates set by the Federal Reserve ultimately brought the rate of inflation down in the early 1980s, but at the cost of sky-high unemployment and business failures. *Source: U.S. Bureau of Labor Statistics; Board of Governors of the Federal Reserve System.*

lasted only a year. Just six months into Ronald Reagan's presidency, in mid-1981, the economy contracted again. Unemployment peaked at 10.8 percent in December 1982, and it didn't drop until the following summer.* And even though the *rate* of inflation declined, consumer prices still increased—by 10 percent in 1981 and 6 percent in 1982.[2] New home sales hit their second lowest level on record, and car sales fell 44 percent in 1982. Businesses failed 55 percent more often in 1982 than in 1981.

"On paper, statistics like these are known as 'unfavorable economic indicators,'" opined Sen. Lowell Weicker, the Connecticut Republican who became chair of the Small Business Committee when the GOP

---

* Economists refer to this economic frailty as a "double-dip" recession. For people living through it, it felt like one big recession.

gained a majority in the Senate in 1981. "In the real world, every one of them marks a living, breathing human tragedy."[3]

The economic despair of the early 1980s ran far deeper than a downturn in the business cycle. The underlying conditions—slow productivity growth, stagnating wages, business failures—pre-dated the anti-inflationary monetary austerity that Volcker triggered, and they endured long after Reagan pronounced "Morning Again in America" when he ran for reelection in 1984. The "living, breathing human tragedy" that Weicker called out became a persistent feature of American life, whether the overall economy was growing or shrinking. Plant relocations—to lower-wage states, as well as to lower-wage countries—restructured the labor market, as service-sector jobs replaced manufacturing positions.[4] Jobs in services were generally less well paid than jobs in manufacturing, where labor unions had historically been stronger. The result of this long-term recalibration was a total reshuffling of employment options. For millions of Americans, work became less permanent, benefits less secure, and wages less gainful. The big, hierarchical corporations that had bestrode the business landscape in the 1950s and 1960s looked like outdated relics, incapable of replicating the growth of the postwar period and stumbling toward a stagnant future.

In response, a powerful new idea about business quickly achieved near-total ideological hegemony and popular consensus: the future would be built not by institutions but by *individuals*. The road to renewed growth would be paved by those brave risk-takers who embraced change and started their own companies. In a stagnant economy, a loud set of voices insisted, regular people with drive, moxie, and ideally some venture capital could shake free of the rigid bonds of corporate America and kick-start the economy. New, homegrown companies would not only be more *virtuous* than big businesses, but they would also prove to be economically *essential*. The United States could recover its lost dynamism, but only by tapping the innovative potential of *entrepreneurs*.

This faith in the power of entrepreneurship has, in the past several decades, become firmly embedded in how we talk about economic life. It is a truth universally acknowledged that new business ventures are the beating heart of modern capitalism. In a political culture that cannot agree on anything, there is virtual consensus that entrepreneurs are the risk-takers, job-creators, and industry-disruptors that make the world go around.

Given the potency of this conviction, we tend to forget that people have not always thought that way. Throughout most of the twentieth century, mainstream economic thinkers did not generally pay much attention to entrepreneurship. They focused on the potential of large institutions, not individual initiative. Economist John Clark of Columbia University, writing in 1942, concluded that "the coming of the large corporation means a splitting-up of the entrepreneur function until it merges indistinguishably into investment and management."[5]

Although that consensus held for decades, interest in entrepreneurship slowly began to grow. From murmurs at a handful of business schools and economics departments, the idea burst full-bore into the public conversation by the early 1980s, propelled by both the collapse of the postwar growth economy and the power of an organized intellectual community. Seemingly overnight, talk of entrepreneurs and entrepreneurship was everywhere. One study of the frequency of the word "entrepreneurship" in each issue of the *Harvard Business Review* found that it rose from the low single digits in the early 1970s to consistently surpass 40 by 1990.[6] Courses on starting a new business exploded onto business school campuses. Whole magazines launched—with names like *Entrepreneur* (1977) and *Inc.* (1979)—providing models and examples of entrepreneurial success stories. "Entrepreneurship centers" emerged at academic facilities around the country. By the end of the 1980s, commentators regularly bragged that they were living in the "era of the entrepreneur."[7]

All that celebration, however, often obscured important debates about what entrepreneurship was or how it affected the economy. Academics offered formal definitions, identifying an entrepreneur as the person who took risks associated with uncertainty or someone who combined economic resources in a novel or innovative way, creating new value in the process. More popularly, the term quickly became synonymous with having the gumption to start a new business, whether or not that business was in any way distinctive from other businesses.[8] (Today, many people would describe the two teenagers I pay to do yardwork for me as "entrepreneurial.") And as the concept spread in popularity, it eventually came to apply to *any* creative, rule-bending, or "disruptive" behavior, even by someone working inside a large organization like a corporation, government agency, or university. The term "intrapreneur," referring to someone behaving in an entrepreneurial way within a preexisting structure, appears to have emerged and gained greater usage starting in the early 1980s.

Prior to the 1980s, most conversations about entrepreneurs focused on their adventurousness and individualism. In 1975, University of Texas management professor Albert Shapero summarized that consensus aptly in *Psychology Today*. Yes, he concluded, the "figure of the entrepreneur stands tall in American folklore and history." But the appeal was deeply personal. Americans naturally pondered "how satisfying it would be to grab control of life, to be more than wage slave, to make events happen instead of waiting for the world to move and shake us." Starting one's own business was, for a certain type of person, a path to Jeffersonian independence.[9]

Yet in response to continued stagnation, academics and policy activists began to promote a different vision of entrepreneurship—as a savior for a sickly economy. As New York University economist William Baumol explained in 1998: "Entrepreneurial activity became a concern to the general public in the 1980's when we all thought that the United States was falling behind, and that the rest of the world, particularly Japan, would sink us." As people grew convinced that "America had lost the spirit of entrepreneurship," Baumol continued, "we began self-consciously to reacquire that spirit."[10]

This widespread embrace of entrepreneurship had important consequences for public policy. Liberal and conservative politicians alike called for more funding for new business ventures, frequently to the exclusion of other economic programs. Political debates over taxes, social spending, environmental regulations, and labor protections were all shaped by the conviction that entrepreneurship had to be fostered first and foremost.

The rapid rise of entrepreneurial culture was the product of deliberate organizational and intellectual work spearheaded by political activists, academics in business schools and management programs, and politicians from both parties. Whatever their approach, all were trying desperately to combat the "unfavorable economic indicators" that lay largely beyond their control. Through their movement-building, this cohort of self-interested parties—all "entrepreneurial" in their own ways—helped reset popular ideas about how the economy worked, where value lay, and what role individual Americans could play in it all.

———

Robert Rosenberg was born into the restaurant business. His father, William, opened the first Dunkin' Donuts in Quincy, Massachusetts, in 1950. In 1963, when the younger Rosenberg took over the company, more than 100 Dunkin' Donuts outlets dotted the Bay State, and Robert—twenty-five years old with a Harvard MBA—set his sights on national expansion. By the time Ronald Reagan became president in 1981, Rosenberg had opened or franchised more than 1,000 locations.* Even in the worst of the stagflationary crisis, people liked doughnuts, and Dunkin' was a *growth* company.[11]

Much of Rosenberg's energy, in fact, was focused on moving into overseas markets like Japan. But expanding abroad meant complying

---

* He also served as chairman of the board of the International Franchise Association, which his father had helped found—more on them in chapter 6.

with complex regulations, such as filling out paperwork required under the Foreign Corrupt Practices Act, which bans bribing foreign officials to gain preferential treatment. Echoing the anti-regulatory animus of business owners like Billy Carter, Rosenberg complained that mid-size companies like his didn't have the kinds of sophisticated auditing or compliance departments that large multinationals did—even though he was successfully growing, while so many large corporations stagnated. "We have had to survive and grow in a kind of hostile environment," he told a reporter. Perhaps, he hoped, the new Reagan administration could do "something about cutting down the paper and the regulations," so companies like his could grow in a more "unfettered" way.[12]

Early in Reagan's term, Rosenberg joined approximately 100 other leaders of mid-size companies to form a new organization, the American Business Conference (ABC), that promised to become the major political advocate for fast-growing firms like his. With founding members that included manufacturers like the Toro lawn-and-garden-machine company, Huffy Bicycles, and accounting firm Arthur Andersen, the new group represented a wide range of industry types as well as firm sizes; members brought in annual revenues anywhere from $20 million to $1 billion. Far more important than their absolute size, though, was their growth: all ABC companies boasted annual growth rates of at least 15 percent during the previous five years. Put another way, during the worst of the economic slump in the latter half of the 1970s, Rosenberg and his fellow ABC members had managed to double the size of their companies.[13]

The driving force behind this new institutionalized voice for entrepreneurs was none other than Arthur Levitt of the American Stock Exchange, who conceived the idea in the late 1970s while planning Jimmy Carter's Small Business Conference. As he surveyed the landscape of Washington politics, Levitt concluded that business's influence on policymakers was skewed in ways that were not only unfair but also counterproductive. Giant companies—the household names that populated the Fortune 500—got plenty of attention from politicians, and major lobbying groups like the Business Council (founded in the 1930s) and the Business Roundtable (created more recently in the early 1970s) made sure that big corporations' concerns were top of mind among legislators. Small businesses had the National Federation of Independent Business speaking for them, and specific sectors, from manufacturing to banking to realtors, all had their trade associations, too.[14] What was missing from that ecosystem, Levitt believed, was someone to represent the companies that held the keys to economic recovery and growth.

"I decided," he recalled, "that if there was going to be a more meaningful government-business dialogue, it would have to be with more risk-oriented, upstart firms."[15]

In February 1981, Levitt formally unveiled his new organization. And while he personally provided the vision and drive, he outsourced the day-to-day leadership to thirty-six-year-old John M. Albertine, who became the ABC's first president. The son of a coal-mining family from Pennsylvania, Albertine had earned a PhD in economics from the University of Virginia in 1975 and taught economics at Mary Washington College thereafter. More recently, he had worked as a staffer on Capitol Hill and directed Congress's Joint Economic Committee, a bipartisan group of senators and House members that evaluates economic conditions and makes policy recommendations.[16]

As the ABC president, Albertine quickly became a loud critic of the status quo. While all business associations denounced traditionally liberal positions on taxes, regulation, and labor, the ABC distinguished itself through its full-throated attack on what Levitt and Albertine called "bureaucratic arteriosclerosis" *within* the corporate world. That focus shaped both the group's policy agenda and how it recruited members to the cause.

The conglomerate wave of the 1960s—the trend of big corporations with names like LTV and Gulf+Western expanding into a wide range of unrelated sectors—had long since crested by the early 1980s, but it left behind an important legacy: the belief that multi-unit, highly diversified companies could be managed like investment portfolios by well-credentialed generalists, shifting resources from division to division in complex arrangements.[17] But in the eyes of the ABC, that type of business-school mumbo jumbo created precisely the stagnation they were trying to fix. Levitt and Albertine didn't want "portfolio managers" in their new club. They wanted strong leaders who were not hoodwinked by the fancy planning tools, growth-share matrices, and complex market analyses that predicted which sector of the economy was ripe for exploitation. The ideal business owner, they believed, embraced "value and innovation, entrepreneurial leadership, common-sense organization," all of which "contradict the false conventional wisdom that once passed as sophisticated management."[18] Unlike the corporate dinosaurs, ABC executives would be "fanatics for fundamentals." Personally involved in their businesses, they sought to "encourage experimentation, not bureaucracy."[19]

Bill McGowan was exactly the kind of "entrepreneurial CEO" that Levitt and Albertine had in mind. Twice a year, the founder and CEO of telecom upstart MCI would lecture his new managers on the importance of leaving old-style corporate bureaucracies behind: "I know that some of you, with your business-school backgrounds, are out there already beginning to draw organization charts and to write manuals for operating procedures," McGowan told his team. "As soon as I find out who you are, I'm going to fire every last one of you."[20]

A study by consulting giant McKinsey, commissioned by the ABC, lent its authority to Levitt and Albertine's quest to root out bureaucracy and unleash the power of the business world. The winning formula, the report concluded, was to capture small firms' energy and adaptability and to deploy those traits at high-growth, mid-size firms. This fixation on energy, adaptability, and relative lack of structure—all trademarks of small companies—amounted to a direct attack on accepted notions of management theory. As business historian Alfred Chandler famously argued in his 1977 Pulitzer Prize–winning book *The Visible Hand*, it was precisely the creation of managerial hierarchies that allowed big corporations to take off in the mid-nineteenth century, generating the scale and scope that small firms could never hope to match.[21] A decade before the computer technology industry would make headlines for its antiestablishment ethos and assault on corporate hierarchies, ABC companies were already turning Al Chandler on his head.

"Winning businesses," McKinsey concluded, fought back against corporate bureaucracy in three ways.

First: "They turn their employees into entrepreneurs." Managers and employees at ABC companies owned more than 30 percent of the stock in their companies, far above the typical levels at large corporations. Some even adopted "no-layoffs" policies, making clear the company's commitment to its employees.

Second: "They shun traditional management overhead functions." Four out of ten ABC companies did not have planning departments, preferring instead to integrate responsibility for planning, personnel, and communications into the purview of the managers responsible for different product lines or business divisions. "The winners," McKinsey argued, "let general managers be general managers."

Finally: "Top management signals clearly that it will not tolerate bureaucratic behavior." Bill McGowan may have been an extreme example, threatening to fire anyone who created an org chart or job title, but he typified a spirit of radical nonconformity that, for Albertine and Levitt, was essential to breaking the grip of corporate bureaucracy and spurring entrepreneurship.[22]

The ABC's distaste for corporate bureaucracy dovetailed with its policy agenda, since its leaders detected the same evils in the political establishment that they saw in corporate America. From the get-go, the group made explicit overtures to the "supply side" wing of the Reagan administration—those policy advisors who argued that the key to economic recovery was always *less*: less government debt that raised interest rates, less taxation that disincentivized work and investment, and less regulation that drove up the costs of doing business.

Two prominent supply-siders headlined the ABC's coming-out party at the Four Seasons Hotel in Georgetown in early 1981. One was Congressman Jack Kemp, a Republican from New York chiefly known—in addition to having been a quarterback for the Buffalo Bills in the 1960s—for championing dramatic cuts in marginal tax rates.* The second was David Stockman, former congressman and newly appointed director of the Office of Management and Budget, who would go on to engineer the sweeping spending cuts that accompanied Reagan's tax reform. Stockman and Kemp's vision of a streamlined, accountable federal government—run like a business—was a perfect match for the antibureaucracy, antiestablishment mood of the charter ABC members.

The now-defeated Carter administration, Stockman told the crowd, had managed to generate an unacceptable $50 billion cost overrun. "If the companies of the American Business Conference, which have realized a 29 percent growth record in 1980, had done such a poor job of projecting their budgets," he concluded, "they would not be here today." The assembled crowd—from Dunkin' Donuts' Bob Rosenberg to Jack Albertine—roared with applause.[23]

Within a few years, Levitt's evangelism and Albertine's public-relations savvy had brought the ABC into the firmament of corporate lobbying. In short order, the group rivaled the Chamber of Commerce,

---

* Kemp's tax cuts formed the basis of the Economic Recovery Tax Act of 1981, which Reagan signed into law later that year. Supply-siders famously promised that lower tax rates "pay for themselves." Their argument was that lower taxes would stimulate economic growth and thus create *more* income to be taxed. Even at a lower tax rate, they claimed, the government could collect the same amount of revenue as before, and therefore tax cuts would not create a budget deficit. This has, in practice, never happened.

the National Association of Manufacturers, and the Business Round-table in terms of clout with Congress and the White House.[24] *Fortune* magazine dubbed Albertine the "hottest lobbyist in town" in the summer of 1983.[25]

President Reagan agreed. "You have achieved a remarkable recognition for an organization established only 18 months ago," he told Albertine. "Those pessimists who think American business no longer has the energy and the creativity to lead this nation into the twenty-first century should be here today."[26]

While no doubt grateful for the compliment, the ABC's leaders and members believed their mission was to transcend the world of corporate lobbyists, not join it. As the economy continued to stagnate, organized entrepreneurs loudly condemned the major business associations and the crusty old industries they served. "The big guns have no credibility anymore," said ABC member George Hatsopoulos, the founder of high-tech firm Thermo-Electron of Waltham, Massachusetts, in 1983. "Now it's up to the small and mid-size companies to take over leadership and educate both the Congress and the public."[27]

Mobilization by ABC firms played a key role in putting a new vision of entrepreneurship on the national agenda. But the campaign to educate Congress and the public also received a vital boost from another corner—the ivory towers of academia.

———

In the early 1950s, only two business-school courses on entrepreneurship were offered anywhere in the country (at Harvard and NYU). In 1970, 16 schools taught it; in 1975, 104 did; and more than 200 did so by the mid-1980s.[28] By the early twenty-first century, 1,600 business schools taught more than 2,200 courses on entrepreneurship, some 277 faculty positions had been endowed, and 44 refereed journals launched.[29]

This growing academic interest had been a long time in the making. Since the rise of modern universities in the late nineteenth century, institutions of higher education had self-consciously devoted themselves to training students for the world of white-collar employment. For business schools, which emerged from the wave of professionalization that accompanied industrialization, this meant teaching the skills students needed to succeed in the bureaucratic hierarchies of large corporations—hence the MBA: master of business administration.* By the post–World War II period, in the heyday of corporate capitalism, it made little sense to spend time studying the practicalities of starting a new company. When 188 students at Harvard Business School enrolled in 1947 in Professor Myles Mace's course "Management for New Enterprises," the first course explicitly on entrepreneurship at a modern business school, they ventured into what many would have considered a history class.[30]

The idea that entrepreneurship was a historical, not a present-day, phenomenon was, perhaps ironically, reinforced by its most famous theorist and the man most responsible for igniting academic interest in it: Austrian-American economist Joseph Schumpeter, then working across the Charles River from Professor Mace in Harvard's economics department.[31] From his early writings at the turn of the twentieth century to his highly influential 1942 book *Capitalism, Socialism and Democracy*, Schumpeter had argued that entrepreneurship—which he defined as "simply the doing of new things or the doing of things that are already being done in a new way (innovation)"—had been central to mass industrialization in the nineteenth century.[32] New firms, new ideas, and new processes, or what Schumpeter called "new combinations," were essential features of the "gales of creative destruction" (Schumpeter's famous phrase, which he borrowed from sociologist Werner Sombart) that had defined the rise of industrial capitalism.[33]

---

* Whether one agreed with business schools' practical mission or not, there was little debate that they existed to create managers. As one critic summarized in 1887, business schools "may qualify a young man to be a good clerk but they do not prepare him to be a merchant in the wider and nobler meaning of the word."

Central to Schumpeter's conception of entrepreneurship, however, was the idea that it was rare. It didn't happen much, so when it did, the consequences were huge. For Schumpeter, in other words, entrepreneurship was a handy way to understand changes *that had already happened*. As if to reinforce the point, a cadre of Harvard professors founded the "Center for Research on Entrepreneurial History" in 1948, two years before Schumpeter died, to expand his theories into a historical research agenda.[34]

Following Schumpeter's death, however, a very different conception of entrepreneurship took root. Building on his explanation for *how* new techniques and new combinations sparked growth, a cadre of economists and business theorists began to argue that entrepreneurship was in fact far more common and more attainable, if only it could be properly nurtured. The implications of this shift were monumental: if entrepreneurship was widely achievable *and* new firms were the font of economic growth, the potential was almost magical. By the 1980s, as large corporations looked increasingly sclerotic and clunky, these neo-Schumpeterians had assembled a vast amount of theoretical scholarship to feed to a public hungry for solutions to a lackluster, low-growth economy.

Business theorist Peter Drucker was the most influential force behind the idea that entrepreneurship was for everyone and that anyone could be an entrepreneur. Austrian by birth (like Schumpeter), Drucker established himself as a prominent public intellectual while working as a professor of management at NYU in the 1950s and 1960s and then, from 1971 until his death in 2005, at Claremont University in California. In 1953, he created the *second* business school course on entrepreneurship (after Mace at Harvard), provocatively called "Entrepreneurship and Innovation."

What motivated Drucker was his observation, reinforced by a coterie of midcentury scholars, that the United States had become a "postindustrial" society. Following thinkers like sociologist Daniel

Bell, Drucker pondered the consequences of a society where technological automation and sophisticated management meant that more
jobs were white-collar and labor was more rooted in knowledge rather
than rote, routine drudgery. For Drucker, this new order meant new
possibilities: more and more workers—whether within large corporations or outside of them—could devote their time to pioneering new
and more efficient methods and techniques. All this new brainpower
meant that companies of any size could profit through innovation, not
just by oppressing their workforces, monopolizing markets, or exploit-
ing natural resources (techniques that had been dominant during the
industrial society).[35]

And since the opportunity to behave entrepreneurially was everywhere in American business, Drucker concluded, it was available to
everyone. Entrepreneurship was "a discipline," he summed up in the
mid-1980s. "And, like any discipline, it can be learned."[36]

Drucker's views had especially pronounced effects at the nation's
business schools. The technical expertise in analytics and management
tools that midcentury programs had specialized in seemed less and less
applicable in a world of stagnation and corporate downsizing. Frustrated by declining opportunities at big corporate employers, a new
generation of Baby Boomer business students began demanding new
types of training in how to start and run their own companies.

In response, the course listings for entrepreneurship exploded. Early
classes tended to be biographical, focusing on the personal characteristics of successful entrepreneurs. But by the 1980s and 1990s, the growing body of scholarship—produced by the swelling ranks of professors
and researchers—provided fodder for more practice-based courses on
things like how to secure venture financing. In addition, students could
now take more philosophical or theoretical courses, like how to develop
an entrepreneurial "mindset."[37]

This explosion in academic interest in entrepreneurship propelled a society-wide rediscovery of Schumpeter's theories, at least in

a stripped-down, easily digestible form. "Creative destruction," which for Schumpeter described a Marxian process whereby capitalism fell in on itself, became in the late twentieth century a celebratory stand-in for economic progress itself. (Its echoes were clear in the famous slogan adopted by Facebook creator Mark Zuckerberg in the early 2000s: "Move fast and break things.")[38] And before long, the appeal of entrepreneurship education spread beyond business schools. Liberal arts colleges, professional schools, and even engineering and agricultural schools all offered courses on entrepreneurship, and undergraduate business majors shot up.[39] By the year 2000, according to one survey, more than 60 percent of young Americans between eighteen and twenty-nine said they aspired to own their own business.[40]

Owning your own business—being an entrepreneur—became deeply engrained in the American psyche during the 1980s. The academic movement, along with the mass mobilization of organized groups like the ABC, offered a hot promise in the face of an otherwise gloomy economic landscape. But the power of this new ideal was not limited to the courses students took or even the decisions individual people made to jump into the entrepreneurship fray and start out on their own. It also reshaped national political battles, both affirming the Republican Party's long-standing image as the party of business and providing openings for new types of liberal Democrats to position themselves as pro-growth capitalists. At the center of those politics was a growing divide between old-style big business and the newer, sleeker companies that enthusiastically embraced the new mantra of entrepreneurship.

———

The recession that killed inflation pushed the economy to the brink in the early 1980s. Mel Boldt, who owned a small machine shop in the Chicago area, spoke not only for fellow members of the Illinois Independent Business Association (where he was the president) but also for business owners nationwide when, exasperated, he complained to a reporter in 1983: "We're bleeding in so many places and Washington isn't providing any answers. . . . It's like a rat being forced into a corner—we've got to bite back. When you drive an entrepreneur to the brink of losing his business, you're threatening his life."[41]

Two years into the so-called Reagan Revolution, the American economy continued to flail. Tax cuts, regulatory reforms, and cuts to social programs—the hallmarks of "Reaganomics"—had all gone into effect, but none stemmed the rising tide of bankruptcies among small and mid-size companies. All the platitudes in the world about the spirit of entrepreneurship did not bring customers to Mel Boldt's door.

The failure was stark, because ever since the beginning of Reagan's presidency, political appeals to small and mid-size business owners had been central to White House strategy. With their focus on growth, innovation, and regulatory reform, organizations like the American Business Conference were "at the heart of the whole Reagan philosophy, the entrepreneurial code," according to White House business liaison Wayne Vallis.[42] But maintaining their political support in a time of economic disaster posed challenges that mere slogans could not solve.

Elizabeth Dole, the Harvard-educated attorney who had led the Federal Trade Commission for five years under three presidents in the 1970s, understood the problem particularly well. As Reagan's director of the Office of Public Liaison, Dole was charged with keeping business in line, ensuring support for the administration's policies not only from chief executives but also from the panoply of lobbying groups that flooded the nation's capital.

"Small business is bedrock Republican," she told Vice President George Bush in the fall of 1981. The "small business constituency" supported "the Republican ticket in overwhelming numbers in 1980, and is vital to our political and legislative success for 1982 and 1984." But that allegiance wasn't ironclad. Reagan had to be careful, she warned, because "segments of the small business community have the general perception that this Administration favors big business and corporate America."[43] In the winter of 1983, White House staffer Red Cavaney, a former energy industry CEO who reported to Dole, shot off a memo to colleagues. Everyone should take note, he warned, of "the effort under-way by the DNC [Democratic National Committee] to wrest the loyalty of small business from the grasp of the Republicans."[44]

For Democrats, the economic travails of the early 1980s created an opportunity to paint the White House as indifferent to indepen-dent business owners. While Dole was certainly correct that the GOP reflected the "traditional" policy preferences of groups like the NFIB—less regulation, lower taxes, weaker unions and worker protections, and a lower minimum wage—the bipartisan, politically rebellious spirit of entrepreneurial start-ups altered those dynamics. The types of firms that Arthur Levitt and John Albertine united in the American Business Conference were "an exciting bunch of companies," according to Sen-ator Lloyd Bentsen, a Texas Democrat for whom Albertine had once worked as a staffer. "And in many cases, these fellows are out on the cutting edge of technology," Bentsen continued. "So we like to hear from them."[45]

Leading Democrats had long embraced a pro-business message, but the prominence of high-profile firms in fields like electronics and com-puting technology created an opening for a new breed of politician—socially liberal but economically more interested in capitalist solutions than government agencies. Journalists took to calling this group "Atari Democrats," a term coined by House Speaker Tip O'Neill's aide Chris Matthews (who went on to a career in cable news). The moniker invoked the popular videogame company that had taken over American living rooms in the 1970s and came to apply to liberal politicians who were moving away from New Deal-era fixations on labor unions and big government programs.[46] Rising stars like Gary Hart of Colorado, Paul Tsongas of Massachusetts, and, perhaps most fatefully, Bill Clinton of Arkansas and Al Gore of Tennessee, all echoed Albertine and Levitt (both Democrats) in promoting a brighter, more entrepreneurial economic future. The key, they argued, was strategically directing government programs—grants, preferential loans, and other plans—toward the right type of growing firms.[47]

To be sure, the political alliance between upstart high-technology companies and the Democratic Party—so long associated with unions and regulations—was far from perfect. Many entrepreneurs remained distrustful of "big government" and the hubris they saw behind economic planning. Even Atari's founder, Nolan Bushnell, was dismissive of Atari Democrats' proposals for incentive grants to upstart technology companies. The problem, Bushnell reasoned, was that such programs would require *government funders* to pinpoint the right places to invest. "I guarantee you that no government agency can target the right industry," he promised. "The problem is that these Atari Democrats would never have targeted Atari."[48]

Bushnell's cynicism reflected political reality: Reagan Republicans had home-field advantage when it came to the business community. The GOP had been the "party of business" since its inception in the 1850s, and Reagan's anti-government, anti-regulatory speeches resonated with owners of companies of all sizes. Nonetheless, given the growing prominence of the Atari Democrats and continued hard times, White House staffers like Elizabeth Dole and Red Cavaney believed now was not the time to take anything for granted.

"If we are unable to keep our populist underpinnings and become too heavily associated with the 'big' at the expense of the 'small,'" Cavaney worried, "this threat could pose some serious problems."[49]

What those Reagan officials understood was that long-standing tensions between large and small firms persisted despite general agreements on policy preferences. Small and mid-size business owners like Mel Boldt routinely complained that government ignored their needs, that the costs of regulatory compliance were disproportionately higher for companies without huge revenues and big accounting departments, and that high interest rates and rising labor costs hurt them worse than they hurt large corporations. Most important, echoing the critiques Albertine and Levitt deployed at the American Business Conference, small-scale proprietors saw themselves as culturally distinct from "corporate bureaucrats."

For Ronald Reagan himself, invoking the rhetoric of entrepreneurship and opportunity came naturally, but actually showing up and addressing business owners' real needs proved far more challenging. Despite his reputation as a folksy and effective communicator, he often displayed pro-big-business instincts that only exacerbated the divide between large corporations and upstarts.

"I was once asked what the difference is between a small business and a big business," Reagan commented to a meeting of minority business owners in 1987. "I answered, 'Well, a big business is what a small business would be if the government would get out of its way and leave it alone.'"

That lighthearted humor betrayed Reagan's single-minded fixation on government overreach and his lack of awareness of the cultural and structural differences between big corporations and small enterprises. Moreover, he fully disregarded the unique social and economic challenges that confronted Black- and Latino-owned companies, telling the mostly African American audience that even the civil rights movement "was in great part a struggle against discriminatory government regulations."[50]

But rhetoric was only part of the disconnect. Policy problems further exposed Reagan's myopia, not only about racial politics but also about the conflicts between big corporations and the other 99 percent of the business-owning community. Those issues came to a head in his administration's ill-fated effort to abolish the Small Business Administration.

The campaign to kill the SBA started as soon as Reagan took office, when advisors like David Stockman drew stark ideological lines in the sand over what they saw as unproductive governmental waste.[51]

And the SBA, Stockman charged, was a prime example of the "social pork barrel" spending that midcentury liberalism had inflicted on the country. Since its creation in 1953, the SBA had expanded dramatically; the volume of business loans that the agency guaranteed grew from $450 million to $3.6 billion over the course of the 1970s. For small-government purists, SBA spending—which included preferential programs for minority-owned small companies—amounted to unfair public subsidies.

In response to pressure from the supply-siders, Reagan's first budget reduced the SBA's funding, cutting the volume of loans it guaranteed in half. After he won reelection in 1984, fiscal hawks pushed him to eliminate the agency entirely. Only a fraction of companies ever availed themselves of its services, they argued. What's more, as Stockman charged, the agency systematically reallocated funds "from more creditworthy to less creditworthy firms." Propping up companies that were so weak as to require an SBA loan was, in effect, throwing good money after bad. Reagan himself embraced this harsh view of the SBA, and especially its minority set-aside programs. The whole thing, he observed, was "another example of government poking its nose into areas where it has no business."[52]

A public battle ensued. The small business lobbying community, particularly the NFIB, remained largely noncommittal—its members and leaders recognized the SBA's symbolic importance, but many agreed with Stockman's anti-government, anti-bureaucracy politics. Big banks, on the other hand, supported the SBA, largely because they profited by administering the low-risk loans.

Politicians from both parties attacked Stockman and Reagan as heartless and out of touch. Lowell Weicker, the liberal Republican from Connecticut who chaired the Senate Small Business Committee, promised Reaganites that "they were going to have a war" if they tried to abolish the SBA. When the White House proposed to do just that in 1985, Weicker forced the president to settle on a compromise—cuts of

$2.5 billion from the SBA's budget over three years. The White House again tried to get rid of the agency the following year, but once again it failed to get enough support in Congress. "The reality," SBA director Charles Heatherly explained, "is that the small business community wants an independent agency, and we accept that."[53]

The brouhaha over the SBA wasn't the only political black eye Reagan suffered by his failure to understand the appeal of independent business and that "anti-bigness" extended to the corporate sector as well as to government. In the summer of 1986, the White House held a second Conference on Small Business, fulfilling a promise made at the previous event hosted by the Carter administration. Fifty-seven state-level meetings brought together some 20,000 business owners. In August, delegates to the national event were feted by Republican legislators and cabinet members, including Elizabeth Dole, who by then was the Transportation Secretary, and her husband, Bob, a senator from Kansas. Out of some 2,200 policy recommendations put on the agenda, delegates selected 60 to forward to Congress.[54]

Despite that fanfare, one luminary failed to make an appearance. President Reagan himself departed for his summer vacation two days before the conference began, and his absence was conspicuous.

"I think the administration has pretty much given this conference a stepsister approach," explained Paul Gravett of Portland, Oregon. The owner of a hearing-aid store, Gravett had traveled across the country to help chart the future for independent shops like his. Even though he had voted for the president twice, Gravett believed Reagan's decision to skip the conference was part of a broader pattern—lots of praise and plaudits, but little in the way of real action.

Another Reagan voter, Maria Maronge of Maronge Electric Company of Louisiana, agreed. "This is a once-in-a-lifetime thing for me, and I was hoping to get a glimpse of him," she said. But in the end, Maronge felt she had been "shoved by the wayside because we're not as important as he tries to make us believe."[55]

While Reagan came across as out of touch, his successor, George Bush, worked deliberately to mend fences with the small and mid-size business community. A former business owner himself (he made a killing as a "wildcat" oil developer in West Texas in the 1940s), Bush fully embraced the political agenda laid out by groups like the ABC and the National Federation of Independent Business.

"I know that excessive regulations and paperwork requirements can strangle a business," Bush told a group of women business owners shortly before the 1988 election. "I oppose mandated benefits, for I know that they can kill small businesses and jobs." Putting a fine point on the matter, he continued: "Mandatory health insurance, in particular, could put many small businesses out of business and many people out of a job."[56]

As president, Bush committed to putting the entrepreneurial agenda into practice. His SBA administrator, Susan Engeleiter, for example, became a prominent voice for cutting the capital gains tax. Although the strongest support for cutting that tax, which is assessed on investments that increase in value, traditionally came from wealthy individuals and large financial institutions, Engeleiter linked capital gains explicitly to the fortunes of small and independent businesses. Smaller enterprises, she argued, relied on "informal investors" like family and friends, who were generally "not millionaires." Reducing the taxes they paid on the returns on those investments was crucial, or else "investors will be less willing to provide the long-term capital that small firms need."[57]

But perhaps no issue showcased the political power of the entrepreneurial agenda as much as the minimum wage. By the time Bush took office in 1989, nine years had passed since Congress had last raised the minimum wage, from $3.10 to $3.35. Inflation since then had reduced the purchasing power of that wage by more than a dollar per hour.[58] When labor advocates in Congress approved a plan to raise the minimum wage from $3.35 to $4.65, Bush found himself in a bind. Workers demanded the wage hike, but business groups denounced the plan as inflationary and unfair to small companies. The NFIB, for example, would have preferred to actually *lower* the minimum wage, but, recognizing the political impossibility of that approach, called on Congress instead to create a series of exemptions—a lower minimum for teenagers and apprenticeships, as well as a full exemption for companies with revenues below $3.5 million.[59]

What followed was high-stakes political poker. As a compromise, Bush proposed a smaller increase, to $4.25, but threatened to veto anything higher. The Small Business Legislative Council (SBLC), an umbrella group of nearly 100 trade and professional groups that represented some 4 million small companies from a range of industries, praised the president for having "struck the right balance with [his] proposal" and pledged its support.[60] Democrats in Congress thought the president was bluffing and passed a bill to raise the minimum to $4.55. A nationwide coalition of unions, civil rights groups, women's groups, and other activists all urged Bush to sign the Democrats' bill into law. But the president followed through on his threat and issued the first veto of his presidency, only fifty-five minutes after the bill passed (while flying in Air Force One, no less).[61]

Congressional supporters of the minimum wage hike failed to override the president's veto, but they ultimately settled on Bush's preferred rate of $4.25. In addition, the compromise law incorporated small business advocates' suggestion of a three-month sub-minimum "training wage" for teenagers. In 1996, Congress made that rule permanent, creating the still-used $4.25 subminimum wage for teenagers for the first ninety days of work (or about the length of a summer job). And in a final overture to the business community, Bush's minimum-wage reform—which he signed in November 1989—created a general exemption to minimum-wage rules for companies that made less than half a million dollars in annual gross sales. That provision was eliminated in 1996.[62]

By the early 1990s, the political and ideological power of business owners—hailed and defended as growth-driven entrepreneurs and innovators—had become fully woven into American politics.

———

George Bush's devotion to entrepreneurs was not enough to rescue his presidency, which faltered in the face of a steep recession in 1991. But it signaled the culmination of a ten-year campaign, spearheaded by activists, academics, and politicians, during which entrepreneurship and the economic promise of independent business ownership captured the American imagination. The mobilization of growth-oriented companies through the ABC, the explosion of academic and popular interest in entrepreneurship, and the complex, often contradictory partisan wrangling all reflected a new set of values.

Yet this revival did not play out the way earlier apostles of small and independent business had expected. Far from a return to mom-and-pop stores and Main Street values, American business in the 1980s bathed in the glitzy light of Wall Street. Those years are often remembered as the "Deal Decade," a time when hostile corporate takeovers, big-dollar mergers, and leveraged buyouts dominated the scene. The "managerial capitalism" of the mid-twentieth century had passed away. What emerged in the wake of giant conglomerates was a world of high finance, of stripped-down, agile corporations fundamentally geared toward achieving maximum short-term stock valuations.[63] The phrase "lean and mean" summed up that corporate culture. "Unlike all prior merger waves," management professor and sociologist Gerald Davis has written, "the 1980s takeovers left the average corporation smaller rather than bigger, as their unrelated parts were spun off or sold."[64] Refocused on their "core competencies," those companies became more streamlined. But they certainly did not become small.

The culture of entrepreneurship fit perfectly into that business environment. According to its most vocal apostles, entrepreneurship meant achieving growth by liberating companies from the stultifying tyranny of "regimentation"—either from government or from their own clunky structures. T. Boone Pickens, the oil tycoon who became one of the most prominent "corporate raiders" in the 1980s, pronounced the arrival of a new, fast-changing world of high-tech and global trade. What it had to overcome, he insisted, were the corporate bureaucrats and their "stifling of the entrepreneurial spirit, disregard for stockholders, and obsession with perquisites and power."[65] The fictional character Gordon Gekko in 1987's *Wall Street* made the same point in his famous "Greed Is Good" speech. Explaining to stockholders why they should sell out to him so he could take over their company, Gekko roared: "You are all being royally screwed over by these . . . these *bureaucrats!*"[66]

Under the new ethic of "shareholder capitalism," what mattered most was market capitalization—economic value, in other words. And that ethic only became more dominant as profits from financial services began their meteoric rise from the middle of the 1980s onward: in 1984, finance made about 11 percent of all corporate profits; by 1992 that figure reached 30 percent. (It topped out at 40 percent in the early 2000s.)[67] And while share prices rose, workers took the hit. Every year during the 1980s, the U.S. Bureau of Labor and Statistics found, between 1.5 and 2 million jobs were lost due to plant closures.[68]

Despite all the celebrations of Wall Street culture, the 1980s were far from an economic paradise, either for workers or for business owners. In 1987, a bipartisan congressional coalition released a sobering report on the state of American jobs and small businesses. Former presidents Ford and Carter served as honorary co-chairs of the effort, lending their imprimatur in hopes of boosting "a renaissance of entrepreneurship and business creation needed to carry America successfully into the twenty-first century." What they concluded was dire. "The era of American advantage is over," the report announced. "Modern management and finance, technology, and the worldwide increase in the education and skills of workers have created a global economy," and global competition had "exposed the shortcomings of our educational system" and "laid bare the lack of corporate readiness to compete."[69]

But if big corporations were failing to create jobs, opportunity, and growth, it was not at all clear that entrepreneurial small and independent businesses were prepared to pick up the slack. Despite all the intellectual, political, and cultural attention heaped on entrepreneurship in the 1980s, the hype far eclipsed the reality. America *wasn't* becoming more entrepreneurial. The rate of new business formation declined steadily, while the number of businesses that closed up shop (the "exit rate") rose, particularly during the relatively prosperous latter half of

Declining Business Dynamism

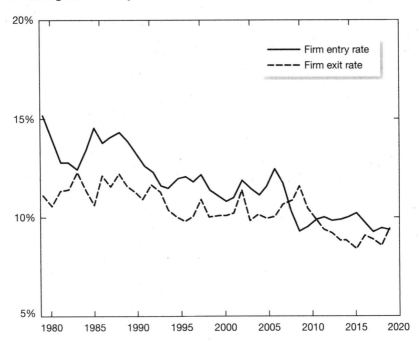

Even as "entrepreneurship" and "innovation" became national buzzwords in the 1980s and 1990s, business itself became less dynamic. A small number of new firms in a few niche industries, notably digital technology, captured headlines, but the overall trend was toward stagnation. The firm entry rate, which measures the percentage of companies less than a year old at any given time, declined by more than a third by the time the Great Recession hit in 2009. The firm exit rate, or the percentage of companies that went out of business or were absorbed by someone else in the previous year, mostly held even until the Great Recession, when it started to trend downward. *Source: Business Dynamics Statistics: "Firm Age by Firm Size, 1978–2020," U.S. Census Bureau*

the decade.[70] What's more, the share of American workers employed by new companies also trended downward, falling from close to 6 percent in 1977 to 4 percent in the early 1980s and 3 percent in 1990. (It got as low as 2 percent during the Great Recession in the early 2010s.)[71]

But it was exactly during this retrenchment that the cultural and intellectual allure of entrepreneurship exploded. As greater numbers of Americans encountered a world of work marked by low growth, stagnant real wages, and greater concentrations of wealth at the top, the promise of entrepreneurship—however far from reality—took on a renewed place in the public imagination. Whether the gospel came from business owners, consultants, professors, or politicians, the promise of going it alone attracted a widening range of everyday people who looked to business ownership as a solution to their economic anxieties.

Share of Employment in New Companies

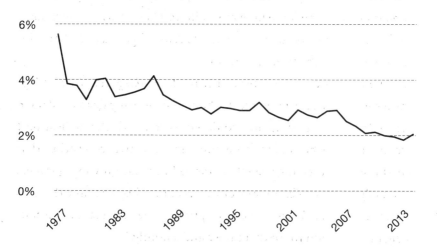

Politicians and boosters love to praise start-up companies for injecting new life into the economy. But talk of "job creators" took off exactly as the actual share of employment at new companies trended downward. *Source: Economic Innovation Group, "Dynamism in Retreat: Consequences for Regions, Markets, and Workers," February 2017, using Business Dynamics Statistics from the U.S. Census.*

5

BRING THE
WORK HOME

For Sarah Edwards, the wake-up call came when she was hospitalized for a stress-related illness. "You almost died here," her doctor told her. Change your lifestyle, or you'll be back.

At the time she fell ill, Edwards was a few years out from her bachelor's degree at the University of Missouri at Kansas City. It was the early 1970s, and she believed she was on the right track—she was married, the mother of a young child, and holding down a demanding state government job. Her employment was steady and her position prestigious, exactly what her Depression-era parents had taught her to shoot for, but she could feel the stress mounting.

As she recounted years later in her book, *Working from Home*: "Juggling a successful career and motherhood meant being dead tired most of the time and not being able to do either job with the dedication I wanted." Despite her doctor's warning and her own conviction that something had to change, she felt trapped in what growing numbers of well-educated, professional women recognized by the mid-1970s as a classic dilemma. "I didn't see any options," she concluded, "without giving up my dream for both a career and a family."

Then one day, during a work meeting at an outside consultant's home, Edwards had an epiphany. "He was doing what, at the time, seemed like a most unusual thing: operating his business from his home," she recalled. A few years later, after earning a master's degree in social work, she took the leap and opened a psychotherapy practice out of her house. The difference, she reported, was transformational: "I felt healthier immediately. For the first time in my son's young life, I could be a real mother and still pursue my career."

What Sarah Edwards came to believe was that working from home offered the perfect solution to the demands of modern life. In the years that followed, she received a PhD in psychology. In time, she resettled to the mountains outside of Los Angeles as a home-based licensed clinical social worker. Her specialties included cognitive behavioral therapy and emotional reconsolidation therapy, through which she helped patients find the emotional balance and peace that she created for herself.[1]

What's more, she did not keep her enthusiasm for her lifestyle to herself. Instead, while still maintaining her psychotherapy practice, she launched a lucrative side business encouraging others to follow her lead and find a way to work from home. In 1985, she and her husband, Paul, published a giant how-to handbook, *Working from Home: Everything You Need to Know About Living and Working Under the Same Roof*. In the years to come, the pair went on to publish more than a dozen books, write countless syndicated columns, and host radio programs on the joys and challenges of merging work and home life.[2]

As apostles for working from home, Sarah and Paul Edwards were on the vanguard of a new movement. Just as entrepreneurship and the promise of small business ownership became all the rage, people also began to turn against the very concept of the office job. Corporate downsizing, slow growth, and "lean and mean" business practices combined to place new stresses on middle-class professionals, creating an opening for new ways of thinking about work, home, and the relationship between them. Decades before the Covid-19 pandemic compelled so many people to bring their work home, Sarah and Paul Edwards were already blazing a trail.

"In the past ten years," they wrote in the introduction to their 1985 book, "people have begun to explore new options for living and working." Earlier generations of middle-class Americans, like Sarah Edwards's parents, had looked to the corporate world for security (especially the white men, for whom it was most accessible). Children of the 1960s, the Edwardses believed, were looking for a change. Working from home promised liberation, a declaration of independence of sorts. It meant saying "goodbye to the daily commute, the dead-end job, the office politics, and the feeling that everyone else was in charge of our lives," they said.[3] Baby Boomers like them had spent their youth marching for civil rights, against war and sexism, and to save the environment. As they entered middle age, many converted that revolutionary energy into a new mission—to restore balance to their lives and free themselves from the constraints of a 9-to-5.

As boosters like Sarah and Paul Edwards pointed out, there were two primary ways people could work from home. The first was telecommuting—keeping a salaried (or, far more rarely, wage-earning) job at a traditional employer but using computing and telecommunications technologies to spend some amount of time "on the clock" while at home. The second, which many enthusiasts argued was a natural progression from the first, was cutting the cord entirely and launching a home-based business.

Either approach, as Nick Sullivan of *Home Office Computing* magazine put it in 1988, represented a profound new understanding of what it meant to live and work.

"In the 1980s, the American Dream is to venture out on your own—as an entrepreneur, an independent contractor, or a corporate employee with an electronic persona," Sullivan wrote. Working from home, people could retain their independence while keeping professional connections and engaging in meaningful work. "You are remote but connected," he concluded. "Your work is national or international; your life, local."[4]

The magazine that printed Sullivan's ode typified the self-reinforcing trend of work-from-home boosterism. Originally launched by publishing giant Scholastic as *Family Computing* in 1983, the publication had first looked to tap into the popularity of Atari-style videogames and computer games. But as popular attention to working from home grew, Scholastic rebranded the magazine first as *Family & Home Office Computing*, and then just as *Home Office Computing* in 1988. Through feature articles, interviews, and mailbag advice columns, it fed the rising demand for work-from-home content even as it proselytized for new converts.[5]

And all that excited rhetoric was rooted in a real phenomenon. In the early 1980s, researchers and journalists reported anecdotal evidence that more and more people were indeed working from home.[6] Getting precise figures is notoriously difficult, and even the most sophisticated surveys could only take a stab at measuring changes in the *formal* workforce. Substantial numbers of people labored at home, as they always had, in an informal sense, doing everything from caregiving and home repairs to illicit activities. Moreover, as with most surveys of employment, the studies done in the 1980s tended to separate agricultural from non-agricultural work. Whether family farms counted as "working from home" or not was not really considered.

Despite those caveats, researchers did uncover important trends. In May 1985, the Bureau of Labor Statistics pegged the total work-from-home population (excluding farmers) at more than 17 million people. Of those, 9 million worked at home one full day per week or more, while 1.3 million worked at home full-time.[7] And in 1988, a New York–based market research firm estimated that the number of people working full-time at home had hit 4.9 million in 1987 and rose to 6 million in 1988, out of a total civilian labor force of 121 million.[8] According to at least one survey, the total number of full- and part-time home-based workers reached 20 million by 1991.[9]

Although it never became the dominant way Americans work, the movement toward working from home in the 1980s left a vital legacy. The rising numbers of home-based workers, even part-time, normalized a concept that Sarah Edwards had originally found so foreign. Abetted by corporate marketers selling the latest high-tech devices, from personal computers to fax machines, the work-from-home movement helped create the concept of the "home office" as a status symbol among middle-class professionals. Ironically, it also created a vocabulary for critiquing corporate culture even as it spread a futuristic faith in the gadgets those big tech companies produced.

The movement's primary legacy, though, was to reinforce a changing set of cultural values about employment and the imperative of going it alone. Its essential ethos was the conviction that "work" and "home" should not be separate spheres of human activity. Those elements would become persistent parts of the way many Americans came to think about their labor and economic opportunities. The loudest voices propelling this vision were self-help authors like the Edwardses, as well as journalists, academics, and professional consultants, all of whom had something to sell. These evangelists, frequently underwritten by major corporations, made their livings by drawing on cultural trends, new developments in communications technology, and a very specific sense of their historical moment to craft their message.

———

The intellectual force behind the arguments that work-from-home boosters made was bestselling author and self-described "futurist" Alvin Toffler. Born in New York to Polish Jewish immigrants in 1928, Toffler grew up challenging the materialistic assumptions of postwar American society. After launching his career as a labor columnist, first for *Labor's Daily* and eventually for *Fortune*, he rose to international prominence in 1970 with his bestselling book *Future Shock*.[10] That book took as a starting point the widespread but faulty premise that culture and technology were changing at an unprecedently rapid pace in the 1960s. Such a belief, of course, was not new in Toffler's time—since the rise of industrial society, members of each successive generation have proclaimed that they were living through historic moments of social and technological upheaval. (This remains true today!) Nonetheless, Toffler affirmed a commonly held notion, and his diagnosis of the disorienting psychological effects of what he called "information overload," or the sense of being constantly bombarded by new and different ideas, gained him a widespread readership around the country, from the counterculture to suburbia.[11]

Although *Future Shock* really put Toffler on the map, it was his follow-up hit that resonated most with work-from-home enthusiasts. In 1980, Toffler's *The Third Wave* laid out a large-scale historical and anthropological typology that captured the uniqueness of the current moment in the history of work. All of human history, he argued, could be viewed as a series of "waves" rooted in how patterns of work and production shaped social structures. The First Wave began with what is commonly called the Agricultural Revolution some ten thousand years ago, when sedentary farming and pastoral civilizations developed alongside, and eventually to the exclusion of, gathering-hunting societies. The Second Wave corresponded to the Industrial Revolution of the nineteenth century. Centered on mass production and mass consumption, industrial life stressed "standardization, centralization, concentration, and synchronization"—the hallmarks of a bureaucratically organized society. The Third Wave, Toffler claimed, was happening now. Going forward, he predicted, the rigid organizational structures of industrial society would continue to become decentralized and atomized. In this new world, old hierarchies and collectivities would become things of past. Here the individual would be king.[12]

Like many writers of the period, including business theorist Peter Drucker, Toffler was deeply influenced by the concept of the "post-industrial society," popularized by the American sociologist Daniel

Bell. As automation reduced the human labor required for industrial production, Bell and other public intellectuals argued, the central dynamics of modern society were more shaped by the production of knowledge and the provision of services than the manufacturing of material goods.

Toffler departed from Bell, though, largely through his ebullient embrace of this new social realignment. A cautious scholar, Bell worried that the consequences of the changes wrought by the postindustrial society would be dramatic and severe. While potentially positive, they also brought new threats to democracy and the social order, and they thus demanded sober, critical analysis. He had little patience with what he considered the naïve and unserious optimism of "futurists" like Toffler. In print, Bell dismissed Toffler as a "popularizer" of "deceptive" oversimplifications. In person, it is rumored, he referred to the bestselling author as "future schlock."[13]

Such ivory-tower criticism had little effect on Toffler's popular reach, however. What made his books so attractive was his ability to offer a historical framework that explained a sensation that Sarah Edwards had experienced directly: that working from home was *unusual*, that it went against the established way of doing things, but that it was also somehow liberating and progressive. Toffler gave people like Edwards a way to understand themselves as revolutionary norm-busters, the wave of the future. "Over the past thirty years," they wrote, in a clear echo of Toffler's view of human history, "the foundation of our economy has changed from an industrial base to an information and a service base." In this new economy, they believed, working from home was not only possible but inevitable.[14]

Underlying Toffler's pop-analysis of human society was an important story about the relationship between capitalist development and the location of work. While we might assume that there is a natural separation between where you live and where you work, that distinction is in fact a relatively recent historical development. For most of

the existence of our species, "home" and "work" were not distinct conceptual spaces of human endeavor. While certain jobs may have taken
people away from their domiciles—on ships, in mines, and in armies,
for example—the bulk of humanity labored where they lived, sleeping
and eating in the same places as they farmed, cooked, wove, and chis-
eled. In colonial Boston, to take a well-known example, Paul Revere's
silversmith shop and John Adams's law office were attached to their
respective houses.

That began to change with the economic takeoff that we call industrial capitalism. Beginning in England around the year 1800, the
factory system of production united labor power, production technologies, and capital—"men, machines, and materials"—under a single roof.
By the advent of the first big businesses in railroads, oil, and steel in the
late nineteenth century, thousands of laborers toiled together on the
same giant factory floor, and nobody called it "home."[15]

To be sure, that stark separation existed much more in theory than
in reality for large numbers of people. Poor and working-class people,
especially women and children, continued to labor for pay inside their
homes. Much of that labor was performed informally—that is, not as
regular employees—and in-house, from caregiving for children and the
elderly to regular maintenance of clothes and equipment to cooking
and cleaning.

Yet in terms of popular ideas about what work *should* be like, the
rise of industrial society marked an important and historic departure.
Among middle- and upper-class families in particular, "work" and
"home" became separate spheres—the former was public, profitable,
and male; the latter domestic, private, and female. Political and economic debates in the twentieth century, including especially efforts to
organize and mobilize working people into trade unions, all proceeded
from the assumption that "work" happened away from home.[16]

What Toffler predicted, and indeed argued for, was an active effort
to subvert that central feature of industrial society. As he predicted,

"our biggest factories and office towers may, within our lifetimes, stand half empty, reduced to use as ghostly warehouses or converted into living space. Yet this is precisely what the new mode of production makes possible: a return to the cottage industry on a new, higher, electronic basis, and with it a new emphasis on the home as the center of society."[17]

Among work-from-home advocates, that rebellious promise struck a chord. Working at home was, Toffler argued, the ultimate expression of an old concept: market differentiation. Since the rise of mass consumption and the advent of branding and advertising at the turn of the twentieth century, companies had sought to expand their appeal to consumers by providing greater choices. Henry Ford's old slogan about the Model T—you can have it in any color "so long as it is black"—faded away as early as the 1920s when General Motors automobiles offered different colors, trims, and updated model designs year after year. That trend only accelerated after World War II, when the mass-consumption society exploded into suburban shopping malls and fast-food franchises. Market researchers targeted ever-narrower groups of consumers, especially young people spending their parents' money.[18]

The Baby Boom generation in particular, Toffler reasoned, had grown up with more and more choices when it came to food, entertainment, hair care, you name it. It only made sense that they'd apply the same expectations to the question of how—and where—they should work.

"You see more kinds of technology, more kinds of work, more family arrangements, more communications channels," he told a reporter. At every level of society, there's an enormous wave of differentiation."[19] And with it, he insisted, came freedom and opportunity.

But the appeal of working from home was fueled by more than the ethos of consumer culture, market differentiation, and shifting social mores. As Toffler noted, new technologies, especially in computing and telecommunications, were rapidly changing how work got done, reinforcing the cultural and intellectual trends he described. Telecommuting—or "telework," as it was commonly known outside the

United States and by scholars—exploded in popularity as new ideas met those new technologies.

———

> It's 7:00 P.M. and Jack Rogers, manager, husband, and father, is arriving home from another ten-hour day at Acme Publishing. Struggling to swim through the crowded waters of middle management, Jack works late most days—only to bring home a briefcase at night and on weekends to work still more. His neighbors all do the same. Once inside, Jack faces a succession of chores: meals to prepare; kids to feed, bathe, and tuck away for the night; a house to clean, straighten, repair, and improve. Then there's that briefcase.[20]

So began *The Telecommuter's Handbook: How to Work for a Salary—Without Ever Leaving the House*, published in 1990 by Brad Schepp. It was Schepp's first book, but there would be many more. Based on its success, he and his wife, Debra, issued a second edition in 1995 and established a successful business together as motivational speakers, consultants, and authors of more than twenty books on everything from online job hunting to genealogy to selling on eBay. Like Sarah and Paul Edwards, the Schepps tapped into the growing public demand for information about working from home, turning their passion into a career.

But it all started with telecommuting, which, as Schepp pointed out in his 1990 *Handbook*, had taken the American workforce by storm.

Schepp's anecdote about the fictional Jack Rogers underscored the new pressures that professional white-collar families faced by the beginning of the 1990s. Modern men like Rogers, Schepp implied, had bid good riddance to the old days of *Father Knows Best*, with its clear division of labor between a breadwinning husband and a housekeeping, child-rearing wife. Instead, the idealized middle-class male was now both a successful professional and an active, involved father who cooked, cleaned, and cared for the kids. His idealized spouse did the same.

The problem wasn't gender equity, Schepp maintained, but rather that the new set of expectations for middle-class professionals meant that *everyone* was overstretched. More and more, he argued, "both men and women spend ten to twelve hours away from home each working day." Home life had become a distant memory.

But as Schepp hastened to point out, a special group of people had solved the conundrum of the modern condition and found a way out. "They have become telecommuters, employees who work for their companies from home," he triumphantly announced.[21]

Outside of the United States, as well as within scholarly circles, people tended to call it "telework," putting the emphasis on the labor. Linguists or Greek speakers might point out that only the term "telework" makes any sense. You can work "at a distance," which is what *tele* means, but you can't really *commute* "at a distance," since the entire idea of commuting involves moving to the place where you work. Be that as it may, "telecommute" became the far more common term in popular conversation in the United States. And the reason was that the concept first came about at a time when Americans were struggling to get to work at all, during the oil crises of the 1970s.

The modern environmental movement was a creation of the 1960s, but the OPEC oil embargo of 1973 and 1974 put a giant exclamation point on its push for conservation and ecological stewardship. In the public mind, the energy crisis united concerns about pollution and overcrowding with the real problem of gas shortages and limits on natural resources. As motorists queued up for petroleum and the price of home heating oil skyrocketed, consumers, business owners, and government agencies—already rocked by inflation in the cost of other products, especially food—all reassessed their consumption habits and looked for ways to reduce their bills. And in crowded urban centers like

Los Angeles, where daily life revolved so intensely around automobiles, the issue of traffic and pollution was an obvious place to start.

Unsurprisingly, therefore, Los Angeles was ground zero for the first major study of automobile commuting and its relation to pollution. In 1974, a former NASA engineer named Jack Nilles led a team of researchers at the University of Southern California to study the issue. The fruit of their research, published in 1976, was *The Telecommunications-Transportation Tradeoff: Options for Tomorrow*. As the report summarized, the growth of large companies with downtown offices in the years following World War II had created structural transportation problems in America's cities. Simply put, moving millions of people to centralized worksites every day created unnecessary pollution and wasted both energy and time. And drawing on Daniel Bell's concept of the "post-industrial society," Nilles's team pointed out that the most egregious examples of wastefulness were found in the "information industry." Unlike at factories or mines or stores, workers in business services, research and development, and other "knowledge"-centered fields were often not really required to physically be at a given production site. For the most part, they only did so because that was the way things had always been done.

The solution, Nilles and his team proposed, was to create *different* sites of work in less centralized places. Their report proposed that firms take advantage of "modern telecommunications and computer technologies"—which in 1976 meant massive mainframe computers and physical phone lines—and redirect workers "to locations much closer to their homes than is the case now." Specifically, they envisioned a new corporate landscape where large firms divided their activities among satellite locations, rather than a single, downtown headquarters. Decentralized, regional worksites would reduce the length of commutes, and thus traffic, pollution, and idleness.[22] Workers could *telecommute* by commuting somewhere else.

The environmentalist legacy of telecommuting far outlasted the

1970s. As the concept gained a greater purchase in the public mind in the 1980s, the possibility of reducing congestion, smog, and road rage all factored into the praise. In 1990, for example, self-proclaimed "Environmental President" George H. W. Bush hailed "commuting to work at the speed of light" as a solution to "congested highways and mass transit."[23]

Yet what is perhaps most notable about Nilles's proposal is that it did not envision that significant numbers of people would work at their *homes*. Regional work hubs made sense in 1976 because of the complex communications infrastructure required to connect people in any meaningful way. Computers in the mid-1970s were giant machines used by big government agencies and wealthy corporations; they were mostly unavailable to everyday people and certainly not in their homes. In the next few years, though, Nilles's notion of regional mini hubs would be largely forgotten, and the concept of "telecommuting" would become firmly associated with working from home. In 1983, researcher Margrethe Olson concluded that "many jobs have the potential to be independent of a particular work location" and that the "most commonly suggested remote work location is the employee's own home."[24]

What had really changed from the mid-1970s to the early 1980s was the technology of computing and communication. In the space of only a few years, knowledge workers acquired a whole new ability to do their jobs without leaving home.

The proliferation of the fax machine marked an important, if often overlooked, development. Although the technology behind the analog facsimile had existed since the early days of photography (the first fax machine was invented in 1843!), the device only burst onto the corporate scene in 1980 once manufacturers adopted a common standard that allowed fax machines from different makers to communicate with each other. In short order, the ability to re-create documents over phone lines reduced the needs for some office workers to meet face-to-face.[25]

By far the biggest development, though, was the near overnight

arrival of the personal computer (PC) in the early 1980s. When Jack
Nilles's report on telecommuting came out in 1976, the only computers designed for home use were "kits" like the Altair 8800 (for which a
young Bill Gates wrote BASIC software code, laying the groundwork for
the creation of Microsoft) and the "Apple I" designed by Steve Wozniak.
But in 1977, Wozniak and his partner Steve Jobs unveiled the Apple II,
which included a screen, keyboard, and disk drive. Commodore and
Tandy followed suit, releasing their versions of personal computers
the same year. IBM—the longtime leader in mainframe computing—
released its first PC, the 5150, in the summer of 1981.[26]

Virtually overnight, these desk-sized, versatile, and relatively affordable machines bulldozed through the business world, overturning all
prior notions of what work was or could be. Writing in 1982, author
John Naisbitt—like Alvin Toffler, a self-described "futurist" frequently
cited by work-from-home boosters—captured the exhilaration that sur-
rounded the advent of the personal computer. "From the beginning
of time through 1980 there were only 1 million computers," he wrote.
"Commodore alone expects to match that figure in 1982."[27]

In her sweeping biography of Silicon Valley, historian Margaret O'Mara affirms that manic growth: "In 1980, Americans bought
724,000 computers from a couple of dozen computer makers. Two
years later, in 1982, the market had ballooned to 2.8 million units."
What made PCs so special, O'Mara concludes, was their intimate connection to daily life. "Americans encountered these machines nearly on
a daily basis, whether at home, at work, or at school."[28]

More than any other technology, the PC changed how Americans
understood the possibilities of working from home. As telework consultant Gil Gordon of Monmouth, New Jersey, summed up in 1988:
"One of the strongest trends in homebased work today is the interest
in using a personal computer (PC) to earn money. Whether it's an inexpensive Commodore 64, a high-powered IBM, or anything in between,
the PC is seen as a potential moneymaker by many people today."[29]

Major corporations, including telecommunications and computing companies, hitched their rhetorical wagons to the new trend. Some
engaged consultants like Gordon, whose eponymous firm advised corporations and other large organizations, such as city governments,
on how to implement telecommuting programs. In 1981, for example, retailer JCPenney began hiring customer-service representatives to
field incoming phone calls for the company from their homes, and by
the end of the decade the company employed more than 100 "in-home
associates" across multiple cities.[30]*

But by far, Corporate America's greatest contribution to the new
ideal of working from home was in the realm of popular culture. Home-
based workers—telecommuters as well as business owners—were, after
all, their customers, and the more of them there were, the more stuff
they needed to buy. Starting in the 1980s, an onslaught of marketing
campaigns targeted this new community of potential buyers, cementing the idea of the "home office" in the American imagination.

In 1990, for example, AT&T's "Home Office Resources" newsletter proudly declared itself an ally to people who were "busy achieving
the freedom, satisfaction and personal sense of adventure that most
'nine-to-fivers' can rarely find." Invoking the image of Alexander Graham Bell—who, after all, invented the telephone from his home office!—
the company proudly declared: "Now, telecommuters travel over the
phone line."[31]

Throughout the 1980s, companies like IBM, Microsoft, and Apple
likewise poured tremendous resources into home-market personal
computers and related software. In short order, they expanded their
reach far beyond gamers and hobbyists to home-based workers. An
advertisement for Apple's Macintosh Plus made the case explicit. Taking the form of a letter to consumers from CEO John Sculley (who

* We will pick up the story of outsourcing customer-service work to home based
"mircropreneurs" in chapter 9.

ousted and succeeded Steve Jobs in 1985), the ad proclaimed: "The Macintosh makes you feel right at home, because the images on the screen look just like items on your desk." And "with a Macintosh Plus in your home office, you can make even better use of the most essential business asset you've got. Your brains."[32]

But corporations selling new tech were not the only movers and shakers propelling popular interest in working from home. As enthusiasm around home-based business grew, a new cottage industry emerged for savvy consultants to market themselves both to home-based workers and to traditional companies alike. Combining professional authority and an ability to translate academic research for the public, these consultants bridged the gap between large companies and the eager home-based workforce. At the same time, they affirmed the mantra of the movement: home-based work promised everything from happier and more productive employees to lower overhead costs to a cleaner environment.

———

Among the cadre of professional work-from-home boosters, none had the reach, audience, and heft to match Joanne Henderson Pratt of Dallas, Texas. A consultant, researcher, public speaker, and, like Toffler and Naisbitt, self-described "futurist," Pratt quickly rose to the top of the national work-from-home scene. In the early 1980s, she authored one the earliest research studies of typologies and characteristics of telecommuters, establishing herself as a highly regarded and sought-after expert on all things home-based. The consulting and research business she ran—from her home, of course—gave her a national platform to shape several distinct but intersecting aspects of the work-from-home movement, from policy debates to cultural and gender politics.

As her star rose, Pratt began promoting not only telecommuting but also home-based business ownership, which she came to believe was a logical progression. In an advisory report to the SBA in 1986, she concluded that the newfound "attention to home-based businesses appears to be part of the current fascination with new job opportunities made possible by home telecommuting."[33] Prior to the rise of telecommuting, no such relationship had existed; most people who worked from home in the 1970s and before had been self-employed. Yet Pratt's research and public advocacy was a foundational part of a growing conviction, reinforced by self-help authors and other champions of entrepreneurship, that step one was to work from home for your old boss, and step two was to branch out on your own.

Pratt's journey to her status as national evangelist for home-based business was a long one. An Ohio native, she attended Oberlin College in the late 1940s before earning a master's degree in chemistry from Radcliffe College (the coordinate women's college of Harvard University until 1999) in 1950 at the age of twenty-two. A trained chemist, she worked in the Boston area for several years, first as a researcher at Beth Israel Hospital and then as a physical chemist at the management consulting firm Arthur D. Little.

In the 1960s, by which time she had moved to her husband's hometown of Dallas, Pratt parlayed her industrial expertise into her own chemical consulting business, working with a range of industrial clients. This being Texas, she specialized in applications of chemistry to the oil industry. Like a latter-day Frederick Taylor—the mechanical engineer-turned-shopfloor-consultant who famously promoted "scientific management" at the turn of the twentieth century—Pratt grew interested in questions of workplace design. In the early 1970s, she and her husband, James, an architect, co-founded a nonprofit research and consulting group for Dallas-area professionals that specialized in custom-designed workshops for educational- and public-oriented clients, including museums. Within a decade, the Pratts' nonprofit had conducted a number of large research projects that focused on "off-premise employment," kindling her interest in new ways of thinking about work and where it happened.

In 1980, she launched Joanne H. Pratt Associates to devote herself fully—and for-profit—to research and consulting in the field of remote work. Her first major research project, a survey of home-based workers for Xerox's Office Products Division, established her expertise in all aspects of telecommuting, from its benefits to workers to the implications of land-use law (such as whether you were violating local zoning ordinances by doing business at home). In her writings, she argued that working at home was better for the environment (since people drove less), that it made workers more efficient and productive, and that it enhanced family life.[34] Over the next twenty-five years, Joanne H. Pratt Associates provided research, analysis, and consulting services to corporate clients, educational institutions, and municipal government agencies on how to implement telecommuting procedures. Some of her largest clients included corporations like AT&T, Apple, and Bank of America, as well as governments like the state of New Mexico.[35]

As Pratt expanded her research interests to include the promise of home-based business ownership, however, she ran into a revenue problem. While her telecommuting research was clearly marketable to companies and public agencies, her research into home-based-businesses did not come with an obvious clientele. Small, home-based enterprises hardly had the money to hire a big-name consultant, so Pratt needed to find more creative ways to make money.

One income stream came from the Small Business Administration, which hired her to produce several research studies and then helped publicize the findings. In the wake of an advisory report Pratt submitted in 1986, for example, the SBA convened an eighty-person symposium to tout the extent to which "home-based businesses have become a critical component of our economy." In addition to serving as an incubator for new business ideas, the SBA stressed, "home-based businesses provide jobs to those who otherwise might be unable to work because of personal handicaps, household responsibilities, or the need to supervise children or elderly members of the household."[36]

In addition to her work for the government, Pratt further enhanced her national standing in the late 1980s as a writer and advice columnist for the "Shop Talk" feature of *Home Office Computing* magazine. Her monthly mailbag addressed a range of topics, from policy to practice, and highlighted the growing cultural fascination with working from home.

For an up-and-coming mail-order specialist in Illinois looking to sell souvenirs to her sorority sisters around the country, Pratt praised the importance of market research and recommended bulk-rate discounts from the post office.[37]

To an accountant in New Jersey concerned about the legality of home offices, she warned of the perils of restrictive zoning ordinances. "Not enough communities have modernized their codes" to explicitly allow home-based businesses, she cautioned.[38]

And for a desktop publisher in New York City looking to master the bidding process for government contracts, she suggested tapping into networks and training workshops from the Small Business Administration, even though "these are frequently geared to minority and female entrepreneurs."[39]

Pratt also used the exposure from "Shop Talk" to build her consulting and research business. Since she received more mail than she could possibly answer, she drafted a form letter to those that didn't make the cut, suggesting that she could work through their specific problem directly. "My fee is $300 with a professional discount to *Home Office Shop Talk* readers of 50 percent," she advised. "To answer your questions takes more research time than you might guess and usually requires long distance phone calls as well. That makes my service expensive. But the cost is tax deductible."

Most notable about the "Shop Talk" feature was the degree to which it showcased the tremendous—if often misplaced—hopes that many Americans had in the magic of computer technology to free them from the daily grind and provide their work-from-home salvation.

Late in 1988, for example, Pratt received a letter from Irving Mardes of Brooklyn, New York. Mardes, a fifty-three-year-old construction worker who made $540 a week and had no savings, explained that he hoped to transfer to an accounting job. He lacked any computer skills, and his boss refused to train him in Lotus software out of fear, Mardes suspected, that he would leave to set up his own bookkeeping and accounting practice from home. Pratt did not publish Mardes's letter, but she did offer to consult for him, since he was "obviously an intelligent person who will succeed in business."[40]

Irving Mardes was not alone. Across the country, people were taking to heart the suggestions of advocates like Joanne Pratt, and the number of home-based businesses rose. Yet they were not all success stories. Many would-be business owners, like Mardes, did not have sufficient savings or technical experience, but had become convinced that investing in computer training and software would provide a clear path out of a dead-end job. The for-profit consulting industry couldn't help but reinforce those dreams, unrealistic though they might be.

Casting some cold light on rising attention to home-based business in the mid-1980s, telework scholar Margrethe Olson of New York University aptly summed up the dilemma at the heart of the movement: "At one end of the spectrum, if a person's skills are in demand and the person has few nonwork constraints then setting up a business at home represents flexibility, autonomy, and probably success. At the other end of the spectrum, if the person's skill is not in demand and he or she has few other work options because of family responsibilities, work at home is a less than ideal choice, is difficult and probably stressful, and may actually represent exploitation of the workers."[41]

———

By the late 1980s, the white-collar work-from-home movement had brought national attention to the world of telecommuters and home-based business owners, even though early predictions of its growth proved wildly over-optimistic. In 1971, for example, AT&T had predicted that all Americans would work from home by 1990; in 1980, the company revised that figure down to 50 percent.[42] In reality, by the late 1980s, the ranks of full-time home-based workers remained small, perhaps 5 to 10 percent of the overall workforce.

Nonetheless, signs seemed to point to growth, at least at the time. In an economy marked by corporate layoffs and plant closings—which affected not only blue-collar but also managerial, technical, and sales workers—the appeal of rethinking work appeared clearer by the year during the 1980s. Major firms rolled out pilot telecommuting programs, and interest in home-based businesses grew.[43] Consultants, researchers, and politicians all echoed a common refrain: working at home increased workers' freedom and autonomy, granting them flexible control over the conditions of their labor; it was more ecological and less stressful than commuting; and it was family friendly, ideal for overtaxed parents who wanted to spend more time with their children.

The appeal of working from home was especially strong among middle-class and professional women. Among the estimated 1 million Americans who worked full-time from home (excluding farmers) in the mid-1980s, women made up about 60 percent, according to one study.[44] What's more, of the 3 million or so home-based businesses that operated more than eight hours per week, the majority were owned by women. As Joanne Pratt summarized in 1987, "The typical home-business owner is a married white woman over 25 years old."[45]

According to many women within that expanding community, working at home offered, at least in theory, a solution to the perceived conflict between professional success and family life. That tension—often summarized as the desire to "have it all"—had been central to debates within feminism for decades. Working-class and poor mothers, of course, had always worked for pay, both inside and outside the home, and they performed substantial unpaid domestic labor as well.

Middle- and upper-class women, on the other hand, frequently faced a stark choice between career and family. Working from home offered a middle path.

Georganne Fiumara of Westbury, New York, typified the view that running a home-based business solved the problem for women who felt "caught between career and motherhood," in her words.[46] In 1984, she founded the Mothers' Home Business Network to connect the otherwise scattered community of women who were actively running a home-based business while mothering young children. Her newsletter and membership outreach provided insights and strategies, and she built that expertise into a national platform, writing for *Family Circle* and other magazines. (In 1997, Fiumara took her analog company online, launching HomeWorkingMom.com, which still existed as of 2023.)

Fiumara's publications drew on the expertise of a range of home-based businesswomen who shared tips on such things as structuring the workday around the kids' school and play schedule. As one contributor wrote: "I still maintain a couple of hours in the afternoon for 'momma to work.' . . . Although my work time is fragmented, I usually average 25–30 hours, more or less, per 7 day week."[47]

"Homeworking Mothers Really Can Have It All," ran the headline on the application to join Fiumara's network.[48]

Network builders like Fiumara were far from alone in hailing the revolutionary potential offered by women running businesses out of their homes. Political activists, particularly those linked with socially traditional and conservative politics, also greeted the growth of home-based women-owned businesses with enthusiasm. Phyllis Schlafly of St. Louis, for example, had long been a leading voice for conservative issues, most prominently those related to women's rights. In the 1970s, her lobbying group Eagle Forum played a key role in the defeat of the Equal Rights Amendment, which Congress passed in 1972 but which failed to gain ratification by enough states before it expired in 1982.[49] During the 1980s, Schlafly's organization expanded its purview, in the words of a spokesperson, to "find some positive, truly pro-family solutions to the problems parents are facing."

Schlafly especially appreciated Joanne Pratt's efforts to promote home-based work, which offered "the possibility of breaking the welfare chain through a whole new approach to work." Staying at home with children while retaining personal economic autonomy, she explained, allowed American women to honor their traditional domestic responsibilities while providing for their families. In late 1987, the two women met at a Dallas hotel to discuss their mutual interests in lobbying to remove legal barriers—including local zoning ordinances and tax policies—that inhibited home-based work.[50]

Yet for all the raucous excitement about the liberating potential of working from home, a more sobering set of political and intellectual critiques challenged the central assumptions of that ebullience. Historian Eileen Boris, an expert in the intersection of labor, gender, and race in American industrial history, played an especially important role in giving voice to the dark side of the work-from-home dream. At a national conference on the "New Era of Home-Based Work" in 1987, Boris compared the recent trend toward home-based work with the historical practice that labor scholars call "homework."[51] Two years later, she and political scientist Cynthia Daniels published an anthology of scholarly essays that delved deeper into homework's exploitative and oppressive history, as well as its present incarnation, and offered valuable perspective on its potential and pitfalls. (Boris solicited input from Joanne Pratt, but Pratt did not ultimately contribute to the volume.)[52]

Homework, which Boris and Daniels defined simply as "paid labor in the home," had been around for a long time, regardless of what Alvin Toffler had to say. And importantly, it was almost always associated with inferior pay, unsafe and oppressive conditions, and exploitation, especially for poor people and disproportionately for women. Centuries before the rise of big factories in the nineteenth century, rural families would take in raw materials, such as wool, from merchants and

spend the winter months confined to their small houses, transforming them into finished goods. (This was the origin of the term "cottage
industry.") Under this "putting out" system, as it was known, the people doing the in-house labor were largely dependent on the traders, who
profited handsomely. The laborers, though, had very little control over
prices, timetables, or the conditions of their work.

Importantly, Boris and Daniels stressed, these types of practices
endured even after the advent of large factories, mines, and eventually office buildings. As industrial capitalism carved distinct spheres
that separated "home" from "work" among middle-class and wealthy
people, homework remained a vital source of income for marginalized
communities. Homeworkers in the industrial period were typically
poor and overwhelmingly female, and their labor remained out of view
to much of society—devalued in a cultural as well as a material sense.
Isolated in their homes, homeworkers were paid by the piece rather
than by the hour, and their compensation was less than what factory
workers earned for the same output. Their physical isolation meant
that homeworkers were largely left out of the labor movement as well,
since a disparate, home-based workforce proved far harder to organize
than people who worked on the same shopfloor every day. The gains
made by trade unions in the early twentieth century, real and important though they were, were disproportionately felt in the factories and
thus among workers who were better off, more likely to be white, and
usually male.

Given this history, Boris and Daniels concluded, the popular view
that working at home was an indisputably good thing was not only
historically inaccurate but also dangerous. People who worked at
home were less likely to benefit from labor-union representation and
more likely to be exploited by unscrupulous and largely unsupervised
employers. And on a cultural and political level, exalting the women
who ran a business from home while *still* doing all the work necessary to
care for children (and, presumably, take care of other domestic chores

like cooking, cleaning, and shopping) threatened to perpetuate the very devaluation of domestic labor that activists within the women's movement had fought against for so many decades.[53]

Worries about the downsides of working from home were by no means isolated to academic corridors. People around the country voiced similar concerns. In 1986, when Joanne Pratt conducted her first survey for the Small Business Administration, she reported that several respondents feared that working from home could "accelerate a trend towards pay for results instead of pay by the hour." Telework consultant Gil Gordon, whose business depended on convincing large employers to develop telecommuting programs, worried that, unsupervised, the trend could lead to "sweatshop" conditions. Organized labor, for its part, recognized the risks that the work-from-home movement represented to the welfare of workers, not to mention the continued ability of unions—which had been losing members and political power for years—to organize. The AFL-CIO, for example, favored an outright ban on "computer homework" of any kind.[54]

Moreover, the idea that substantial numbers of women chose home-based work so that they could simultaneously be professionals and "traditional mothers" did not stand up to scrutiny. Just under half of women who ran full-time businesses from home, according to the Current Population Survey in 1985, cared for children younger than school age. And a significant number of those relied on childcare providers—both paid and unpaid, either at home or in a daycare facility—to allow them to work. Contrary to what Georganne Fiumara's newsletter suggested, most of those women were not caring for their children *while* working.[55]

According to one study of home-based women business owners, only 13 percent of respondents listed "being home with kids" as the primary reason for starting their home-based business. Financial opportunity and need were far more important motivators, followed by gaining a greater sense of control over one's time and not wanting to work for somebody else anymore. Importantly, several studies found that women were more likely than men to list "greater income" as the driving factor in their decision to go it alone.[56]

———

As computer and communication technology continued to advance, and as the costs of traditional employment continued to outpace profits at major corporations, the forces that drove the work-from-home movement in the 1980s only accelerated. The advent of the Internet in the 1990s and, in the following decades, high-speed broadband connectivity and interactive teleconferencing platforms like Skype and Zoom made remote work even more feasible. And yet the same questions remained. Was work-from-home economical? Was it exploitative? Was it good for women, or children, or the environment?

Ultimately, the massive "wave" predicted by Alvin Toffler—in which the formal boundaries between work and home were forever erased, taking society back to preindustrial times—did not materialize. Telecommuting faced blowback, especially among major employers like IBM, Bank of America, and AT&T, all of which scaled back their remote-work programs in the 2010s. By 2019, only about 5.7 percent of American workers (or 9 million people) worked primarily from home.[57]

By contrast, one of the most important trends of the early twenty-first century was the expansion of massive corporate "campuses" created by large employers, especially in computer technology fields. Rather than appeal to the comforts of home, these work environments were deliberately constructed to make their employees feel included, creative, and entertained *at work*. In 2013, when an executive at Google was asked how many of the search giant's workers telecommuted, he answered: "As few as possible."[58]

The Covid-19 pandemic marked a clear turning point, as millions of people around the world scrambled to find ways to work from home, whether they liked it or not. And while the long-term consequences of that experience have yet, as of this writing, to work themselves out, the cultural legacy of the work-from-home movement of the 1980s has clearly left its mark. In late 2021, more than a year into the pandemic, a colleague of mine came face-to-face with the persistence of the very ideas boosted by people like Sarah Edwards, Joanne Pratt, and Phyllis Schlafly decades earlier. The occasion was a visit to her doctor to confirm that she was pregnant. Making her way through the reams of information and paperwork that newly expectant mothers confront, she took note of some strategically placed flyers from the U.S. Career Institute. Greeting her was the image of a smiling young woman holding a toddler and sitting in front of a computer. "Train to be a Medical Billing Specialist," the flyer proclaimed. The field was growing, and demand was high. But most important, there was no need to come into a hospital or doctor's office. Instead, the "greatest job opportunity of your life" was the chance to work from the comfort of your own home. "Be your own boss; set your own hours," the flyer promised. What's more: "Be home for your family." Although the millions of people who had to work from home with young children around during the Covid lockdowns of 2020 might have disagreed, the cute infant on her mother's lap made a heart-wrenching case. Invoking the child's voice, the headline read: "I'm Glad You Work from Home, Mommy."[59]

6

LAND OF FRANCHISE

With a franchise, you're in business
for yourself, not by yourself.

—International Franchise Association slogan

Michelle Gobert was twenty-three years old when she quit her job. It was the spring of 1990, and the U.S. economy was teetering on the brink of recession. (The downturn would formally begin in July.) Gobert, a recent graduate of historically Black Xavier University of Louisiana, had been making slightly north of $25,000 a year as a staff accountant at the consultancy KPMG in New Orleans. But the promise of stability and professional advancement that corporate life offered was not enough to keep her tied to an office job. She longed for the independence that came from taking control of her own labor and reaping the benefits directly.

"With the amount of time and effort you put into it," she reasoned in an interview with *Black Enterprise* magazine, "you might as well do it for yourself rather than somebody else."[1]

Yet rather than start a totally new business, Gobert was drawn to what was becoming an increasingly popular alternative: opening a franchise outlet of an existing company. In the fall of 1990, she and her husband, Norman, purchased a franchise license from the Signs Now Corporation of Austin, Texas, which itself was only four years old, and they opened their own shop.[2] Bringing the Signs Now system to New Orleans, the Goberts got off to a strong start, producing computer-generated banners and vinyl lettering for about five hundred clients, including the New Orleans Saints football team. Michelle became the full-time president, while Norman, then thirty-one years old and a systems engineer for International Business Systems, kept his day job and served as vice president.

"We caught the football season and the political campaign season in full swing," explained Norman. Within a month of opening, the Goberts brought in $21,000 in revenue, nearly doubling the national monthly sales record for Signs Now franchises.

Striking out on their own brought challenges, to be sure. Their rapid growth soon leveled off, and Michelle Gobert reported that she worked far longer hours than she had at her corporate job. Setting up their Signs Now franchise had cost the couple approximately $100,000, including fees paid to the parent company that granted the franchise as well as start-up and operational costs for their shop. And, as a family, they also lost Michelle's steady income from KPMG. To make it work, the couple arranged a bank loan for most of what they needed and relied on personal savings for the rest. Yet when they were profiled in *Black Enterprise* magazine a year after their launch, they had no regrets. Franchise ownership was difficult and less secure, they admitted, but the work was personal and meaningful. It was *theirs*.

By getting into the franchising game in a service and retail-oriented business, Michelle and Norman Gobert joined a growing trend in the 1980s and 1990s. The modern franchise system dated to the nineteenth century, but its scope had, until recently, been relatively limited. Throughout the postwar period, most franchises had been confined to product-based distributors (such as car dealerships) and fast-food restaurants. In the late twentieth century, though, the franchising model spread to a broad range of business types. By some estimates, twice as many companies sold franchises by the mid-1990s as had in

1980.[3] Changes in the macro-economy, and especially the proliferation of service-oriented companies at the expense of manufacturers, created a new world for franchising. As a reporter for the *Wall Street Journal* observed in 1987: "almost all of today's major demographic trends are fostering growth in the products and services most suited to franchising."[4]

Franchising, boasted author and "futurist" John Naisbitt, was "the wave of the future" and "the single most successful marketing concept ever." It was, according to the International Franchise Association (IFA)—"*the* success story of the 1990s."[5]

Michelle and Norman Gobert shared that excitement, and in many ways they typified the new trend. They were both college educated and had logged some professional experience before opening their Signs Now franchise. What's more, they set their sights beyond the most familiar type of franchise, the fast-food restaurant. In some ways, of course, opening a Signs Now store was similar to starting a McDonald's franchise—the Goberts, as *franchisees*, got the benefits of a nationally known company (the *franchisor*) that supplied a clear business plan and a well-defined suite of products. Yet by eschewing fast food in favor of a marketing and advertising business, the Goberts pushed the horizons of franchise relationships into the fast-expanding business- and consumer-service sector.

At the same time, the Goberts were also quite exceptional in important ways. First, they were notably successful. Michelle Gobert went on to own several signage franchise units in New Orleans with a company now known as Image360.[6] The same could not be said of many others who followed the franchising dream. Moreover, as African American franchise owners, the Goberts were part of a distinctly underrepresented group. Only about 3 percent of franchise establishments, according to some estimates, were Black-owned in the early 1990s.[7] The figure rose to 6 percent by the early twenty-first century, where it has remained. (African Americans constitute roughly 12 percent of the national population; they are therefore significantly underrepresented among franchise owners.)

What drew people like the Goberts to franchising was the same set of ideals that "work-from-home" and self-employment boosters used: promises of unlimited opportunities and personal independence. And underlying that push was a tremendous public-relations campaign by the growing numbers of corporations who sold franchising agreements, as well as their chief organized representative, the International Franchise Association (IFA).

The key to the pitch was forging a link between franchising and both long-held ideals on the one hand, and newer economic uncertainties on the other. In a 1993 book sponsored by the IFA, authors and consultants Carrie and Robert Shook explained that owning a franchise "was the epitome of the American dream." In troubled economic times, "it relieves the anxiety of being laid off" and provides "the opportunity to attain financial security and, for the most successful, the accumulation of wealth." In short, franchising meant "independence—the freedom to be your own boss." Most important, they argued, it took the guesswork—and, they implied misleadingly, some of the risk—out of entrepreneurship. By teaming up with an established corporate franchisor, franchisees gained "the freedom to own, manage, and direct their own business."[8]

The expansion of franchising thus coincided with, and in turn helped perpetuate, a new definition of the American Dream as something rooted in entrepreneurial risk-taking. Ironically, that new vision of the dream was deeply tied to large corporate entities. Despite the cultural fixation on small enterprise, big companies were still the ones that manufactured and transported most of the country's goods, and that provided financing for small operators. And vitally, in contests between franchise owners and corporate franchisors, the corporations always came first. The franchise boom, in other words, drew on the rhetorical power of independent business ownership while largely perpetuating the very economic inequities it promised to redress.

———

From its early history, the franchising system—and its offshoots, including arrangements like "multi-level" or "network" marketing—has been driven by the economic interests of the people at the top.

Baby Boomers who grew up in post–World War II America usually associated the term "franchise" with the McDonald's restaurants and Howard Johnson hotels that dotted the country's cities, towns, and highways. But the business model went back much further than the fast-food craze. In fact, the concept dates to medieval Europe, when a feudal ruler would grant a special monopoly right to an individual or group to do something like build a bridge and collect tolls, or to organize a market and charge admission. That privilege was called a "franche," Old French for "free" or "exempt." In exchange, the recipient of the privilege paid a share of the proceeds back to the sovereign, which is where we get the term "royalty payment."[9]

The modern version of the franchise relationship took shape far more recently, but, like its ancestor, developed to serve the interests of the already powerful. At the core of the arrangement is the franchisor, an established company that sells a set of rights—branding, process, products—to a smaller outfit, the franchisee. Such agreements generally break down into one of two types: *product/trade-name franchising* and *business-format franchising*, although scholars point out that the technical boundaries between the two forms can be somewhat blurry. Business-format franchising, which we associate with companies like McDonald's, is perhaps more familiar, but product/trade-name franchising emerged earlier (and is thus sometimes called "traditional" franchising).[10]

Product franchises, which focus on a single company's product line, originated with the rise of big corporations in the mid-nineteenth century. In the United States, two of the most famous franchising pioneers were the McCormick Harvesting Machine Company and the Singer Sewing Machine Company. Singer, founded in 1851, still exists today. McCormick, launched four years earlier, merged into International Harvester in 1902; that multinational dominated the agricultural equipment market for much of the twentieth century before eventually disintegrating in the 1980s.

Both Singer and McCormick produced relatively complex mechanical devices that required expertise to repair, in addition to well-trained salespeople to teach buyers how to use them. To reach, serve, and retain customers in far-flung parts of the country, the companies created networks of authorized dealers and sales agents, all of whom had defined territories that they were allowed to work in. At first, those relationships were somewhat loose, but as Singer and McCormick grew, they exerted more control over their respective agents. Singer, for example, put in writing to its sales and repair agents that "all business should be done in the name of the company." Each company set prices centrally and organized its advertising at the national level. Within a few decades, each had established clear rules governing territories, prices, and other aspects of the relationship between corporate headquarters and their networks of sellers, distributors, and service technicians.[11]

The franchise system got its next kick with the arrival, at the turn of the twentieth century, of that signature consumer product—the motorcar. From its meager beginnings in the 1890s, the automobile industry quickly revolutionized not only how people lived and moved but also nearly every aspect of American business, from the arrangement of factory floors to credit-lending practices, from safety regulations to the franchise relationship.

As automobiles rolled out of factories and onto city and town streets, carmakers recognized how useful it would be to have specially licensed retailers sell their vehicles. Detroit's William Metzger, often described as the country's first car salesman, launched his automobile retail showroom in 1897 and brokered deals between car buyers and automakers like Cadillac and Oldsmobile (both of which were later absorbed into General Motors).[12] In 1907, Ford Motor Company created a network of authorized dealers who, while formally independent, entered into restrictive agreements with the mother ship—generally, they had no control over prices and no right to sell non-Ford products. By the 1920s and 1930s, those preferential dealer arrangements became formalized into product franchise contracts.[13]

Other industries followed suit. Large petroleum refiners—the descendants of John Rockefeller's Standard Oil Trust—applied the carmakers' logic to what was a relatively simpler product: gasoline. As car culture grew in the early decades of the twentieth century, individually owned filling stations entered franchise agreements with major oil producers.[14] At the same time, food and beverage production also became big business as brands consolidated and went national, beating out smaller, local producers. As early as 1899, Coca-Cola began setting up bottling franchises. By outsourcing the work of injecting the fizzy water into its patented syrup, the sugary drink maker quickly grew into an iconic global corporation.[15] From Coke to cars, product franchising proved to be a beneficial way for mass producers to move into distant markets, keeping the profits flowing to the top.

Although product franchising emerged first, the second type—*business-format franchising*—eventually became more familiar. Like its predecessor, this arrangement developed to suit the needs of *franchisors*, even as the mystique around it tended to focus on the opportunities it presented to *franchisees*. Credit for early adoption goes to Martha Matilda Harper, whom the *New York Times* hailed as "one of the pioneers in the beauty business in the United States." Born in Ontario in 1857, Harper founded her eponymous Harper Method Hair Parlour in upstate New York in 1888. In the 1890s, as chain stores like A&P and Woolworths were transforming the retail world, she took the unusual step of creating franchise agreements with salon owners—nearly all working-class women like her—whom she trained and supplied. At its peak, up to five hundred franchise owners in the United States, Canada, and Europe were part of the "Harper Method."[16]

For several decades, only a handful of companies followed Harper's lead in creating franchised operations. Cosmetics tycoon Annie Turnbo Malone, for example, became one of the country's first female African American millionaires by producing and selling haircare products targeted specifically at Black women. After setting up shop in St. Louis in 1902, Malone recruited and trained licensed sales agents, including Madam C. J. Walker, who later launched a rival cosmetics empire and became one of the wealthiest people in the country. In 1918, Malone created Poro College, which educated cosmetology students and established franchise operations throughout the world. Her legacy, in the words of her biographer, was "a merging of women's health and economic independence."[17]

By the roaring 1920s, business-format franchising became more common. During the boom that preceded the Great Depression, the expanding consumer economy spawned thriving service-oriented industries in restaurants, hospitality, and retail, and a few large firms began experimenting with business-format franchising. Howard Johnson's, founded in 1925, began selling restaurant franchises in the 1930s.[18] A&W Root Beer, following the Coke model, initially franchised its production and, in 1924, created one of the first fast-food restaurants, which it also franchised. According to one scholar of franchises, though, those early adopters kept their traditional focus on their products—soda and food—much in the way that Harper and Malone focused on their haircare products. Only in the 1950s did franchisors more fully embrace the idea of selling a *process*.[19]

The golden age of the business-franchise format overlapped the golden age of American consumer capitalism in the postwar years, and it flourished under the Golden Arches. Although hamburger chains had been around for several decades—since the first White Castle opened in 1921—franchises were relatively uncommon when Maurice and Richard (Mack and Dick) McDonald entered the restaurant business in the 1940s. Based in San Bernardino, California, the McDonald brothers initially cooked a variety of barbecue products, but they quickly decided that a stripped-down burger-and-fries operation would allow them to control quality and costs better. As they streamlined their processes, they started looking for franchisees to whom they could license their model. But the going was slow. Between 1953 and 1955, the McDonalds sold fifteen franchises, only ten of which opened restaurants.[20]

Things began to change when the brothers met Ray Kroc, a sales representative for a malted-milk mixer company.[21] Looking at how popular the McDonald brothers' store was, Kroc had an epiphany: "I thought, 'Well, jeepers, maybe the way for me to sell multimixers is to open up these sure-fire hamburger units all over the country myself.'"[22] In 1955, he and the McDonalds signed a deal that allowed Kroc to establish McDonald's System, Inc., and begin setting up new franchises. In 1961, Kroc formally bought out Mack and Dick for a million dollars apiece and quickly transformed the company into the most recognizable franchise "opportunity" in the world.[23]

What Kroc understood immediately was that he was not in the *hamburger* business—he was in the *restaurant format* business. Building on the McDonalds' original methods, he quickly settled on a set of standardized, replicable practices. Everything was consistent, he explained in 1968, down to "the exact size of the bun, three and three-quarter inches, and how much onions go on it—one fourth of an ounce." At the central level, he coordinated marketing, rationalized supply chains, and constructed an elaborate training program for franchisees and employees. The secret, he claimed, was to carefully select potential franchise owners, to make sure they would represent the quality he wanted people to associate with the brand.

At the same time, he also insisted that there were no barriers to franchise ownership. No prior business experience was required, he explained, and anyone could succeed if they had the right drive and temperament. "We put our franchisees through a training school. Then we open the store for them, help them get it going and do everything under the sun to help them boost their sales."[24] Anybody could do it.

———

McDonald's and its imitators—Burger King, Wendy's, and many others—were the public face of the franchise concept in the 1950s and 1960s. But starting in the 1970s, and then with greater speed in the 1980s and 1990s, business-format franchising expanded well beyond fast food. As U.S. manufacturing shrank and the service sector expanded, all manner of service and retail industries became hotbeds for franchise arrangements—from tax preparation to specialty retailers, from real estate to travel agencies, and from convenience stores and motels to car rentals and pest control.[25]

This expansion into new domains was matched by a growth in the number of franchisors and the number of franchise establishments, particularly business-format franchises. The total number of units rose from just below 200,000 in 1972 to more than 300,000 in 1988. In the early 1990s, one study reported that 9,000 new business-format franchises were created each year. Counting the precise number of franchise units is a notoriously difficult endeavor, though, and estimates vary widely.[26] According to the U.S. Census, there were approximately 500,000 franchise operations in the United States in 2017, representing about 6 percent of all business establishments.[27]

Driving that expansion was growing interest in selling franchises. The system, after all, brought tremendous advantages to successful franchisors. First, from the perspective of labor-management theory, franchising helped resolve a thorny dilemma known as the "principal-agent" problem within a firm. Under a traditional structure, a company's owners can have trouble getting the people who have control over the company's day-to-day operations—the managers—to put in the necessary work to make the company thrive. The reason is that managers' incentives came through earning their salary, which was only *indirectly* affected by how well the company was doing. Under a franchise relationship, on the other hand, the managers *were* the owners, at least of the franchise unit, and thus had a much more direct stake in the establishment's performance. Franchisees could always hire their own salaried store managers, but then the principal-agent problem became their concern, not the franchisors'. In the language of business theorists, the franchise relationship better aligned the interests and incentives of the franchisees with those of the franchisors. (The practice of compensating high-end corporate managers with company stock options, whose value reflected the firm's performance, is another example of an effort to resolve the principal-agent problem.)[28]

Second, selling franchises provided a potential competitive boost for relatively small companies looking to grow quickly and compete with national chains. Although we may think of companies like McDonald's as "big business," many companies that got into the franchising game were relatively small and cash-strapped. Under the franchise arrangement, the task of raising capital for expansion fell to the *franchisees*, ambitious people like Michelle and Norman Gobert, who put their personal savings and credit into developing restaurants, motels, or Signs Now stores. Franchisor companies could thus expand using someone else's money.

Yet business theory only provides part of the explanation for the franchise boom. On a more fundamental and structural level, franchising expanded in the late twentieth century because the country's courts stepped in and resolved several pesky legal questions about the system. From its early years, franchising had always occupied a murky status in the law. Just as the general public sometimes associated them with "big business" and sometimes with "small business," so, too, did the legal system not know quite what to make of the relationship between franchisors and franchisees. Were they the same entity? Or different? Settling that question had important ramifications for antitrust, labor, and tax law alike.

The U.S. Supreme Court weighed in on many of those questions in a series of decisions that directly precipitated the upsurge in franchise formation. In 1977, the Court ruled that product franchisors could lawfully restrict the geographic areas in which franchisees could sell their products. That decision reflected a consumer-oriented view of antitrust law that had gained intellectual heft through the writing of legal scholars like Robert Bork at the University of Chicago. In essence, the Court concluded that restrictions on *intrabrand* competition—such as preventing franchisees from directly competing for the same territory—would increase competition *between* brands, and thus reduce prices and benefit consumers.[29]

In other words, it was OK for McDonald's to prevent two different McDonald's restaurants from opening across the street from each other, because that would encourage Burger King to open there instead, theoretically increasing competition in the burger market and benefiting hungry consumers.

Just as important, the Court resolved a legal fuzziness about employment that had made franchisors nervous since the advent of national labor protections during the New Deal in the 1930s. Simply put, the question was whether companies that sold franchises were the legal employers of workers at those franchises. Could McDonald's workers unionize nationally and negotiate a wage contract that individual franchisees would have to honor? In 1968, the Court ruled that no, they couldn't. Even though franchisors controlled the nature of the work done—from production processes (like how many onions to put on the hamburger) to the design of the uniforms—their employees were considered to work only for the *franchisee*. Exemptions to labor laws that applied to small businesses would thus apply to franchise establishments. In the words of one prominent scholar, "franchisors have largely succeeded in keeping franchisees outside the legal boundaries of the firm."[30] In practice, this created a weaker regulatory environment that benefitted both franchisors *and* franchisees, though not so much the folks who worked at the franchises.

———

Those legal and political wins were largely the fruit of organized activism by franchising's most effective lobbyist, the International Franchise Association (IFA). From its early days in the 1960s, the IFA institutionalized the voice of franchisors in American public life. From political action committees and legal briefs to far-reaching public information campaigns, it not only strengthened franchisors' legal standing but also cemented the notion in the public mind that franchise ownership was a key part of a redefined "American Dream."

The idea for a franchisors' association came from the man who brought you Dunkin' Donuts. Born in the Boston, Massachusetts, neighborhood of Dorchester, William Rosenberg (whose son Bob we met in chapter 4) dropped out of high school during the Great Depression to help provide for his family. During World War II, he ran a catering service that sold lunches and snacks to factory workers out of old telephone trucks, and he eventually expanded to vending machines and workplace cafeterias. What he noticed, as he later recalled, was that two items seemed especially profitable and made a natural pairing. "Coffee and doughnuts," he concluded, "are like husband and wife." And a business idea was born. In 1948, at the age of thirty-two, Rosenberg launched the Open Kettle in Quincy, Massachusetts, an outfit that he renamed Dunkin' Donuts two years later.[31] In 1955, the same year Ray Kroc began franchising hamburger restaurants for the McDonald brothers, Rosenberg inked his first franchise agreement.

Four years later, as he told the story, Rosenberg was attending a franchisors' convention in Chicago when he conceived another new idea: create a national organization to defend the good name of franchising and franchisors.[32] And it needed defending. Not long before, the Better Business Bureau had listed shady franchise deals as second only to false advertising when it came to major sources of business fraud.[33] Between a bad public image and the system's relative novelty and legal uncertainty about the "restraints" franchisors put on franchisees, franchising needed a PR makeover.

The International Franchise Association's explicit purpose, according to the by-laws that Rosenberg and another conference-goer drew up, was, first and foremost, to "maintain a high standard of integrity and efficiency" among franchisors. What's more, the organization promised to help franchising "maintain its proper standing with all respected industries." Perhaps most important, the group explicitly embraced its role as a lobbyist. It promised to "represent its members as required before legislative bodies" as well as to "assist in the enactment and enforcement of local, state and federal laws to the best interest of the members."[34]

Over the next several decades, the IFA established itself as the loudest voice in the public square speaking out for franchisors. It directly lobbied elected officials, filed amicus briefs in key legal decisions, and engaged in well-funded and effective PR blitzes. In 1978, a few years after Congress officially sanctioned corporate political action committees (PACs), it became one of the first business groups to mobilize campaign contributions to franchise-friendly candidates. And it led the legal campaign that permitted franchisors to exert control up and down a production and distribution chain without being subject to antitrust laws, all while letting franchisees claim the privilege of being separate entities for the purposes of receiving small business loans and special small business exemptions to tax and labor policies.[35]

When it came to public debate, the IFA joined with national business groups during the Carter and Reagan administrations in blaming the nation's economic woes, from inflation to slack growth, on government bureaucracy and heavy-handed regulations.

"There are 41,000 federal regulations controlling the American hamburger," IFA executive vice president Joe Koach declared in 1980. "It costs the average businessman ten times more to file a form with the Securities and Exchange Commission than to go to MIT for four years, including all of his expenses."*

"So what is IFA's goal?" Koach continued. "Our goal is to create an environment in which franchising can be refounded to grow and to survive; to regain the recognition that entrepreneurship is the soul of the free economic system."[36]

While the IFA's policy fights and legal activism focused primarily on franchisors, its public outreach tended to stress the perspective of franchisees. Part of that strategy involved deliberate collaboration with government agencies at the federal and state levels. In the mid-1980s, for example, it began working with the Small Business Administration to co-sponsor one-day regional conferences on franchising. As James Sanders, the SBA administrator under Reagan, explained, the conferences aimed to "provide practical guidance and advice for current owners of franchise opportunities," as well as for prospective franchisees.

"Franchising," Sanders continued, "is a vibrant and growing industry and provides a wide variety of opportunity for the small business owner."[37]

Vitally, the IFA promoted the benefits of franchise ownership for people who might otherwise be left out of economic advancement. As early as the 1960s, franchising had been deeply implicated in the nation's tumultuous reckoning with racism and discrimination. From sit-ins to boycotts to economic uplift programs and the push for Black-owned business, debates over what was then called "Black capitalism"

* Please note: I was unable to independently confirm the figures cited by Mr. Koach comparing the relative cost of SEC form filing and four-year tuition at MIT.

frequently centered on the role of franchise companies.[38] Beginning in 1976, the Office of Minority Business Enterprise joined with the Department of Commerce to publish a detailed "Franchise Opportunities Handbook," singling out more than six hundred franchisors that the government judged to be "nondiscriminatory franchisors"—that is, companies that (following the law) did not deny franchise opportunities on account of race.[39]

The IFA, for its part, also publicized efforts by its member companies to promote minority business ownership. In 1992, its "Minorities and Women in Franchising Committee" issued a report hailing franchisors that had started recruitment, job-training, and business-financing programs deliberately aimed at racial and ethnic minorities. PepsiCo, for example, launched a policy of purchasing supplies from certified minority-owned businesses, while managers and franchisees at 7-Eleven convenience stores ran trade fairs to introduce minority business owners to ways they could work with the corporation. According to the survey, however, only 41 percent of franchisors actively targeted racial minorities in their search for franchise owners.[40]

Reporting on another IFA survey in 1994, *Black Enterprise* magazine lauded the possibilities franchising offered for people of color. Black would-be franchisees, the magazine suggested, should look beyond restaurants to consider business and professional service franchises. Compared with more familiar franchises, many service-oriented fields were "not as capital and real estate intensive as, say, fast-food or construction outlets."[41]

The IFA's primary responsibility, as a trade organization, was to serve its dues-paying members. Those were the people who relied on the organization to defend their reputation and, where possible, help drum up business. From its early years, the organization released a membership directory, a sprawling publication that included not only lists of names but also detailed descriptions of how their businesses operated. The IFA's public-facing magazine, *Franchising World*, which it began publishing monthly in the late 1960s, contained feature pieces about the joys and freedom that came with buying a franchise. By the 1990s, it regularly released a compendium of several thousand franchise companies in its *Franchise Opportunities Guide*.

The *Franchise Opportunities Guide* (known internally as the FOG) captured the essence of the IFA's pitch to potential franchise owners. Hundreds of thousands of franchise establishments did business around the country, from your favorite burger and pizza joints to housekeeping, exterminating, and hair-styling companies. And most important, the FOG explained, franchising was "drawing people from every walk of life." From those fresh out of college to retirees, franchising offered "a good opportunity to people with various levels of capital and experience." In a business world marked by prejudice and glass ceilings, the "number of women and minority franchise owners is increasing dramatically," it reported. And since franchises sat at the secure nexus of big business and small business, the people who owned them "can be in business for themselves but they're never left by themselves."[42] Running "a proven franchise system," the IFA announced in an invitation to its International Franchise Expo in Washington, D.C., "is their key to financial freedom, job security and personal satisfaction."

Franchisors themselves reinforced this messaging.

"It's Your Turn to Be the Boss," ran an ad for Kwik Kopy Printing.

"Taste the Sweetest Opportunity," suggested the Great American Cookie Company.

"Don't Let This 'Almost Perfect' Business Pass You By," said Molly Maid.

"We're Looking for a Few Good Presidents," pronounced the Closet Factory.[43]

Through clever politicking and marketing, the IFA created a glowing impression of franchising: a fast-growth, relatively low-risk, and equal-opportunity path to advancement for anyone. To be sure, nearly every magazine feature, congressional hearing, and published ad issued a caveat—franchising "isn't for everyone" and it required a tremendous amount of effort and real risk. Nevertheless, the boosters behind the franchise boom of the 1980s and 1990s went to great pains to accentuate the positive and minimize, if not eliminate, the negative.

The reality, as an emerging body of critics proclaimed, frequently didn't live up to the hype. As franchising expanded amid the larger "go-it-alone" ethos of the 1980s, public criticism likewise grew, throwing cold water onto those utopian dreams.

———

The fiercest source of dissent came from within the franchising arrangement itself, rooted in the inherent tension between franchisees and franchisors. Despite franchisors' long-standing rhetoric about "independence" and "being your own boss," franchise owners often didn't see it that way. Complaints about lack of autonomy arose from the early days of McDonald's in the 1950s and grew louder amid the legal battles of the 1970s. Franchisee associations frequently challenged the rigid rules of the franchise agreements, which put nearly all the control, but little of the risk, in the hands of franchisors.

Even people with generally positive views of franchising cautioned that the promises of true independence were usually overblown since, by design and by contract, franchisors held all the cards. The entire concept, after all, was premised on the franchisor's business model, which typically included control over prices, locations, processes, and suppliers.

"You don't have the freedom to do anything and everything you want," noted William Swift, owner of multiple Jack-in-the-Box restaurants in San Antonio, Texas, in 1987. "It's the franchisor who establishes the guidelines and if you don't like them, you shouldn't be in the business."[44]

That lack of control, coupled with real financial risks and the difficulty of getting out of a franchise agreement, frequently led to conflict. In the late 1970s, for example, a group of Burger Chef franchisees mobilized out of frustration with corporate-level decisions. "We don't have the kind of advertising and marketing help that Burger King and McDonald's have," said William Michot, head of the association of Burger Chef owners. Fed up with corporate mistakes, Michot's group demanded "to be involved from the ground floor in programs affecting sales, profitability and major expenditures."[45] (General Foods Corporation, which owned Burger Chef, gradually began selling the company off to Hardee's in 1982; the last restaurant called Burger Chef closed in 1996.)

Moreover, academic and governmental research studies also cooled off the overheated rhetoric. Most tellingly, several reports in the early 1990s challenged the widely repeated claim that franchises did not fail very often and thus represented a much less risky way of going into business. In his critical but ultimately sympathetic guide to franchising, published in 1994, Robert Purvin of the American Association of Franchisees and Dealers explained that statistics about franchise failure were invariably misleading. The problem was that, by design, franchises were business contracts that could be sold back from the franchisee to the franchisor, and then resold again to another franchisee—no matter how much money the first franchisee lost on the project. In such a case, the "franchise" itself continued to exist, at least on paper, and the franchisor could claim it didn't fail. In reality, of course, somebody lost their shirt.

"The popular perception that only 5 percent of franchises fail after five years is not only incorrect, but is used by many franchisors as a marketing statement even when their own company has much larger franchisee attrition," Purvin explained.[46]

The disconnect between the lofty rhetoric and complex reality was especially stark for traditionally underrepresented business owners. Despite the odes to minority business owners on the pages of *Black Enterprise* and the public reports of the IFA's Minorities and Women in Franchising Committee, most franchise buyers were wealthy, professional, and white. In the early 1990s, the average franchisee was forty years old, had a net worth of approximately $330,000, and had made $66,617 in annual income before buying the franchise.[47] (Those figures correspond to roughly $767,000 and $155,000 in 2023 dollars.) Moreover, the overall trend in the franchising world was toward a concentration of wealth: the rich got richer. By the early 2000s, about 40 percent of the people who owned a major-chain franchise owned more than one. At McDonald's, for example, 81 percent of franchisees ran multiple locations.[48]

It may have been disproportionately the province of white professionals, but as a concept, franchising played a key role within the evolving culture of the hustle for a wide range of Americans. And it had vital consequences for how millions of people approached the idea of independent business ownership.

———

In the same years that franchising expanded into an ever-wider range of fields, a different—but conceptually related—business arrangement blossomed: the form of direct sales known as multi-level marketing (MLM). While MLMs, often called "network marketing" companies by their proponents, differed in form from franchise relationships, they shared vital characteristics in common. First, they used promises of individual opportunity and relatively low risk to entice participants. As important, they capitalized on growing economic stagnation and declining upward mobility by focusing their recruiting efforts disproportionately on women and the poor. Finally, they successfully—and with little obvious sense of irony—tapped into anti-corporate, anti-bureaucracy sentiment to bring people in, even as the real profits of their ventures flowed up to corporate headquarters. Walking a fine line between legitimate and fraudulent, MLMs relied on energetic, charismatic founders whom they hailed as visionaries, and they promised easy money and stability if only you did what they did.[49]

As with franchising, modern direct sales descended from the early years of mass production and mass distribution—the era of the "travel-ing salesman" of the type depicted in the 1950s musical *The Music Man*. Economically, the logic of direct selling was that independent contrac-tors could bring products to customers who lived far away from major production centers, allowing people to buy directly from an agent of the company rather than a store, theoretically reducing costs.

In the early years, most traveling salespeople were men.[50] In 1886, however, the California Perfume Company—a precursor to Avon—began to recruit women to distribute perfume door-to-door, deliber-ately shifting the sales strategy to reflect a personal touch known as "socializing." After World War II, Avon and other pioneering compa-nies like Amway, Mary Kay, and Tupperware expanded dramatically, promoting direct sales as a boon to middle-class women, who could maintain "a foot in both worlds" as businesswomen and homemak-ers. In short order, women came to predominate within the ranks of distributors, conducting door-to-door sales and hosting house parties where friends, family members, and guests could sample products like cosmetics and kitchen goods.[51]

As direct selling grew, a significant number of its practitioners came to use a multi-tiered, or "network," model. Leading companies compen-sated independent distributors not only for the sales they made per-sonally but also by paying them a portion of those sales made by others whom the distributor had recruited to the venture—typically known as the "downline." As with the selling itself, the recruiting process usually happened through personal contacts, reinforcing the operation's class and gender dynamics.[52]

What most attracted would-be business owners to MLMs in the 1980s and 1990s was the specific appeal to personal independence. If buying a franchise was pitched as less risky than opening a new, origi-nal business, then signing on as an MLM distributor took that logic to an extreme. After all, MLMs promised not only low entry costs but also unlimited potential income.

In addition, MLMs offered a personal connection that pushed back against the cold world of business. Pioneers like Amway and Tupperware learned early on that personal relationships and networks made participants feel connected and supported. Many of the products MLMs specialized in appealed to people's most intimate needs, from beauty and hygiene to weight loss, fitness, and combatting the effects of aging. And echoing work-from-home advocates like Joanne Pratt and Sarah Edwards, many MLMs explicitly told women that they could "have it all." Health product company Melaleuca (founded in 1985), for example, proclaimed itself "on a Mission" for "Stay-at-Home Moms." "Would you like . . . to stay at home with your children? . . . contribute to your household income? . . . have time for what is most important? You can!"[53]

That message permeated the highest reaches of American political culture. Recording a private video message for the trade group known as the Direct Sellers Association in September 1996, President Bill Clinton praised the nation's direct sellers—distributors and recruiters—for embodying the central economic message of his presidential reelection campaign: personal responsibility and opportunity. People who engage in direct sales, the president effused, "help our economy grow and help keep the American Dream alive for millions of Americans." As MLMs expanded across the country and across the world, the president affirmed, they brought opportunities to women, to older people, to people with disabilities. "Your industry gives people a chance, after all, to make the most of their own lives. And to me, that's the heart of the American Dream."[54]

———

The boom in franchising—as well as direct sales through multi-level marketing—was central to the new cultural ideal that insisted on independent business ownership as the wave of the future. Nurtured by self-interested companies, including the franchisors and the MLMs who found new ways to grow and profit while outsourcing risk down the chain, this mythology of going it alone blossomed in the latter decades of the twentieth century. Whether one opened a franchise, a downline, or a home-based business, growing numbers of people became convinced that by working for themselves, by being their own boss, they were achieving, as Bill Clinton put it, the American Dream.

A new conviction spread within American culture: Starting a new business was the right thing to do, both for yourself and for the national economy. Yet the chasm between ideal and reality was wide. For many people, the lived experience of self-employment was often a far cry from the rosy scenario painted by its most eager boosters.

7

BE YOUR
OWN BOSS

One day in 1989, my father came home from selling industrial machine equipment all day and announced that he had quit his job. At forty-five years old, he was sick of commuting to work in a jacket and tie every day, only to work for someone else and draw the same paycheck week after week. He was a good salesman, he figured, and he knew the local market for small-scale industrial machinery. So from that day forward, he would answer only to himself. He would be self-employed.

I don't recommend my dad's approach as a model of marital responsibility. My mom was somewhat put out to learn, without warning, that she would now be the family's sole breadwinner for the indefinite future. Nonetheless, my family's story is a poignant example of how pervasive the ideals of self-employment and independent business ownership had become by the end of the 1980s. The virtues of individualism, of breaking with the established order, and of taking advantage of an opportunity to develop something new all had become thoroughly baked into American culture. The siren call of starting your own business seemed to sing louder than ever.

The national press breathlessly perpetuated that message. Throughout the 1980s, reporters paid particular attention to the apparent trend of high-ranking corporate executives walking away from the rat race. A fifty-nine-year-old financial executive named Robert Ritchie, for example, seemed to embody an idyllic, if somewhat stereotypic, dream. Facing the imminent threat of being laid off, Ritchie decided to redefine his circumstances on his own terms—by taking an "early retirement" and buying a country inn in Vermont. There, he reported, he finally found his bliss. He was "earning less money, working longer hours, and enjoying it more."[1]

Combining corporate skills with a lifelong passion—that became a running motif as be-your-own-boss stories proliferated.

In 1985, after seven years as a consultant for Boston Consulting Group (BCG), thirty-six-year-old Jim Koch decided to change things up. "Being a consultant makes you cocky," he told a reporter from the *Wall Street Journal*. "You think you can do anything." In Koch's case, "anything" meant starting the Boston Beer Company, whose signature Samuel Adams beer is often credited with launching the craft brewing movement in the United States. While Koch's success was unusual (and delicious), his determination to go it alone wasn't. His former bosses at BCG estimated that some 30 percent of people who left the consulting firm in the mid-1980s went on to start their own companies.[2]

These folk tales played critical cultural roles. First, they linked the old reverence for small business ownership with the new excitement around entrepreneurship. After all, both Ritchie's Vermont inn and Koch's brewery were prototypical small business ventures, even if the latter became an internationally recognized brand. And second, they gave the impression that successful, liberating self-employment was widely achievable. If the top dogs of corporate capitalism were getting into the independent-business game, the thinking went, then so should everyone else.

But men like Koch and Ritchie were no more the norm than high-technology firms like Microsoft and Apple, which exploded from their humble beginnings in dorm rooms and garages to remake an entire industry. More typical were people like my dad, who plugged away from his basement office for twenty years, never hiring any employees and only rarely paying himself anything at all. Being self-employed—he never identified as a "small business owner"—allowed him the time to go to lots of gymnastics meets, school plays, and soccer games, but he never regained the income from the job he'd left behind.

Moreover, the idea that "everyone" was becoming self-employed was overblown. The data are incomplete, and methodologies for counting self-employment varied over time, so the best we can do is make broad generalizations. What appears to be the case is that the long-term decline in self-employment—which began with industrialization and continued through the post–World War II years—began to slow and even stop in the late 1970s. After that, self-employment ticked up modestly, perhaps a percentage point or so between the mid-1970s and the early 1990s. By 1990, approximately 10 percent of the American workforce was self-employed (whether or not they employed other people), and that figure has remained roughly the same ever since.[3]

What did change in subtle but important ways were the characteristics and demographics *within* the community of business owners, as well as their rationales and motivations. The people most likely to work for themselves were white and Asian men, generally on the older side and financially somewhat comfortable. In the latter years of the twentieth century, however, that caricature became less accurate. The self-employment rate among African Americans, for example, rose from 3.8 percent in 1989 to 5.5 percent in 2005, although it remained lower than the rate for Latino (7.4 percent), white (11.2 percent), and Asian (12.2 percent) people. Women also opened companies at faster rates than men; the bulk of that increase occurred between the mid-1970s and the early 1990s.[4]

The notable, if slight, democratization of business ownership in the 1980s and 1990s seemed to affirm the message preached by business groups, politicians, academics, and journalists: here was a chance to earn more income, to attend to parenting responsibilities, or simply to tell the boss to shove it. Such a narrow focus on the *opportunities* that came with working for yourself, however, ignored the role that economic *necessity* played in many people's decisions. It overlooked the motivations of those who were marginalized, impoverished, and excluded from wealth and power, and especially those who were discriminated against for their race, gender, or national origin. For people who were unable to support themselves and their families through wage or salaried work, business ownership could offer a better path, but certainly not a cheerful one. For immigrants confronting language barriers, social exclusion, and racism, or for women faced with sexist expectations and corporate glass ceilings, the "opportunity" to get around an economic and social system stacked against them was indeed a "necessity."

When work-for-yourself boosters acknowledged those hardships, they typically did so to praise the individual strength and spirit required to overcome them. Their adulation of scrappy entrepreneurs effectively normalized the unequal and oppressive conditions that pushed many people to business ownership in the first place, reaffirming the conviction that individual risk-taking was the best solution to collective and structural economic problems.

Actual business owners knew better.

———

Consider the case of Dinesh, whose story I learned from a study by scholars who did not use his last name.[5] In 1980, at the age of thirty, Dinesh moved with his wife and young child from Gujarat, India, to New York City, with a visa sponsored by his brother-in-law (an IBM employee). He held a mechanical engineering degree from his home country, but he did not speak English comfortably and looked for work for a while. After a two-month job search, Dinesh took an entry-level job with an engineering company in New Jersey. His wife (whose name was not published) eventually began working at a sewing company as Dinesh ascended to higher-paying positions. In 1986, the family moved to the Dallas–Fort Worth area when Dinesh took a job at a nuclear power plant. Two years later, he was laid off, but he managed to get another job in the same industry. Five years after that, however, he found himself out of a job again.

Corporate life rubbed Dinesh the wrong way. Big companies, he complained to the researchers who documented his story, were full of "dirty politics" that he had no desire to play.

"There are people who network to get ahead and those who actually do the real work," he explained.

What's more, corporate life seemed precarious and unpredictable. As a man entering his mid-forties who had, by then, two children to support, he worried about bouncing from layoff to layoff. "There is a lot of job turnover in the United States," he reflected, "and even though people say there is no age discrimination, there is."

The solution, he determined, was to pursue a lifelong dream by owning his own business. His father in Gujarat had owned a restaurant, but Dinesh wasn't interested in that. And the prospect of parlaying his professional experience—in engineering and the nuclear power industry—into a small business did not seem feasible. Dinesh went another route: he opened a motel.

Motel ownership seemed a natural step for an Indian immigrant. According to estimates at the time, approximately 60 percent of mid-size hotels and motels were owned by Indian immigrants or their descendants. On a more personal level, Dinesh heard testimonials from people he knew who owned motels in the Dallas area, and they suggested that it was a relatively simple business to set up and run.

For two months, Dinesh worked alongside a friend to learn the ropes. He then used his savings to put a down payment on a motel that had previously been run by another Indian business owner and took out a loan to cover start-up costs. For two years, he even moved his family into the motel to save money before they could afford to buy a house nearby.

For Dinesh, getting into the motel business was an opportunity born of necessity. In his mind, it provided a type of security that an industry job did not, since it depended principally on something he could control—the effort that he was willing to put in. In addition, he appreciated being part of a community of people who, like him, had emigrated from India and used their social networks to help each other grow their businesses.

"There is a good fit in this sector between the willingness of Indian immigrants to work and the availability of opportunity," he reported. "People who are born in India and come here are willing to work these long hours."

In many ways, Dinesh's journey from unemployed new arrival to working professional to small business owner reflected a classic American tale. His hard work and personal sacrifice allowed him to break free of the limitations imposed by his immigrant status, his weak English proficiency, and the strictures of corporate life. And by tapping into networks of fellow immigrants, he found his way into a new business niche. As scholars of immigrant entrepreneurship note, the bonds of family, community, and ethnic group have been central to many success stories. The fact that we commonly associate certain groups with certain types of businesses, from nail salons to dry cleaners to minimarts, is a testament to the importance of social capital.[6]

Immigrant entrepreneurship has always been a central part of American culture, and immigrants have long been over-represented among the ranks of business owners.[7] To be sure, there is no such thing as a "typical" immigrant experience; differences in wealth, education, ethnicity, national origin, and historical timing, not to mention personal idiosyncrasies, have all shaped individual experiences. Nonetheless, higher levels of immigration from a wider swath of the world—a result of the liberalization of immigration law in the 1960s—coincided with rising interest in self-employment among immigrants.[8] During the 1980s, the proportion of self-employed immigrant men rose from 11.6 to 12.2, about a full percentage point higher than for U.S.-born men (which rose 10.4 percent to 11.2 percent).[9] And in 2003, foreign-born people accounted for 12.9 percent of all incorporated and unincorporated self-employed workers, while making up about 12 percent of the national population.[10]

The mythology of immigrant business owners spread, from laudatory political speeches to tropes in popular entertainment such as the racist depiction of Apu Nahasapeemapetilon, owner of the fictional Kwik-E-Mart store on TV's *The Simpsons*.[11] Amid rising public enthusiasm for entrepreneurship and business start-ups, writers and commentators invoked a range of common clichés about immigrants. To take but one example, author Steven Solomon provided a typical backhanded compliment of new immigrants in his 1986 book *Small Business USA*. Struggling new arrivals, he wrote, were well suited to entrepreneurship because they were "better prepared than the average native American to work the long hours at difficult, dirty work" and to put up with "initial low pay and grueling hours."[12]

Even efforts to strike back against xenophobia and anti-immigrant sentiment often wound up perpetuating the mythology of the immigrant entrepreneur. In 2010, for example, authors Richard Herman and Robert Smith singled out Google co-founder Sergey Brin (born in the Soviet Union) and Intel CEO Andy Grove (born in Hungary) for their contributions to computer and Internet technology. Immigrants, they argued, should be welcomed and praised for "building the New Economy and creating jobs for American workers."[13]

That attention to immigrant success stories, no matter how well meaning, had an unintended consequence: it obscured the very real social injustices that propelled so many immigrants to go into business for themselves in the first place.

Take the Kims, for example.[14]

Hei and Tae-Jon Kim moved from South Korea to the United States in 1987. Hei, who at thirty was five years younger than her husband, had finished high school but had no higher education. Tae-Jon had completed two years of college in Seoul but, according to the researchers who interviewed him, "perceived very limited employment options in the United States." As a result, he "decided business ownership was his only choice." In 1991, Hei took a job at a factory to provide the family income while Tae-Jon opened a business in a flea market mall.

Or consider Antonio Perez.

Perez moved from Mexico to the United States in 1979. With only five years of formal education, he found work in a factory in the Chicago area. But after being fired from that job, the best he could do was to work for himself as a street vendor. For three months, he later reported, he operated without a license because he didn't know that he was supposed to have one until a fellow street vendor told him. After several years, he opened a grocery store in Little Village, Chicago, catering to the local immigrant community. When grocery sales were low, he would load his truck with merchandise and sell on various streets around the city, as he had when he first started out. That kept him true to his roots, but it also reflected the precarity of his situation.

People like the Kims and Perez found themselves in circumstances where necessity was a bigger driver than opportunity. Like Dinesh, the motel owner, they confronted the perils of layoffs and a weak economy with little in the way of a social safety net. They faced unfamiliar environments, a different dominant language, and trouble transferring skills and education credentials to a new country. Social networks and ethnic ties helped grease the wheels of their budding businesses, but despite the optimism of entrepreneurship boosters, "being their own boss" was less about achieving the American Dream and more a way to make the best of an unjust situation.

On the one hand, the struggles that Dinesh, Hei and Tae-Jon Kim, and Antonio Perez faced echoed those of earlier generations of immigrants. Yet on the other, their experiences reflected the specific economic conditions of the late twentieth century. Growing instability in the job market, stagnant low-end wages, and corporate downsizings all exacerbated the exclusion and discrimination they faced. They heard and even echoed the hype around entrepreneurship, self-employment, and being your own boss that came from the mythmakers, and no doubt the power of those cultural ideals fueled their sense of opportunity. But above all that, economic precarity defined their entrepreneurial experiences. Making a virtue out of necessity didn't change the underlying unfairness they faced.

———

"A business revolution is underway—and women are leading the charge," proclaimed the "Women's Work '94" conference in Waco, Texas. Sponsored by McLennan Community College's Small Business Development Center, the event brought together speakers and panelists from around the business community, including consultants, professors, small business owners, and corporate executives, to hail the rapid advances women had made in the business world. In addition to discussions of women's leadership development and advice for securing government contracts, the conference included a special session for "the woman entrepreneur who wants to 'go it on her own.'"[15]

By the mid-1990s, a celebratory tone pervaded discussions of women's role in business, and especially as business owners. The trends kickstarted by the political, legal, and cultural gains of organized feminists and associations like NAWBO in the 1970s continued apace in the years that followed. From 1980 to 1986, the number of women-owned sole proprietorships grew 64 percent, from 2.5 million to 4.1 million.[16] Of the 700,000 start-ups launched in 1987, women owned a quarter of them.[17] Overall, in the last fifteen years of the century, the number of women-owned sole proprietorships increased at nearly double the rate of men, about 4.1 percent annually compared to 2.2 percent.[18] By the late 1990s, women owned close to 40 percent of all firms—a statistic that remained largely unchanged in the decades that followed.[19] That figure counted companies with employees (approximately 6.1 million in 2019) as well as the far larger number of firms that did *not* employ anybody besides the owner (approximately 27 million in 2019).[20] If we count only *employer firms*, women's business ownership increased less dramatically to about 20 percent (1.2 million) by the late 2010s.[21] In other words, women took on an especially pronounced place among business owners when they worked alone for themselves.

That growing representation of women among the self-employed reflected the double-edged nature of this phenomenon. As with immigrants who opened their own businesses, many women felt compelled to become entrepreneurs not so much out of a sense of endless possibility but in response to structural repression and social injustice. While many women found business ownership liberating, many also admitted that it represented a work-around, a least-worst alternative to systemic sexism, discrimination, and a series of glass ceilings that blocked their upward mobility in corporate life. Amid all the celebrations, an important cohort of women dared to point out that the boom in women's business ownership was substantially more complex and conflicted than its enthusiastic boosters might have suggested.

The remarkable uptick in women's business ownership followed, by about ten years, the historic rise in women's participation in the paid labor force—the phenomenon that economic historian Claudia Goldin has called the "grand gender convergence" of the late twentieth century.[22] Importantly, that increase was most evident among middle-class whites, for the simple reason that poorer women and women of color had *always* been more likely to work for pay outside the home. And for the same reasons, the rise in women's entrepreneurship was also largely a white and middle-class affair. According to U.S. Census reports in the 1980s, women business owners were disproportionately white, typically came from middle-class backgrounds, and usually had a college education. About half were married. And like men, they were far more likely to have started their first business when they were over the age of thirty and had kids who were school-age or older.[23]

In many respects, the "typical" women business owners in the 1980s looked very much like those of previous eras. In the nineteenth century, as historian Angel Kwolek-Folland has noted, most women business owners had been "probably over the age of 30, married or widowed, slightly better educated than most women, and operated their businesses with the assistance of family members."[24] Just as important, women typically concentrated their business efforts in what Kwolek-Folland calls "traditionally female-dominated fields," and that trend continued. Between 1977 and 1987, women's businesses ownership rose fastest in the service sector (from 8.7 percent to 38.2 percent); the finance, insurance, and real estate (FIRE) sectors (from 4.7 percent to 35.6 percent); and wholesale and retail sales (from 8.8 percent to 32.9 percent). Women's ownership of manufacturing, transportation, and construction companies likewise saw a boost, but not to the same levels: 6.6 percent to 21.7 percent, 2.9 percent to 13.5 percent, and 1.9 percent to 5.7 percent, respectively.

Breaking through all those statistics, what was happening is that women became better represented among business owners exactly as the overall economy became more oriented toward the types of businesses that women had traditionally owned. In a business landscape where service companies—in caregiving, hospitality, retail, and food services, for example—came to occupy a bigger place than manufacturing, women took on larger roles as both laborers and business owners.[25]

The rapid increase of women-owned businesses met with criticism as well as applause. Many feminists rejected the idea that climbing the entrepreneurial ladder was a panacea for the sexism women confronted.

Writing in *The Nation* magazine in 1983, journalist Suzanne Gordon decried the new spirit of "corporate feminism" that taught women "how to 'network,' cut deals, make killings, be the boss and get to the top of the corporate heap." In the heyday of the women's liberation movement, Gordon reminisced, "the subordination of one's personal life to one's professional life and the delight in wielding authority were not highly regarded." But by the 1980s, the message seemed to be: "now every woman can attain wealth, prestige and power by dint of individual rather than collective effort."[26] The struggle for real equality and social progress, it seemed to her, had been sacrificed on the altar of materialism.[27]

And cynicism wasn't limited to feminist activists. Just as NAWBO's founders mixed enthusiasm and pride in their accomplishments with a recognition that their advocacy was *necessary* to confront sexism within the business world, many business owners in the 1980s and 1990s pushed back at the unabashedly positive spin. The decision to "be your own boss," they pointed out, was about more than individual uplift. In many cases, it was a response to the persistence of sexist assumptions about women's abilities and priorities, not to mention harassment and explicit discrimination—the "glass ceiling" that blocked professional advancement.

"The 1980s," as writer, lecturer, and financial counselor Jeannette Scollard summed up in 1991, "were a decade when entrepreneurship became a desirable option for capable women who, for myriad reasons, opted against working in corporate America."[28] The author of books like *Risk to Win: A Woman's Guide to Success* and *The Entrepreneurial Female*, Scollard was an international voice for women entrepreneurs—and she identified herself as one, having started multiple companies and served as resident financial expert for the daytime talk show *Home*, which ran on ABC from 1988 to 1994. As she took pains to point out, the flow of professional, white-collar women into self-employment could only be understood in the context of the failures of the male-dominated business world.

"What you find," she told the House of Representatives' Small Business Committee in 1988, "is the cream of women executives are leaving the larger corporate structures and opting to start businesses of their own." Decades into the women's movement, she explained, "not one single woman is among the power brokers in the financial community, and there still is no ladies' room at the New York Stock Exchange." Quite simply, professional women "have figured out that if they want to be president, they are going to have to own the business themselves."[29]

For Scollard, the liberation of being your own boss came from escaping, not scaling, the corporate ladder. Tellingly, she noted, "women have won far more respect in the business community as entrepreneurs than they have in the corporate arena."[30]

The rise of women's business ownership, Scollard observed, coincided precisely with the collapse of midcentury corporate capitalism and the onset of an increasingly fragile and unequal business climate in the 1980s. "While we've been gaining credibility," she noted, "male-dominated corporate America has been mismanaging itself into a shambles."

Plant-closures, offshoring, bankruptcies, and financial scandals plagued the world of Wall Street. "The image of corporate America has become sadly tarnished, and 'job security' is widely regarded as an oxymoron," Scollard wrote in 1991. "In short, big business has lost critical credibility and we, who once had none, have rapidly gained a great deal."[31]

Jeanette Scollard typified the strange amalgam of excitement and resignation with which many feminists approached the question of entrepreneurship. On the one hand, she recognized the persistent injustices perpetuated by a male-dominated, patriarchal business climate. On the other, she argued that the solution was not to push for structural change but rather for women to declare independence from that system and blaze their own path. Critics like Suzanne Gordon continued to argue that this embrace of entrepreneurship amounted to more "corporate feminism," a tacit endorsement of the system it allegedly sought to reform. Despite those protests, the language of empowerment and individual opportunity became ever more dominant. And among a certain type of well-heeled liberal in the 1990s, it represented a strategic reconsideration of values with a specific political agenda.

———

The year is 1993. Eight teenage girls sit at a table, in teams of two, facing a board game. Each team starts with $10,000 in play money—a "bank loan." As they move their tokens around the game board, they keep track of their gains and losses. Depending on where they land, they pick up cards containing different business-related questions. Correct answers add more money to the ledger; errors go in the loss column.

Some questions test their management know-how—How do you pull together the best team? Others deal with financing and debt—Does this situation represent a cash flow crisis? And in many cases, players have to work collaboratively with other teams. "A friend designs a flyer for her product and wants your endorsement. You don't like the product. What should you do?" The more the partners agree, the more they earn.

The first team to make it to the center earns $30,000, pays back the bank, and wins the first round. Yet unlike most board games—and more like real life—everyone keeps playing, and the game goes on.[32]

The game was called An Income of Her Own: The Fast-Paced New Game for the Next Generation of Business Owners, and it was dreamed up and produced by entrepreneur Joline Godfrey. "Nobody's ever designed a business game for girls before," she explained when the product launched. But now, in living rooms and classrooms across the country, young women could roll the dice—as it were—on entrepreneurial glory.

An Income of Her Own, the board game, was sold by Godfrey's non-profit organization of the same name, a clever nod to Virginia Woolf's essay about women's independence, "A Room of One's Own." Founded in 1992, the nonprofit aimed to empower teenage girls from diverse racial and socioeconomic backgrounds and instill in them the dream of owning a business—of controlling (not just earning) their own income, and as a result, their lives.

At seminars and workshops around the country, Godfrey used the board game to capture girls' attention before engaging them in discussions about making those dreams into reality. Echoing people like Jeannette Scollard, she taught seminar participants about the glass ceilings that women in Corporate America confronted. "Maybe the only place to be on par with your male counterparts," she offered, "is to start your own business."[33]

Jeanie Barnett, founder and editor of subscription newsletter *Women's Business Exclusive*, loved the idea behind Godfrey's game. "When I was growing up, we didn't have board games that rewarded girls for becoming entrepreneurs," she said. Instead, she had "Barbie's prom game," which "showed little girls how to compete against each other for the prettiest dress, the flashiest car, the coolest boyfriend. . . . And if you needed some money? Just ask Daddy."

But if women like Godfrey could inspire teens early, Barnett reasoned, "the next generation of working women won't have to remain vulnerable to glass ceilings and economic discrimination."[34]

Godfrey's mission with An Income of Her Own combined the popular faith in entrepreneurship with decades of social activism. For economically and socially marginalized women in particular, she believed, owning a business created opportunity for independence and uplift. A large percentage of the young people who participated in her seminars in the greater Los Angeles area, for example, came from African American, Latina, and Indigenous communities. "By working with young girls before they become trapped in low-paying, low-opportunity jobs, we hope to decrease their economic vulnerability and make them job *makers* instead of job *takers*," she explained.[35]

Godfrey was on a crusade to help young women overcome the obstacles a sexist world threw in their way. Born amid the postwar baby boom in 1950, she earned a bachelor's degree from the University of Maine and a graduate degree in social work from Boston University. For women who grew up in the 1960s, she recalled in a 1992 book, "it seemed that social work, education, or library science were the only real 'professional' possibilities."[36] Against type, she took her training in social work into the corporate sector and launched a ten-year career at Polaroid. There, she became an early model of what business schools call an "intrapreneur"—a corporate employee who acts like an entrepreneur, creating and pushing innovative techniques to shake up old practices. In Godfrey's case, intrapreneurship meant developing a project that helped Polaroid expand from its traditional product focus into a service orientation by marketing a "creative educational program" to vacationers at fancy resorts, who would participate in structured activities with their Polaroid cameras. Her success there led her to launch a successful spin-off company, Odysseum, which provided employee training programs (including board games) for Fortune 500 companies.[37]

After five years running her own firm and advising companies about how to train their workforces, Godfrey's life took an unexpected turn in 1989. In her telling, the impetus came when she encountered a story in *Inc.* magazine that listed "Dream Team" entrepreneurs—Steve Jobs of Apple and the like—without mentioning a single woman.

"I don't know if I was naïve, idealistic, or stupid, but I opened the magazine expecting to see some of my friends in there," she recalled. And in fact some people she knew *were* profiled—they just happened to be men. "Wonderful guys," Godfrey explained, "but no women."[38]

Frustrated, she wrote to the editors at *Inc.*, a relatively new magazine that prided itself on being more tech-oriented and less stodgy than other business publications. "*Inc.*, you let me down," she told them. "*Inc.*, my modern pal, my new age partner, my old friend, you're sexist." In the previous ten years, she knew from personal experience, millions of women had taken the plunge into business ownership in a wide range of fields and sectors, including some of the hottest around. Yet despite being "the most hip, sensitive, feminist group to come along in generations," the editors at *Inc.* apparently only had eyes for men when they compiled their "Dream Team."

The problem, she concluded, was visibility. Women had made huge strides in a very short period of time, but mainstream business leaders—even putative allies like the *Inc.* editors—weren't seeing them. And women business owners felt the snub as strongly as Godfrey had.

"Most of the women I spoke with during that time," she recalled years later, "listed 'not being taken seriously' as one of the greatest obstacles faced by women business owners."[39]

The editors at *Inc.*, apparently chastened, invited Godfrey to help raise the public profile of women business owners. The magazine sponsored a series of dinners with women from different racial and ethnic groups and from a range of age cohorts—from those who had started their businesses before the women's movement to those, like Godfrey, who "had the psychological support of consciousness-raising and feminist politics to buttress their dreams," to young women "of the postfeminist era." Building those networks and hearing those stories, which she wrote about for *Inc.* and in a book, *Our Wildest Dreams*, inspired Godfrey to leave the private sector behind and devote herself to promoting financial fluency and entrepreneurial education for American women, and especially young ones. In 1992, she founded her nonprofit; three years later, she published another book, *No More Frogs to Kiss: 99 Ways to Give Economic Power to Girls*. She launched a financial education company, Independent Means, Inc., in 1996.

Throughout her thirty-plus-year career as a financial counselor, author, and executive at companies she founded, Godfrey both highlighted and, ironically, typified the inherent contradiction within the community that was boosting women's entrepreneurship. Unlike radicals who called for smashing the patriarchy and ending capitalism—

which, they argued, were intimately connected to each other anyway—liberals like Godfrey generally accepted the business world as it was and strived to advance women within it. Entrepreneurship, in her eyes, offered a way for women to make an end run around the injustices of the corporate world.

———

My father wanted to work for himself because he never liked having to answer to somebody else, and because being around for his kids was more important to him than selling industrial equipment. (The fact that his own father died unexpectedly when he was fifteen probably had something to do with that second point.) My wife, on the other hand, opened her own business out of a sense of pride in bringing cultural products from her home country Brazil to North Carolina, and because, as an immigrant, she had a hard time parlaying her professional experience and legal education into the American workforce. My friend Amie from college was excellent at teaching students to take standardized tests and loved the idea of working on her own terms, so she founded a test-prep company and published books on the SAT.

It's likely you know people who have made similar decisions. Or perhaps you are one of the 10 percent of Americans in the non-farm workforce who work for themselves. What's clear is that there are as many reasons for going into business as there are people who go into business. Terms like "opportunity" and "necessity" are imprecise descriptors that frequently overlap and cannot capture the complexity of those experiences.

The language we use to describe business ownership—the idealized vision of self-employment and opportunity—took on its modern form in a time of economic flux and uncertainty in the 1980s and 1990s. The millions of people who walked away from traditional employment to work for themselves, whether they considered themselves small business owners or independent hustlers making ends meet on their own terms, were part of a substantial change in the way we think about work—why we do it, where we do it, and for whom we do it. From parents looking to spend more time with their children to immigrants finding hope in ethnic enclaves to professional women who thought the surest path to being the boss was to own the company, the people who heeded the call to go it alone helped perpetuate a set of cultural values that would only become more firmly entrenched as time went on.

As the American economy stratified in the final two decades of the twentieth century, business owners played key roles in the culture of going it alone. Some bemoaned and challenged the systemic forces that made entrepreneurship a better option than wage or salary work. Others tacitly accepted them and simply pushed ahead. In either case, the women and men who decided to be their own bosses helped perpetuate the notion that there was something distinctly entrepreneurial about the United States. They reaffirmed the conviction that being your own boss was central to the national promise.

8

THE
BACKBONE

n October 2008, as the financial crisis upended the world economy, Barack Obama made a campaign stop outside Toledo, Ohio. Working the crowd, the Illinois senator and Democratic nominee for president shook hands with a thirty-four-year-old man named Joe Wurzelbacher, who wanted to talk about the American Dream.

"I'm getting ready to buy a company that makes about two hundred fifty, two hundred seventy, two hundred eighty thousand dollars a year," Wurzelbacher explained. "Your new tax plan's going to tax me more, isn't it?"[1]

To his credit, the Democratic candidate spent more than five minutes with Wurzelbacher, who explained that he was a plumber. Perhaps choosing his words carefully as the cameras rolled around him, Obama explained the finer points of his plan to provide universal healthcare coverage and make changes to the tax code in the process. Small businesses (like the plumbing company Wurzelbacher suggested he might buy) would receive a 15 percent tax credit to help pay for the costs of healthcare for their employees. Moreover, Obama waded into the complexities of the progressive taxation system, which, he well knew, are easily misunderstood. Under his plan, only income over $250,000 would be subject to higher taxes, and then only an increase from 36 percent to 39 percent, the rate it had been in the

1990s. If Wurzelbacher's company had $280,000 in taxable net reve-
nue, Obama's plan would raise his total corporate tax by $900 a year,
or $75 a month.

Obama couldn't be expected do that calculation in his head, of
course, so the point was somewhat lost. What's more, he neglected to
push Wurzelbacher to specify whether he expected his future business
to earn $280,000 in gross or net revenue. The difference was huge. In the
first case, the business was quite small indeed. After deducting the costs
of doing business, including equipment and labor, Wurzelbacher would
probably be left with a slight profit and little federal tax obligation.
But if he meant he would make that much *after expenses*, then Obama
could have pointed out just how big a take-home profit of $280,000
was. Although reporters later learned that Wurzelbacher had no plans
to buy the business, had no plumbing license, and had made $40,000
in 2006, the hypothetical situation he suggested to Obama would have
made his income five times the national average.[2]

Instead, the Democratic Party's standard bearer offered a long and
wonky rationale for progressive taxation. Although he conceded that
he wasn't likely to get the vote of someone like Wurzelbacher, Obama
took pains to detail how small increases in the top marginal tax rate
on upper-middle-class earners were a trade-off for lower taxes on the
less well-off. "Ninety-five percent of small businesses make less than
$250,000," he explained, and he wanted to help them, as well as "all
these folks who are bus drivers, teachers, auto workers who make less."
Boosting their spending power, he argued, would allow small businesses to grow faster and buoy the entire economy.

"If you've got a plumbing business, you're going to be better off if
you've got a whole lot of customers who can afford to hire you," he concluded, neatly summarizing the basic tenets of Keynesian economics.
"When you spread the wealth around, it's good for everybody."

Wurzelbacher wasn't interested in talking about specific figures, and he certainly did not like the idea of "spreading the wealth around." In his view, higher taxes on his business (again, a hypothetical purchase that he never made) were a punishment and a disincentive.

"I'm getting taxed more and more for fulfilling the American Dream," he told Obama.

Wurzelbacher's campaign-trail encounter with Barack Obama revealed—perhaps without either man realizing it—a distinctly updated and modern version of the old concept of the "American Dream." The term dates from the 1930s and had always evoked an aspiration of upward mobility through individual effort. Originally, and throughout the middle decades of the century, living the "American Dream" meant holding a steady job with rising pay, and all the stability and creature comforts that came with it, from home ownership to higher education. Only in the 1980s and 1990s, when upward promotion at a traditional job became out of reach for so many people, did the American Dream take on Wurzelbacher's connotation: building a business yourself (or buying one), and reaping the rewards.

Although it does not appear that Wurzelbacher was a campaign plant, he did become an overnight political celebrity, particularly among conservative opponents of Obama's policies. Arizona senator John McCain, the Republican presidential nominee, hailed "Joe the Plumber" as a hardworking, everyday citizen *and* an energetic entrepreneur. In a time of economic crisis, McCain argued, politicians shouldn't be taking money away from men like him only to redistribute it. "I want Joe the plumber to spread the wealth around," he declared.[3]

Barack Obama's "Joe the Plumber" moment, as well as the media tempest it provoked in the waning weeks of the 2008 campaign, typified the high-profile place the politics of individual business ownership had achieved in American public life by the early years of the twenty-first century. Although Obama and McCain differed on taxes and most other issues, they agreed wholeheartedly on the need to nurture small, upstart entrepreneurs. For McCain, that meant amplifying the old conservative call to reduce taxes, regulations, and labor power. For Obama, it meant focusing on the 4.8 million employer firms with taxable income below $250,000, even if doing so entailed a slight tax increase for the quarter-million employers whose profits were higher.

Obama, who went on to defeat McCain in the 2008 election, remained committed to providing tax advantages to small companies throughout his presidency. The Affordable Care Act of 2010, known commonly as Obamacare, provided tax credits for companies with fewer than twenty-five employees whose average salaries fell below $50,000. The Small Business Jobs Act, passed the same year, made it easier for small companies to deduct start-up expenses and the costs of mobile phones.[4]

By the 2010s, whether the business cycle was swinging up or down, whether the country was on the roller-coaster ride of a speculative investment bubble—in tech stocks, in real estate—or licking its wounds in the aftermath of a crash, it went without saying that small-scale enterprises, entrepreneurial start-ups, and individual initiative were, or should be, the centerpieces of American economic life. That consensus, of course, had its origins in the economic dislocations and political struggles of the 1970s and 1980s, as globalization, corporate consolidation, and the dominance of finance and service work destabilized the labor market and undercut the traditional, steady job. But it truly crystallized across American public life in the 1990s, when a political ideology rooted in antipathy to market regulation met the near-overnight arrival of the Internet. Embraced by politicians who couldn't agree on anything else, the virtue of going it alone became, by the dawn of the twenty-first century, an unquestioned part of the national creed.

———

The business-ownership ideal reached full bloom in the 1990s, and perhaps nothing reflected its power as poignantly as the unlikely presidential campaign of H. Ross Perot. A diminutive Texas billionaire who had founded several corporations but never sought elective office before running for president in 1992, Perot grabbed national attention by insisting that entrepreneurial business savvy would provide the cure for America's economic dysfunctions. With his folksy, homespun style, he upended the standard two-party political calculus and ran one of the most successful third-party bids in U.S. presidential history.

Perot's quixotic political life took off as the United States came to grips with economic stagnation. After a period of uneven growth in the 1980s, the economy fell into recession again in 1990. Large manufacturers, most notably the "Big Three" automakers General Motors, Ford, and Chrysler, suffered massive losses and laid off thousands of workers. AT&T let 100,000 employees go. This continued a trend: Over the previous ten years, the three biggest American companies by market capitalization—AT&T, Exxon, and General Electric—had lost a combined 723,000 jobs, or 53 percent of their 1982 workforce. In June 1992, unemployment topped out at 7.8 percent, a figure not seen since early 1984 (when it was on the way down).[5]

On paper, the recession wasn't as bad as those of the 1970s or early 1980s. Yet observers at the time noted that it somehow seemed existentially distinct and much worse. "There is a big difference between the public's reaction to this recession and the last one," political pollster Daniel Yankelovich wrote in 1992. "The public experienced the recession of 1981–1982 as if it were a giant traffic jam: once it was over the nation could resume normal speed." But this time was different. "Even though they cannot quite put their finger on it, they fear something is fundamentally wrong with the US economy," Yankelovich concluded.[6] Even if the statistics weren't as bad, the downturn spawned a deep pessimism about the future of work in a precarious and unequal economy.

Professional economists agreed. "This is not just a short-term glitch," Nobel laureate Robert Solow explained. "Family incomes used to double every 30 years" during the height of the growth economy, reported the *New York Times* editorial board, summing up Solow's analysis. Yet "at current rates they'll double in 200."[7]

It was amid this culture of pessimism that Ross Perot entered the political fray. A former IBM salesman, Perot started a computer services company called Electronic Data Systems in Plano, Texas, in 1962. He soon earned a fortune through government contracts, working on programs like Medicare and Medicaid. In the early 1990s, he entered politics, styling himself as a no-nonsense reformer—a successful business owner with a Texas twang and a knack for folksy turns of phrase. And he started to gain a national following. In February 1992, Perot appeared on the CNN program *Larry King Live* to announce that he would run for president as an independent, on the condition that his supporters could get him on the ballot in all fifty states.[8]

Perot's campaign was entirely about economics. Indeed, he had very little in the way of a social agenda or clear foreign policy positions. Rather, he argued for eliminating the budget deficit, cutting government bureaucracy, and reining in what he perceived as wasteful spending. He also understood the unease many voters felt over the expansion of global trade and its hobbling effects on U.S. domestic manufacturing. Competition from countries like Japan, the freer flows of products around the world, and a strong U.S. dollar all combined to put American factories on their back heels. Perot's anti–free trade positions, especially his opposition to the North American Free Trade Agreement (NAFTA), reflected that deep angst.[9]

Yet over and above Perot's policy stances, what distinguished his campaign was how he captured the mood of business owners—not the global elite who ran the mega-corporations but the heads of small and independent operations. In an economic landscape that was becoming more complex and more cutthroat, he argued, those types of companies were getting left behind. Politically, this was an astute way to garner support. While well-heeled corporate executives and managers favored the Republican incumbent, President George H. W. Bush, by large margins, owners of smaller and younger companies turned to Perot, particularly in parts of the country hardest hit by the recession, like the northeast and the west. And what attracted them most of all was his critique of incompetent government officials who just didn't get it.[10]

The American people "were led to believe government could solve our problems," Perot asserted in a Reaganesque tone. But government had failed, he declared, "and it made some problems worse." As a business owner and entrepreneur, Perot promised to bring real business know-how to the presidency. "The United States is the largest and most complex business enterprise in the history of mankind," he said. And yet, among the political class, "officials like to say that government can't be run like a business."[11] Perot proposed that it could.

"I'm just a businessman," he claimed with false modesty at the second presidential debate in October 1992. "I was down in Texas taking care of business, tending to my family. This situation got so bad that I decided I'd better get into it."[12] Government had created America's problem. As a businessman, he averred, he alone could fix it.

In the fall of 1992, Ross Perot won 19 percent of the popular vote, although he carried no states in the Electoral College. Bush got 37.5 percent of the vote and 18 states, and Bill Clinton, governor of Arkansas and nominee of the Democratic Party, took the rest, winning the election with 43 percent of the popular vote and 32 states (plus the District of Columbia). Although most political scientists agree that Perot's candidacy did not ultimately determine the outcome—his supporters would likely have split equally between Clinton and Bush in a two-way race—his pro-business and anti-bureaucracy brand of American populism left a clear mark on American political culture.[13]

Just as important, Perot profoundly shaped the victorious Clinton camp by amplifying attention to a particular set of issues. His attacks on wasteful bureaucracy, both at big corporations and at big government agencies, made it harder for Clinton to propose major structural reforms within the government. His opposition to budget deficits and free-trade deals—notably NAFTA—likewise reinforced the idea that clueless American policymakers could do nothing to improve the hostile climate for business ownership. He lost the election but succeeded in reshaping the political terrain that Bill Clinton had to navigate.

Clinton also faced headwinds from a weak economy. Officially, the early 1990s recession ended well before the 1992 election, but regular people were still feeling its effects when the new president took office. Major corporations continued to downsize and lay off large numbers of workers. IBM, which had reduced its workforce by more than 100,000 jobs between 1986 and 1992, announced tens of thousands more layoffs in early 1993.[14] After plaguing the final year of George Bush's presidency, the phenomenon that became known as the "jobless recovery" continued.

The cultural cachet of business ownership—so clearly on display during the Perot campaign—remained one of the most powerful forces in national politics. The ideal of independent business ownership and the implicit critique of government social policy it contained thwarted much of the new president's agenda.

———

Bill Clinton had come up politically in the world of Atari Democrats in the 1980s. For him, the bleak national economy of the early 1990s created an opportunity to craft a resonant message that merged the promise of new technologies and entrepreneurship with effective, compassionate government policy to build a robust, expansive, and business-centered economy. That combination, for Clinton, was the essence of being a "New Democrat." Instead of old-style liberal talk about "spending," he promoted what he called "investments." In lieu of a traditional welfare system, Clinton called for financial incentives to help people do it themselves. Invoking a phrase he had used since the 1970s, he called for "a hand up—not a hand-out."[15] His political language stressed "personal responsibility" rather than "collective action," reinforcing the values of independence and hard work long associated with entrepreneurship.

In his rhetoric, Clinton positioned himself as the champion of the "little guy"—the hardworking people who had been marginalized, oppressed, and left behind. In his mind, this group included not only the poor and working-class, who had been the Democratic Party's traditional base since the New Deal, and the large swath of middle-class consumers, whom both parties had fought over for decades, but also the owners of small and independent businesses. For the brand of politics Clinton espoused, there was no conflict. Even though the political wing of the small business community mobilized through groups like the NFIB, the ABC, the Chamber of Commerce, NAWBO, and others to push policies mostly associated with the Republican Party, Clinton saw them all as an obvious part of his constituency.

Clinton's efforts to appeal to independent business owners shaped his policy preferences. His first major agenda item, for example, was the budget deficit. Adopting longstanding Republican arguments (also promoted by Perot), Clinton argued that deficit spending by the federal government drove up interest rates and thus raised borrowing costs, disproportionately hurting smaller companies. "As small business owners will testify," Clinton wrote in his first *State of Small Business Report* in 1993, "the best thing the government could do for small business and the economy is to reduce the deficit." The president also pushed for reductions in complex paperwork and regulatory requirements for small firms, as well as tax credits for very small companies that purchased new equipment and a plan to exclude from taxation half of any capital gains made from investments in small firms.[16]*

---

* As was usually the case with political rhetoric, Clinton was vague about whom he had in mind by the term "small business."

Perhaps nowhere was the influence of independent business ownership—as an ideal, as a political constituency—so obvious in the 1990s as in the debates over universal healthcare. Reforming the country's employer-centered healthcare system to extend coverage to all people had been a goal of liberal Democrats for decades, and, once a budget bill was pushed through Congress on a party-line vote, it became the Clinton administration's top domestic agenda item toward the end of 1993. Clinton's strategy, from the outset, was to muster support for reform from the small and mid-size business community, whom he believed had every reason to support it. The costs of healthcare were disproportionately higher on companies with lower revenues. (As with regulatory compliance, big companies could more easily absorb the extra costs.) Moreover, smaller firms *wanted* to be able to afford coverage for their employees. The fact that so many couldn't made it harder to recruit and retain employees, giving larger companies yet another advantage. In theory, at least, they stood to benefit from a system of universal healthcare that leveled the playing field between them and the big corporations.

Business owners were central to the politics of healthcare reform because of the peculiar history of health insurance in America. Unlike most advanced industrial countries, the United States relied on a decentralized, employer-based model for providing healthcare coverage to its citizens. The roots of that system lay in the post–World War II period, when large corporations made deals with insurance companies to provide private healthcare coverage for their employees, with the explicit goal of diluting the power of labor unions and binding workers more tightly to their employers.[17] The structure of healthcare financing, and in particular the prevalence of the insurance model, thwarted competition and inflated prices ever since.[18] Until the early 1980s, medical costs increased at or only slightly above the overall rate of inflation. But during the low-inflation years of the mid- to late 1980s, a complex combination of factors led real healthcare costs to increase rapidly. As a share of GDP, overall health spending rose from 8 percent in 1980 to 10 percent in 1985 to 13 percent in the early 1990s.[19]

And business owners took note. A survey commissioned by National Small Business United (a lobbying group modeled on the NFIB) found that the share of business owners who named "health and medical benefits" as one of their greatest challenges nearly doubled between 1992 and 1993.[20]

As one executive from the National Association of Manufacturers told Congress in 1993, business owners held "a growing belief that as a result of increased spending on health care, less is being spent on upgrading plants and facilities, research and development, training/retraining and other critical business investment."[21]

In his effort to build a coalition for reform, Clinton appealed directly to the image of the virtuous, striving business owner. In a speech to Congress laying out his plan, he singled out the importance of independent business owners, affirming all the ideals that business groups had promoted for years.

"These rising costs," he said, "are a special nightmare for our small businesses, the engine of entrepreneurship and our job creation in America today."

To make the case, he offered a particularly touching story of one such striver:

> Kerry Kennedy owns a small furniture store that employs seven people in Titusville, Florida. Like most small business owners, he's poured his heart and soul, his sweat and blood into that business for years. But over the last several years, again like most small business owners, he's seen his health care premiums skyrocket, even in years when no claims were made. And last year, he painfully discovered he could no longer afford to provide coverage for all his workers because his insurance company told him that two of his workers had become high risks because of their advanced

age. The problem was that those two people were his mother and father, the people who founded the business and still work in the store.[22]

Clinton's appeal to this imagery was deliberate, because his staff knew how important small business support was to the reform agenda and how tough that road would be. "Many small businesses may fiercely resist the proposal," acknowledged advisor Ira Magaziner, who, along with First Lady Hillary Clinton, led the task force on healthcare reform. Health and Human Services Secretary Donna Shalala agreed, noting: "We have to have a package for small business." With that goal in mind, Hillary Clinton called public hearings to gather input from dozens of interest groups, including lobbyists for small and independent firms such as National Small Business United, the Small Business Legislative Council, and the National Association of Women Business Owners.[23]

Unfortunately for the Clinton healthcare initiative, their wooing was for naught. By substantial margins, business owners objected to the central pillar of the plan: a so-called employer mandate that required companies to pay for and provide health insurance as a benefit for workers.

Boston-based restaurateur Stephen Elmont expressed the prevailing view among many business owners. An employer mandate, he told Vice President Al Gore, would be "un-American." The problem, as Elmont saw it, was that government-mandated benefits would create a slippery slope that would suppress business formation. "If I give an inch, I am terribly concerned about that inch," he explained. The Clinton plan would "discourage people from opening up restaurants, it will force marginally profitable restaurants to shut down, and it will mean fewer jobs."[24]

Among business groups, the NFIB—so long a bastion of conservative anti-regulatory politics—took the lead in denouncing the entire project. Rejecting Hillary Clinton's invitation to work collaboratively, the group's president, John Motley, declared that the employer mandate was simply "non-negotiable."

"I might as well spend my time getting ready to fight," he explained.[25]

The NFIB opted for massive resistance because it concluded that every reform proposal in the offing contained "provisions that will require industry to expand its role in providing and paying for health care insurance for employees." Shunting costs onto employers, the group argued, would do the same thing as every other government program—from OSHA regulations to the minimum wage: it would compel small companies to redirect money from some other business function.

And in a political climate where small and mid-size companies had acquired—at least in popular culture—a special responsibility for job creation, the NFIB had a trump card to play.

"If the resulting labor cost increases are large enough, employers will compensate by changing other components of their employees' compensation and benefits package or their employment status," Motley said.[26]

In other words, they would cut pay and start laying people off.

As the healthcare debate stumbled forward in late 1993 and into 1994, the collapse in business support became more widespread. Tarred by its association with "big government" and disowned by the politically popular and powerful community of business owners, the entire reform program collapsed. Clinton's proposal never came up for a vote in Congress. Democrats allowed it to die in committee in August 1994.

Watching Bill Clinton's signature domestic policy proposal wither on the vine, Georgia Republican Newt Gingrich could not contain his glee. The demise of national healthcare reform and the resurgence of a political culture committed to business and capitalism marked a welcome shift, the House minority leader claimed, in "the entire tide of Western history." The Cold War was over and the Soviet Union was no more. For Gingrich, this augured the possibility that stultifying government regulations could also soon be a thing of the past. "I mean, centralized command bureaucracies are dying," he concluded.[27]

Just a few months later, Gingrich would lead a political coalition in the midterm elections of 1994 that recaptured both houses of Congress for the Republicans. Under the banner of a "Contract with America," Gingrich Republicans seized on the long-standing critique of liberal government that had animated supply-siders during the Reagan years and, more recently, the Perot insurgency.[28] Government, according to this vision, was bureaucratic, wasteful, inefficient, and unaccountable—everything that spry, competitive, and entrepreneurial businesses were not.

Under leaders like Gingrich, the Republican Party found itself in a much stronger position than the Democrats to take advantage of both the cultural embrace of business ownership and the rising clout of organized small and independent companies. As the chair of the Republican National Committee put it, the GOP had a historic chance to fulfill its long-standing promise to be "the party of small business, not big business; of Main Street, not Wall Street." Small business leaders agreed. After years of struggling, John Motley of the NFIB declared, "Small business is going to be, as a group, more the apple of the Republicans' eye than big business."[29]

Many Democrats saw the writing on the wall as well. "I've felt first hand the difference between the activism of the Republicans and the passiveness of too many Democrats," wrote Joline Godfrey—the feminist entrepreneur behind An Income of Her Own—to Jim Johnson of the SBA's Office of Advocacy in 1995. "The people who have made real outreach to me have been in the other party." Support from Democrats, she explained, "has been more in spirit than action and in the end that doesn't pay the rent!"[30]

The Clinton White House held out hope that Democrats might regain some ground with the independent business community, but it was an uphill climb. One chance for a reboot came as planning began on the third—and, to date, last—White House Conference on Small Business. Continuing the tradition launched by Jimmy Carter and reinforced by Ronald Reagan offered President Clinton a chance to combine his populist appeals to everyday people with a new vision of markets and capitalism that put a premium on innovation, risk-taking, and entrepreneurship.

At the helm of the effort stood Alan Patricof, a venture capitalist and founder of private equity giant Apax Partners. Job one, Patricof believed, was pushing back against the widespread view that "the Republican Party has become the 'party of small business,' and that the Democrats are for big business." Despite his early enthusiasm, though, he grew frustrated as the planning process wore on.

"There is a *large* potential positive element in *small* business to which someone should pay attention," a discouraged Patricof told White House chief of staff Erskine Bowles. But in too many cases, he believed that he couldn't "get adequate support from the White House" and was "unable to secure high level speakers from the Administration for the regional conferences."[31]

Clinton was determined to shore up his appeal to the independent business community, though, and put more of a personal touch into the event's planning. Perhaps having learned a lesson from Reagan's misstep in blowing off the previous conference nine years earlier, Clinton made a prime-time appearance when the event finally took place in June 1995.

"We know that small business is the engine that will drive us into the twenty-first century," he told the crowd. To that end, he made three vague pledges: to "give new life" to the SBA, to make credit easier to obtain, and "to cut Government regulations that didn't make sense so you could grow faster." (On the last point, Clinton's political headwinds became audibly clear—one audience member shouted "IRS! IRS! IRS!" whenever the president mentioned regulations.)[32]

In the end, Clinton failed to persuade owners of small and mid-size companies that Democratic policies were better than Republican ones. Nonetheless, his steadfast commitment to that community affirmed its centrality within public life and political debate. By the mid-1990s, the national economy recovered from the early-90s recession, and Clinton found himself presiding over a new moment of economic optimism. For a time, public faith in the prospects of long-term economic growth seemed to recover, and the spirit of individuality reigned supreme in political culture.

Throwing fuel on that cultural fire was the near overnight arrival of the system of interconnected networks of computers that revolutionized how people communicated, how business was done, and how Americans thought about work, jobs, and opportunity: the Internet.

———

In a few short years, the Internet leapt from the esoteric corners of computer science departments and government research facilities to completely permeate all aspects of modern life. Only 2.3 percent of people in North America had used the Internet in 1993; ten years later, more than 61 percent had. Internet access in the United States plateaued around 75 percent between 2007 and 2015, and it has since risen past 90 percent.[33] If the Internet had arrived a generation earlier, its outside-the-house effects would likely have been concentrated in major corporations. But coming in the 1990s, in the wake of a major political and cultural shift toward entrepreneurialism and independent business ownership, it quickly became emblematic of new ideas about work and the allure of working for yourself.

For Elenor Cole, it meant a closet full of bras.

In 1998, Cole worked in the lingerie section of Lord & Taylor at the NorthPark Mall in Dallas, Texas. Then in her late fifties, she found retail work exhausting. She got only two breaks a day, and that was only if the store wasn't too busy and there was someone to cover for her. But at least the work was predictable, she reasoned, and she knew her paycheck was coming. Previously, she had owned a manicure shop, so she knew too well the stresses of running a business, but she still missed it. If only she had a niche—something profitable and new, where she wouldn't be undercut by large, established companies. Someplace where she could experience the upsides of self-employment but minimize the uncertainty.

And one day, inspiration struck.

"Plus-sized women couldn't find bras that fit" in stores like Lord & Taylor, Cole explained. "I felt really sorry for them."

If she had had that realization ten or twenty years earlier, Cole might have decided to open a specialty shop to cater to this underserved demographic. Or maybe she would have started a mail-order company out of her home. But in the fall of 1998, she had a new option. She could sell big brassieres online.

So she got to work. Toward the end of 1998, Cole began stockpiling plus-size bras from a handful of suppliers and stashing them in her hall closet. Her son David, then in his late thirties, designed a web page: biggerbras.com. And the new upstart business, Big Girls' Bras, Etcetera, made its first sale in February 1999. By May, when sales reached $3,000, Cole quit her job at the mall. David soon quit his $50,000-a-year job to work full-time for his mother. Within a few years, the company boasted hundreds of online pages of merchandise and thousands of daily users, spent up to $10,000 a month on advertising to drive web traffic, and brought in close to $100,000 a month in revenue.

Big Girls' Bras succeeded in the way that countless small enterprises have, by finding an underserved niche and acting as a middleman. By using the Internet, Elenor Cole was able to locate and target a narrow subset of a larger market and carve off some profit for herself. Within two years, in early 2001, she reported that she was able to pay herself three times what she had made at Lord & Taylor. What's more, she worked fewer hours per week at a schedule of her choosing. She was a far cry from the young tech billionaires who drew the biggest headlines during the "dot-com" craze of the late 1990s, but the early days of Internet-based business treated her well. At a time when Jeff Bezos's Amazon.com was a little-known bookseller, when Google had only begun to replace Lycos and Excite as the search engine of choice, and when future Facebook founder Mark Zuckerberg was still in high school, Elenor Cole—whom a reporter for the *Dallas Morning News* described as a "61-year-old grandmother"—had become, in the paper's words, "the perfect example of why the Internet has captured the imagination of so many wannabe entrepreneurs."[34]

From its earliest days, the Internet promised liberation from stultifying bureaucracies and exclusive hierarchies. That mythology was belied by the quick ascent of a handful of large and powerful corporations, but it proved stubbornly resilient. The "slow human handling of most information," wrote MIT professor Nicholas Negroponte in 1995, "is about to become the instantaneous and inexpensive transfer of electronic data that move at the speed of light. In this form, the information can become universally accessible."[35] The possibilities appeared endless. Little wonder it appealed to the imaginations of entrepreneurs.

Advocates for small and independent business ownership saw enormous potential in the new technology. The Internet allowed newcomers like Elenor Cole to parlay a passion or niche expertise into a viable business, taking advantage of low entry costs—running a website was cheap if, like her son, David, you knew how to do it—and locating far-flung customers. In this new world, upstarts could break down the structural advantages that large, scaled-up retailers had long enjoyed. In a 2002 research brief for the Small Business Administration, Texas-based home-business consultant Joanne Pratt summed up the pervasive view. "Technology, telecommunications, and the Internet are changing the way businesses market and provide products and services," she wrote. "The Internet offers unparalleled new opportunities for small businesses."[36]

At the same time, Internet culture created a vexing set of anxieties and misplaced dreams. The opportunities for a small number of lucky or exceptionally talented entrepreneurs and early investors contributed to a growing sense that *everyone* should be able to make a killing—and quickly. The most immediate and consequential manifestation of that ebullience came in the inflation of the "dot-com bubble" in the second half of the 1990s. It all started, symbolically anyway, in August 1995 with the initial public offering (IPO) of Netscape Communications Corporation, maker of the most popular web browser.[37] In short order, the world of Internet stock investing embarked on a five-year roller coaster that reached its feverish peak when the bubble popped in the spring of 2000.[38]

Yet by then the psychic damage was done. The Internet's inherent promise that new technology, combined with an entrepreneurial spirit and willingness to break out on your own, would lead to personal riches had metastasized into a widespread "get rich quick" culture. One of the darker and most perilous manifestations of this culture took root among the most vulnerable: the proliferation of online scams.

In November 1999, Madeleine Vallieres of Lenexa, Kansas, dashed off a message to the "Working Options" email address at the national headquarters of AARP, an advocacy organization that lobbied on issues of interest to older Americans. What, she wondered, did the organization think about home-based businesses in the Internet age? "I would like to work at home using my computer," she noted. "But all the ads for this seem like scams."

Lindy Doty of Arnold, Nebraska, was looking for an answer to a similar question. "Due to health problems," she wrote, "my husband is no longer able to commit to a full time job, but could work at home setting his own schedule according to how he feels each day. Is there anything to the ads for computer work at home?"

Down in Efland, North Carolina, Louise Francke had an even more specific concern. She had seen an online ad for a Florida-based company called American Success Products that promised to pay people to stuff circulars and print ads into envelopes ($1 per mailing) and even threw in a bonus $30 for any sales that came from a mailing. But the opportunity, likely in an unsolicited email, seemed too good to be true. "Have not been able to get info online from BBB [Better Business Bureau] on this co[mpany]. . . . IS THIS A SCAM??? OR LEGITAMIT [*sic*] BUSINESS???"[39]

Work-from-home gurus Sarah and Paul Edwards had the answers. In the roaring 1990s, when "everyone" seemed to be making it big fast, the market for marks was ripe. In response, updated editions of the Edwardses' how-to manual on running a home-based business called particular attention to how con artists used the new world of computer and Internet technology to prey on people trying to boost their income. Watch out for "everyday work-at-home Schemes, Scams, and Rip-Offs," they warned. Simple tasks like stuffing envelopes, clipping newspaper coupons, tracking your television or radio consumption, "renting time on your computer," or "any too-good-to-be-true" offer was likely someone trying to swindle you.

A typical ad, flooding into an email inbox in the days before spam filters, might read: "COMPUTER—do you own or have access to a personal computer? Up to $35/hour. Full/part time, starting immediately." But if someone asked you to send money first, on the promise of getting more information later, you should stay away.[40]

Fraud has always been a feature of capitalism, from currency counterfeiters to fly-by-night sales outfits to knock-off "Louis Vooton" bags sold on the street.[41] During the 1990s, though, age-old hucksterism ran headlong into the get-rich-quick culture of immediate gratification. And it was bolstered by the new and often-misunderstood world of the Internet.

The most pernicious types of Internet scams involved business opportunities like the ones Sarah and Paul Edwards cautioned against. Particularly common were "pyramid" or "endless-chain distribution" schemes, whereby a would-be investor made an initial payment and was then told to seek out other people to buy into the alleged "business opportunity." Early entrants were paid handsome returns with the contributions of later participants, but at no point did the operation generate any income or *do* anything productive. Such pyramids would inevitably collapse, with the few at the top making off with the money invested by the many in the middle and bottom. Such ploys had existed for centuries, of course, and were most famously identified with Charles Ponzi, a Boston-based fraudster from the 1920s. But the quick spread of Internet access elevated the threat they posed. In 1996, according to a report by the National Consumers League, pyramid schemes were the most common type of Internet fraud.[42] In March 1998, the Securities and Exchange Commission sued International Heritage Inc.—purveyor of luxury items like jewelry—in the largest suit alleging a pyramid scheme to that point in American history. (The head of the SEC, as it happened, was Arthur Levitt, longtime booster of independent companies and founder of the American Business Conference.) And in the five years after 1996, the Federal Trade Commission prosecuted more pyramid schemes than it had in the previous seventeen years.[43]

From brassieres to bamboozles, then, the Internet boom of the 1990s built on and expanded a pre-existing culture of going it alone for which people had been primed for years. Just as the fax machine and personal computer had fueled the work-from-home movement in the 1980s, so, too, did the Internet help convince a wide range of Americans to break free of the confines of traditional work. Faith in the power of individuals—as entrepreneurs, as innovators, as individual wealth generators—was stronger than ever.

———

That devotion never waned, even as a vicious boom and bust cycle consumed the American economy. First the dot-com bubble burst. Then came the dramatic inflation and even more spectacular bursting of the real-estate bubble in the first decade of the 2000s. The trend lines from the 1970s continued—middle- and lower-class wages barely budged, even as people at the top got richer and richer (mostly in financial services), healthcare costs rose, and workplace benefits remained slim to nonexistent for millions of workers. Even when *employment* numbers were good, jobs were bad.

All the same, in the early years of the new century, the phrase "small business is the backbone of the American economy" became one of the most well-trod clichés in public rhetoric, peppering speeches from all over the political world. If you don't believe me, look up an episode of comedian John Oliver's HBO program, *Last Week Tonight*, from September 2017 on the topic of "Corporate Consolidation." In eighteen seconds, Oliver showed thirty-four different American politicians repeating the phrase, nearly verbatim.[44]

That bipartisan commitment to business ownership reflected a much broader set of values that had become firmly integrated into political culture. Owning a small business represented only one path—a notably virtuous one, according to the politicians—toward a society rooted in individual initiative, of taking personal responsibility for one's economic fortunes. And as we'll see in the final chapter, this message only became further amplified as smartphones, app-based services, and other new Internet-related technologies took over everyday life.

Although those values were prominent across the political spectrum, the Republican Party benefited most. Drawing on its long history as the "party of business," the GOP reaped the benefits of its pro-market, anti-regulatory, and anti-tax message in 2000, retaking the White House and narrowly keeping control of Congress. Running for reelection in 2004, President George W. Bush put his own stamp on the prevailing ethic when he proposed the "Ownership Society." Bush's vision explicitly sought to offer an updated and conservative corollary to the "Great Society," President Lyndon Johnson's phrase for his basket of liberal policy proposals (including civil rights, immigration reform, the War on Poverty, and public funding for the arts and sciences) in the mid-1960s.[45] For Bush, "ownership" encompassed a wide range of things, from home ownership (a disastrous proposition for many, as the world found out when the housing bubble burst in 2007) to investment to entrepreneurship. The biggest policy initiative under the auspices of the Ownership Society was a failed effort to privatize Social Security and replace it with personal retirement savings accounts linked to the stock market. When that proposal went up in smoke in 2005 and Bush's political popularity sank, the phrase "ownership society" quickly disappeared from public conversation. Nevertheless, it neatly captured that broader worldview in which everyone took individual responsibility—ownership—for every aspect of their lives and livelihoods.[46]

So when Joe the Plumber accused Barack Obama of shortchanging the American Dream by proposing marginally higher tax rates on business owners whose annual after-expense incomes exceeded a quarter of a million dollars, he was speaking a familiar language. And when Obama countered that *most* small businesses deserved a tax cut because they represented the hardworking, virtuous entrepreneurs who made the country work, he was likewise affirming a well-established orthodoxy.

Ironically, Obama would encounter the consequences of a political culture rooted in the promise of business ownership during his presidency. The fierce partisanship on display during the Gingrich Revolution of the mid-1990s only grew sharper in the years to come, exacerbated by the profound social trauma created by the financial crisis. In the spring of 2009, early in Obama's first term, that partisan rancor manifested in the formation of the Tea Party movement within the Republican Party. First sparked by outcry against proposals for government aid to struggling homeowners, the Tea Party quickly expanded into an attack on all aspects of the Obama presidency.[47] Funded by corporate lobbyists and traditional Republican political groups, the Tea Party also spawned grassroots activism, most notably among older, white Republicans who, not surprisingly for that demographic, generally had higher-than-average incomes. And perhaps most tellingly, a disproportionate number owned their own businesses.[48]

Tea Party activism drew on the business community's age-old critiques of government bureaucracy, waste, taxation, and regulation. (Some clever protestors declared that "TEA" stood for "Taxed Enough Already.") Their organized opposition threw a wrench into the Obama administration's legislative agenda, helped Republicans regain control of Congress in 2010, and pushed the GOP significantly to the right. Before that happened, Obama was able to pass the Affordable Care Act in 2010, succeeding where Bill Clinton had failed and putting the United States on the road toward universal health care coverage. Yet even that legislation, which Republicans would weaken in the years to come, carved out exceptions and tax benefits for companies that employed fewer than fifty people, who were not required to offer affordable health insurance options.

In an era when Democrats and Republicans drifted further apart and agreed on less and less, the virtue of entrepreneurship and independent business ownership rose to the status of sacred cow. For Democrats, appeasing business owners meant readjusting policy aims toward a more conservative vision. For Republicans, it meant continuing to demonize government, regulations, taxes, and a welfare system that, they argued, rewarded "takers" and not "makers."

And even as this political transformation reached its fulfillment, the cultural power of this go-it-alone ethic reached far from the Washington Beltway to recast the ways many individuals understood their work options and their chances at a better life. From technology hubs like Silicon Valley to city streets to the living rooms of suburbia, the dream of independent work became a constant feature of modern life.

9

THE NEW GIGS
ARISE

No shifts. No boss. No limits.

—Uber ad on a billboard near the

Taxi and Limousine Commission's

office, New York City, 2014[1]

n May 2010, a small service calling itself UberCab launched in San Francisco. Three years earlier, the Apple iPhone had hit the market, spurring a rapid uptick in smartphone usage and the proliferation of third-party applications, or "apps." And UberCab was there to take advantage. Making use of new scheduling and payment software as well as global positioning system (GPS) satellites, it offered its users a new way to summon and pay for a taxi ride in the Bay Area. Within three years, the company—by then known simply as Uber—had kickstarted what became known as the "ridesharing industry." Silicon Valley's tech world was abuzz with excitement over the potential for Uber and companies like it to "disrupt" antiquated and tired business models.[2]

By the early 2010s, the Internet was in your pocket. A bevy of new companies exploded onto the scene, providing a wide range of services that dramatically changed what people could do with their phones— order food, rent out a spare room, sell home-made items, and, of course, hail a ride. In short order, these app-based enterprises, no matter what business niche or industry they served, joined the pantheon of firms collectively known as "tech companies," alongside computer makers, software designers, social media websites, search engines, and the like. And virtually overnight, they seemed to promise new ways of moving through the world—an "Uber for Everything."

These companies made a twofold promise to their investors as well as to the general public. First, they would fundamentally change how consumers acquired goods and services, making it easier and cheaper to get what you wanted, especially while on the go. Just as important, they promised an exciting revolution in the act of work itself. The billboard described at the beginning of this chapter—quite un-coincidentally posted outside the municipal agency that licensed and regulated taxis in New York City—made clear that driving for Uber meant something worlds better than a regular job. Uber drivers were independent con-tractors, not employees of the company. This meant unprecedented opportunities for personal freedom and wealth, Uber claimed. Work when you want, as much as you want. Make as much as you want. No boss. No schedule.

The rapid proliferation of companies like Uber, Airbnb, DoorDash, TaskRabbit—the list goes on—appeared to augur a new age. A pano-ply of terms emerged to describe what was happening. As awestruck journalists and self-interested venture capitalists breathlessly insisted, these apps promised to cut out traditional middlemen. Cabbies, pizza deliverers, and even hotels would all become things of the past as a new "sharing economy" replaced the old way of doing things. Equally cheer-ful, if less common, monikers included "peer-to-peer" economy, "on-demand" economy, and even the "collaborative-consumption" economy.

Of course, the idea that Uber and other such companies "cut out the middleman" was demonstrably false. Those companies were the mid-dlemen. Their job was to connect someone who needed a service with someone who provided that service—whether delivering your groceries, writing code for your software, or giving you a ride home from the bar. Their revenue came from taking a cut of the cost of that transaction.

While many observers greeted the arrival of this new style of company with unbridled joy, critics emerged, and quickly. Naturally, the industries being "disrupted"—the taxi drivers, the hotel operators—voiced their displeasure. So, too, did advocates for workers. The labor that propelled this new system, they pointed out, was outside the traditional system. Because the workers were not formal employees, they received none of the perks or benefits of regular jobs—stability, predictability, healthcare, even a statutory minimum wage. They had far more in common with musicians hustling from show to show than employees at traditional companies. Far from a "sharing economy," this new order was really a "gig economy."[3] The term stuck, largely because it highlighted the essential feature of these new arrangements: the impermanence of the work.

Yet for all the hype about its revolutionary potential, Uber didn't invent the gig economy's central creed, that you were better off working independently through a series of gigs. Yes, the specific communications technologies—the smartphones, the GPS, the apps—were newly available, but technology doesn't make change all by itself. What really allowed the gig economy to take off was how those new technologies meshed with a set of cultural assumptions and economic conditions that had been marinating for decades.

Between the late 1990s and the early 2010s, two forces came together: the hustle-culture ideal of being your own boss and an increasingly precarious work environment, which was exacerbated by wild swings in the economy. The spread of the Internet, the cultural embrace of investing and ownership, and the chaos of a roller-coaster economy all conspired to recalibrate people's expectations about what the world of work could offer. What emerged, with a lift from the coding geniuses of Silicon Valley and the disruptive, app-based upstart companies, was an economic vision based simultaneously on instant access and atomized labor.

And while that go-it-alone ethic had a long history (eight chapters long, at this point), it got a particularly powerful boost in the late 1990s.

———

The way Daniel Pink told the story, his moment of clarity came shortly after he threw up in the vice president's office. It was the summer of 1997, and he had been working as a speechwriter for Al Gore for two years. But following a particularly public bout of exhaustion at work, the young writer decided to leave his job.

"Indeed," he wrote later, "I left *all* jobs for good. I became a free agent."

Pink hung out his shingle and became a freelance writer. He was, he recalled, "writing speeches and articles for just about anyone whose check would clear." Among his early clients was *Fast Company*, the two-year old tech, business, and design magazine that published a major cover piece he wrote just six months after leaving Gore's office. In that article, Pink diagnosed and gave a name to the trend that he himself had become part of: the revolt against a regular job and the decision to strike out on your own. What America was experiencing, Pink announced, was the arrival of "Free Agent Nation."[4]

In the late 1990s, Pink argued, a collection of professionals, consultants, innovators, and entrepreneurs were redrawing the road map of work. Some 14 million self-employed Americans made up this community, as well as 8.3 million independent contractors and more than 2 million people who regularly worked for temporary staffing agencies across a range of fields.[5] No matter the type of work they did, the members of this disparate group were united by a shared conviction that the old social compact of Corporate America was dead. The economy of the mid-twentieth century had been rooted in steady jobs, worker loyalty, and stability, Pink explained. Now something new had replaced the loyal, workaday Organization Man: "the footloose, independent worker—the tech-savvy, self-reliant, path-charting micropreneur."[6]

Sara Horowitz, whom Pink profiled in the full-length book that followed his original *Fast Company* article, was especially excited about new ways of working. A labor lawyer from a family of union activists,

Horowitz founded a nonprofit organization called Working Today in 1995 to provide services to independent workers—people who could not avail themselves of the benefits that traditional employers provided. By the time she met Pink in 1997, her organization counted among its ranks nine professional groups and 35,000 total members. For a fee, those members received access to group health insurance as well as discounts on supplies, training programs, and other types of support.[7]

Despite her origins in the labor movement, which had long fought for workers to receive benefits from their employers, Horowitz envisioned a new system that left employers on the sidelines. In the past, she explained to Pink, people became employees of large institutions and then fought (with varying degrees of success) for their rights and benefits. But in the 1990s, she believed, work had become atomized. It was everyone for themselves.

"This is the new structure of work," she explained, drawing unlinked circles on a piece of paper. "Any rights you have come from being an individual. This job notion, which used to undergird everything, doesn't exist here."[8]

Daniel Pink and Sarah Horowitz were convinced they were onto something new. The reality, however, was far more complicated.

On the one hand, the notion that "everyone" was suddenly an atomized, independent worker was an illusion. Class privilege acted like a set of blinders, leading journalists and trend spotters to see a phenomenon that was more prevalent among *people like them* and extrapolate to the broader public. According to data from the U.S. government's Current Population Survey, the percentage of the non-agricultural American workforce that reported being "self-employed" was virtually unchanged between 1990 and 2008, hovering just above 10 percent. More people did appear to be *incorporating their* businesses (although the majority of companies remained unincorporated), but the actual number of people who reported that they got their income primarily through self-employment didn't rise.[9] As a result, critical readers of Pink's article and book argued that he might be overstating the case. The long-term growth in what scholars call "alternative work arrangements"—independent contractors, on-call workers, temporary help agency workers—appeared to slow and even decline a bit during the roaring dot-com economy of the late 1990s, when official unemployment fell below 4 percent for the first time since the 1960s.[10] Perhaps, critics charged, what had appeared in the 1980s and early 1990s to be a trend toward independence had actually just been a predictable response to economic hard times: plant closings in the wake of outsourcing and automation in manufacturing, combined with the recession of the early 1990s and the "jobless recovery" that followed.

"High levels of self-employment," journalist Kim Clark suggested in a harsh review of Pink's first article, "aren't so much proof of a creative and courageous work force as evidence that a desperate population doesn't have job opportunities. It's no accident that Venezuela has triple and Indonesia quadruple the self-employment rate of the U.S. As flimsy and meager as they are, cubicle dividers and paychecks, it seems, are the strongest building blocks for a healthy economy."[11]

At the same time, some longer-term trends suggest that Pink may have had a point. The number of people in "alternative work arrangements" may have remained roughly constant from the 1990s onward, but the number of people who opened microbusinesses that they ran by themselves rose dramatically. Officially called "non-employer businesses," these one-person or family-owned enterprises do not hire any workers, but they still generate at least $1,000 in revenue a year and are subject to federal income taxes.* Starting in the 1990s, the number of non-employer businesses grew quickly, from about 15 million in 1997 to more than 26 million twenty years later. Meanwhile, the number of

---

* The leaf-raking "business" I operated as a teenager didn't count as a non-employer firm; the company my father owned in the same years did.

employer firms that met the SBA's definition of "small" remained mostly flat, at about 6 million. (For comparison's sake, about 20,000 companies counted as "large.")[12]

What's important about non-employer firms is the motivation of their owners. As my UNC colleague Dr. Dawn Rivers has shown, the main driver for many non-employer business owners is *not* entrepreneurial ambition or the desire to make a fortune and build a business empire. Rather, many are motivated primarily by a desire to control their own time and the conditions of their labor, and they will frequently limit the work they do to accommodate their lives. Working independently, in other words, allows many non-employer business owners to achieve that precious thing that folks in the corporate world call "work-life balance."[13]

Numbers aside, Pink put his finger on a key cultural notion—the growing enthusiasm among the technically inclined, news-consuming middle classes that working for oneself was the wave of the future. In the years before Uber started recruiting drivers by redefining labor as entrepreneurship, authors like Pink and the many "free agents" he profiled had already become apostles of going it alone. And as the trend continued, a particular domain of "free agent" work began to attract more attention. Independent contracting, a longstanding work practice with a nebulous legal history, would eventually prove foundational to the business model of gig-economy companies.

———

In 2009, the U.S. Labor Department sued Cascom, Inc. for violating the 1938 Fair Labor Standards Act (FLSA). The lawsuit, brought and eventually won by the newly elected Obama administration, was based on the somewhat dry-sounding legal issue of "worker misclassification." Boring though the case may have appeared, it cast a harsh and critical light onto the seedy underside of work in America.

"Misclassification" meant, in essence, that a company treated workers as independent contractors when it should have treated them as employees. The distinction might seem minor, but it was central to the business model of companies like Cascom.

Here's how it worked: If you were a new Time Warner Cable (TWC) subscriber in southwestern Ohio and you needed someone to install your cable, you made an appointment with the cable company. You might reasonably expect the provider to send one of its people out to do the job, and indeed, in the past, that is exactly what would have happened. But by the 2000s, TWC (the second largest cable company in the country, which was formerly a subsidiary of telecommunications giant Warner Media, later acquired by Charter, and as of 2022 known as Spectrum) changed the way it did things. Instead of hiring its own workers to do cable installation, it began subcontracting installation projects out to smaller companies like Cascom. So far so good. Companies outsource functions to a specialist, often a smaller, sleeker, more efficient, or more local company, all the time. That's how they keep their eye on the thing they do best—what the business professors call their "core competency."

So Cascom, not TWC, became the "cable guy" you waited for at your house. But that's not what happened either. And here's where it got litigious.

The person who arrived at your house wearing the Cascom uniform, driving the Cascom van, and beholden to the Cascom dispatcher for information about where your house was and what you wanted installed . . . that person didn't work for Cascom. And they certainly didn't work for Time Warner Cable, with whom you had set up the appointment in the first place. Instead, the cable installer was an *independent contractor*.[14]

The trouble was that "independent contracting" is a very specific type of work arrangement that is spelled out in the law. The Obama Labor Department sued Cascom precisely because it was violating that law. It was misclassifying its cable installers, who were *not* in fact independent but rather should have been considered employees. And this mattered, because employees are entitled to certain protections, including minimum wages and overtime pay, that independent contractors are not.

Cascom argued that it was merely paying people to perform work on their own time. In a callback to the "piece rate" system associated with sweatshops and the home-based cottage-industry work of an earlier era, the company paid its installers by the job, rather than by the hour. In fact, it did not even keep records of their hours. Yet the claims that installers were truly independent of Cascom turned out not to be true. Instead, the company dictated the time, place, duration, and nature of the installation jobs. What's more, installers had to use Cascom vehicles and tools (which they had to pay for). They were forbidden to hire assistants without permission. They could not take on new clients other than those assigned by Cascom. And if their work was found to be substandard after the fact, they would be fined.[15]

Nothing about this arrangement was "independent," the judge for the Southern District of Ohio determined. This was employment, and by misclassifying them, Cascom had cheated 250 installers out of a total of $1.5 million, which it was ordered to pay.[16]

The Obama administration's suit against Cascom was the fruit of a campaign by labor activists to finally crack down on abuse within the independent contracting system, which had quietly become a mainstay of the modern workscape in the 1990s and early 2000s. In exactly the period in which Daniel Pink identified the rise of "Free Agent Nation," the numbers of independent contractors trended up and more and more companies began outsourcing work to them. Yet for the most part, the public paid little attention. When Barack Obama, during his brief pre-presidential stint as a U.S. senator, introduced the Independent Contractor Proper Classification Act of 2007 to rein in the practice, the bill went nowhere.[17] In a culture that hailed independence and the go-it-alone spirit, putting limits on independent contracting was a non-starter.

While independent contracting became more prominent in the late twentieth century, the fundamental legal questions at stake—whether and how to classify a worker's relationship to the workplace—had deep roots. Prior to the 1930s, there had been no particularly clear definition of the relationship between the person who did the work and the person who paid for that work to be done. In fact, in the nineteenth century, the most common legal question was how to protect a factory owner from liability if a worker did something negligent—like cause an accident that hurt someone. The legal system was not especially concerned with defining the relationship to safeguard the *worker*.[18]

The modern labor movement succeeded in turning the question around during the Great Depression. The most important development came with the Fair Labor Standards Act of 1938 (FLSA), the centerpiece of American labor law passed shortly before the Roosevelt administration ran out of reform steam and shifted to a war footing. (Franklin Roosevelt famously said that "Dr. New Deal" gave way to "Dr. Win-the-War" in the 1940s.) To protect workers from exploitation and unsafe conditions, as well as to enforce rules about minimum wages, overtime, and the prohibition of child labor, the FLSA for the first time offered a legal definition of what an employee actually was. Although defining "employee" might seem obvious in everyday life, as a legal matter it proved tricky, and the statute defined it rather opaquely. An "employee," it said, was "any individual employed by an employer," where an "employer" was anyone "acting . . . in the interest of an employer in relation to an employee."[19] The framers of the law clearly did not have my ninth-grade English teacher, Ms. O'Malley, who taught us never to use a word in its own definition.

That circular and capacious definition left plenty of room for interpretation and, ultimately, controversy. In 1944, for example, the U.S. Supreme Court ruled in *National Labor Relations Board v. Hearst Publications, Inc.* that "newsboys" who sold newspapers on the street on commission were employees of publishing giant Hearst and thus entitled to labor protections.[20] In response to *Hearst* and similar cases, anti-labor conservatives mobilized a political and legal campaign specifically designed to exclude certain categories of workers from the definition of "employee." The 1947 Taft–Hartley Act, which dramatically scaled back labor protections, made "independent contractors" distinct from "employees."[21]

Even after Taft–Hartley, though, the law remained murky on how to draw the line between employees and independent contractors. Those distinctions mattered, since the former enjoyed protections not only under New Deal–era laws like the National Labor Relations Act (which legally recognized unions), the Fair Labor Standards Act, and the Social Security Act but also under legislation passed in the 1970s, like the Occupational Safety and Health Act (OSHA) and the Employee Retirement Income Security Act (ERISA), which governs 401(k) accounts and the like.

The precise definitions of "employee" and "independent contractor" have never been codified in law. Instead, the legal system has relied on an uneasy morass of tests, generalities, and assumptions to determine who is who, usually on a case-by-case basis once a given arrangement is challenged in court. Courts typically use two types of tests, either separately or in conjunction with each other. The "control test" asks how much say a worker has over the nature and condition of the work. Or, in the wonky words of the Internal Revenue Service: "an agent is an employee only when the principal controls or has the right to control the manner and means through which the agent performs work." The "economic realities test," on the other hand, asks how much workers depend on an individual company for their livelihood. The more you count on income from a single source, the more you are an employee. The more you treat any given job as one client among many, the more you are in business for yourself as an independent contractor.[22]

For decades, the ambiguity of independent contractor law and the challenges of classifying workers remained a marginal problem for most Americans. But by the turn of the present century, both the practice of independent contracting and the legal problems it entailed became more common. Getting exact counts of the "non-traditional" workforce is a daunting and imprecise task, but researchers have documented a notable uptick in multiple categories of alternative work, with independent contracting leading the way.[23] By one count, approximately 6.4 percent of workers identified themselves as independent contractors in the 1990s; about 7.4 percent did so by 2009.[24]

Looking at the question slightly differently, another study noted the rising number of people receiving 1099-MISC tax forms from the IRS in the early years of the twenty-first century. Such forms, generated when someone earns between $600 and $20,000 outside of traditional (Form W2-receiving) employment, increased by 22 percent between 2000 and 2014, while the number of W2s declined by about 3.5 percent.[25] If anything, this type of study undercounts the number of people engaged in independent work, since it cannot account for informal and illicit economic activity.

In the early twenty-first century, in other words, a modestly higher number of Americans earned a greater amount of their income through irregular types of employment. In 2019, one analysis of multiple surveys and studies suggested that, after accounting for business-cycle fluctuations, the "incidence of alternative work arrangements" increased by about 1 percent, or between 1.4 and 1.6 million people, from 2000 to 2017.[26]

The gig economy did not invent the appeal of working independently, even though it came to depend on it. In fact, the arrow of causation likely went the other way: the changing labor landscape and the cultural vision that underlay that shift paved the way for app-based companies to thrive. Long before anyone had heard the word "uber" outside of German class or had thought to spell "Lift" with a *y*, an increasing number of Americans had ventured—by necessity, in search of opportunity, or both—into the world of independent contracting. A 2015 study by researchers at George Mason's Mercatus Center concluded that the proliferation of "sharing-economy firms" was itself "a response to a stagnant traditional labor sector and a product of the growing independent workforce."[27] By 2021, according to one study, some 9 percent of Americans, or 30 million people, reported earning at least some income from an online gig platform in the past year. Of those, nearly one-third said gig work was their "main job."[28]

In the early 2000s, economic life was becoming increasingly precarious. Living costs rose even as lower- and middle-class wages barely moved in many sectors. Jobs became less steady, and work itself became less regular and more contingent. And that was before the world economy went to hell.

––––––

The global financial system melted down, to use the common nuclear-age metaphor, in 2007 and 2008. The crisis became full-blown with the bankruptcy of investment bank Lehman Brothers in September 2008, and the world plunged into the worst economic contraction in seventy-five years. During the Great Recession that followed, official unemployment in the United States topped out at 10 percent in 2009 and 2010; accounting for the underemployed, underpaid, and those who abandoned the workforce entirely, the true level of suffering was much higher.*

The crisis years of the early 2010s exposed both the economic precarity and the new cultural assumptions that had come to define work

––––––

* According to the official declaration by the National Bureau of Economic Research, the American economy was in recession between December 2007 and June 2009; thereafter, it was in recovery. However, as a matter of lived experience, the "Great Recession" endured until at least 2013 or 2014 for the hardest-hit people—those who lost their homes, their livelihoods, their savings. As a point of comparison, the U.S. economy was in "recovery" between 1933 and 1937, yet those years are commonly, and correctly, remembered as the "Great Depression."

in modern America. While investors and homeowners may have lost speculative gains when the market crashed, the real pain was experienced by people further down the ladder. Low-wage service-sector workers lost their jobs when consumer spending collapsed. Debt-addled college graduates saw their future job prospects dry up. Blue-collar workers watched factory jobs quickly complete their post-NAFTA slide abroad. A multipronged crisis—of resources, of hope, of faith in institutions and democracy itself—engulfed the country.

All the while, the boot-strapping culture that promised economic independence and the virtues of going it alone sang with a louder voice than ever. Burned by the greed and incompetence of slick bankers and massive corporations, Americans turned inward, doubling down on the promise of independent work. It was precisely in this despondent economic environment that app-based companies began to proliferate.

Gig-economy firms were well placed, amid a global economic catastrophe, to take advantage of a fragmented workforce that valued the go-it-alone spirit. When Uber first launched in San Francisco, its drivers picked you up in company-owned luxury sedans; in 2012, the company's "UberX" service allowed drivers to use their own cars.[29] Under both systems, however, the company engaged its drivers as independent contractors. An Uber driver, as the journalist Sarah Kessler put it in 2018, "supplied his own car, gas, and overly pungent air fresheners." Moreover: "He paid for his own coffee breaks and his own health insurance. All of the responsibilities of being in business, including taxes, rested on his shoulders."[30]

In 2013, 35,000 current and former Uber drivers filed a suit against the company for misclassifying them as contractors instead of employees.[31] That suit was settled privately, but others followed. In 2015, a year that saw the number of U.S.-based Uber drivers double, the company faced fifty lawsuits in federal courts—three times as many as its rival, Lyft. Some alleged misclassification, while others accused the company of misrepresenting (or, as non-lawyers say, lying about) other aspects of the work experience. In one case, the Federal Trade Commission accused Uber of recruiting drivers by fudging the terms of its leases and loans and inflating estimates of their expected earnings. Uber settled the case in January 2017 for $20 million.[32]

Public policy debates about worker classification continued without obvious resolution. In 2018, the Supreme Court of California ruled that hiring companies should bear the burden of proving that independent contractors were truly independent—that they worked on their own terms and schedule; that the work they did was *not* the company's principal activity; and that the worker typically did that sort of work for a range of clients. By that logic, nearly all app-based "sharing" or gig-economy companies would *not* qualify and would have to treat their workers as employees. That meant offering a minimum wage, overtime, and workers' compensation, reimbursing expenses, and supplying the tools necessary to do the job (such as a car).[33] The California State Assembly codified and expanded that decision in 2019. Yet the next year, voters approved a ballot initiative called Proposition 22, which undid the new law. The repeal campaign, funded and supported, unsurprisingly, by app-based companies that sought exemptions for their businesses, encouraged Californians to put their love of cheap prices ahead of the well-being of drivers. A suit challenging the constitutionality of Proposition 22, which could shape the future of gig work in California, was making its way through the courts as of this writing.[34]

Abuse of independent-contractor status and the exploitation of people suffering through the Great Recession was not limited to app-based "sharing" companies, of course. In the mid-2010s, janitorial services franchising companies like Jan-Pro and Coverall made headlines and sparked lawsuits over their work arrangements. Such companies typically promoted themselves as opportunities for hardworking people to control their own destiny and own their own business by buying a franchise. Franchisees would pay tens of thousands of dollars in start-up fees, as well as royalty fees and management fees (5 and 10 percent of revenue, respectively, for Coverall). Their income would then come from cleaning offices and other spaces, but the list of clients came directly from the franchisor, who was also their only supplier for the required cleaning materials. Any new client a franchise owner might solicit first had to contact the corporate office, who would then assign the client to a cleaner *of its choosing*. Since they could not even be sure they would get the work, franchisees had no incentive to market themselves as a normal business would. Perhaps most damning was the flow of payments. Franchise owners received their checks not from their clients but from the franchisor, once all their fees and charges had been removed. According to franchisees, those checks could work out to as little as a few dollars an hour, well below the statutory minimum wage.[35]

Another field that took advantage of atomized work was customer-service phone support. A little-known but massively interconnected company known as Arise Business Solutions typified the trend. Founded in 1994, the company launched its "Arise Platform" in 1997, creating a novel way for major public-facing corporations to outsource the task of communicating with the public.[36] Rather than hire their own customer-service representatives, large companies—big clients included Disney, AT&T, and Amazon—routed their customer calls to Arise representatives, who gave callers the impression that they worked for whatever client the callers thought they were dealing with. Most Arise workers operated from their homes, through special communications hookups that allowed them to mimic a call-center atmosphere all on their own. "They were saying as long as you're wearing your polo shirt, you can rock out in pajamas if you wanted to," one worker explained.[37]

In the 2010s, Arise added a new wrinkle to this system: rather than hire its own representatives to pretend to work for Disney or whoever, it instead engaged independent contractors. Arise bragged about the new plan to its clients. Using independent contractors, CEO John Meyer explained, allowed the company to "squeeze wastage out of a typical day." Under normal work arrangements, Meyer continued, "a typical employee has a utilization rate of 65 percent because you're paying for their lunch, breaks, and training." Not so with independent contractors, who paid for training and materials themselves—in some cases up to $1,000 over multiple months.[38] His fixation on efficiency and implicit opposition to corporate bureaucracy recalled the evangelism of business-school seminars and groups like the American Business Conference in the 1980s, updated for the new communications technologies of the day.

To attract workers—whom the company referred to as "agents," since it could not legally call them employees—Arise promised the independence and freedom that came from being your own boss and working from home. The joy of working for Arise was the joy of being an independent business owner. "Set your own schedule," the website proclaimed. "No commute, no suit!"

In fact, Arise took this approach a step further—its independent contractors did not even contract directly with Arise. Instead, the company subcontracted with very small businesses known as "independent business operators," or IBOs. The IBOs then worked directly with the independent contractors who answered the phones and allegedly, according to independent contractor law, retained complete control over the terms, nature, and conduct of their labor. In this way, Arise promised, it was able to "provide entrepreneurial opportunities to many underserved populations, where small business owners have the ability to create flexible schedules based on their lifestyle needs."[39]

The reality was far different. While precise figures are impossible to obtain and litigation is pending as of this writing, many agents reported significant unpaid labor and below-minimum-wage income. Paid by the call (a modern-day version of the "piece rate" system), many found themselves wasting time, unpaid, waiting for the phone to ring. "Sometimes I wouldn't get a call for 30, 40 minutes, sometimes an hour, and I'd just have to sit there," former worker Tami Pendergraft recalled.[40] Federal class action suits were filed in 2011, 2012, 2013, and 2016, and the District of Columbia announced a wage theft lawsuit in 2022.[41]

Yet in a culture predisposed to hail the hustle, Arise achieved soaring success: President Obama heaped praise on the company's CEO at a White House jobs summit in 2009, and in 2017 the company boasted $40 million in quarterly revenue and nearly 30 percent gross profit margins. By 2020, its network of agents reached 70,000 in number.[42]

———

In June 2018, the House of Representatives' Committee on Small Business convened a hearing so its members could better understand "Millennials and the Gig Economy."[43] The youngest members of the so-called Millennial generation (those who were born before but had not yet become adults by the turn of the twenty-first century) entered adulthood in the late 2010s to confront both exciting opportunities and frightening new realities. One-third of the workforce, or north of 50 million Americans, worked something other than a traditional 9-to-5 job, the hearing reported. And that trend was even more pronounced among younger workers. A decade removed from the financial crisis, some 47 percent of people in their twenties and thirties were freelancers or gig workers.*

Young people had mixed feelings about the new world of work. According to a study by consulting giant McKinsey, 72 percent of the young people who held nontraditional employment asserted that they "voluntarily entered the gig economy because of the freedom it affords

---

* Statistics like this vary considerably, depending on survey methodology. Estimating the status of workers is notoriously difficult, and these figures should always be taken with a grain of salt. Some evidence suggests that the especially tight labor market of the late 2010s led to an unusual degree of freelance and gig work, but that those numbers receded a bit thereafter. What is clear, though, is that nontraditional work played a much larger role in young people's lives than it had for earlier generations.

them." The remaining 28 percent, on the other hand, worked "out of necessity as opposed to choice." Across the board, younger workers endured a higher-than-average unemployment rate of 8.5 percent in 2018, compared with 4 percent overall. What's more, a full 50 percent of Millennials reported "feeling underemployed."

The ethic of the gig economy, and its fixation on the magic of mobile app technology to make life easier, certainly appealed to young people. Some of the witnesses called to testify before the House Small Business Committee—they were charged with giving the "youth" perspective to a far older group of politicians—painted a glowing picture. The personal freedom and opportunities that gig work brought, they explained, were worth the trade-off in job stability, paid sick leave, and other benefits. As one former U.S. Marine who started a dog-training business put it: "I don't honestly know if we are thinking of retirement or Medicaid, Medicare, whatever, because, you know, we are young, we are healthy and, you know, we are not worried about those things right now."

Other witnesses, however, raised concerns about the long term. Steven Olikara of the nonprofit Millennial Action Program, for example, acknowledged that freedom is great when you are young, but that economic stability would become more important when today's go-getter gig workers got older. What would happen, he asked, when they begin "thinking about starting families and buying cars and buying houses"?

Democratic representative Yvette Clark of Brooklyn, New York—who, at age fifty-four, had been born at the very tail end of the Baby Boom generation—added to the skepticism. Was the gig economy really the next logical step in promoting business ownership? she wondered. Or was it just a way to enrich big companies? Gig workers might resemble business owners because they had to bear the costs of their labor, Clark noted, "but they gain neither loyal employees nor control over the product or business that they want to grow." Given that, maybe it made sense to talk about providing healthcare benefits or retirement savings or disability insurance to gig workers rather than let the unencumbered enthusiasm for going it alone go unchecked.

Steven Olikara agreed. Gig work, entrepreneurialism, and a do-it-yourself economy might be the wave of the future. But those workers deserve to "have some basic security that undergirds that type of work."

"In short," he concluded, "the social contract that we created in the 20th century needs to be updated for the 21st century."

Epilogue

THE WAY WE WORK

Eighteen months after the House Small Business Committee heard testimony about "Millennials and the Gig Economy," the first cases of Sars-CoV-2—better known as the novel coronavirus, Covid-19—were detected in Wuhan, China. By March 2020, the Covid pandemic had emerged in full force around the globe, and the U.S. economy quickly fell into a tailspin. Inside a week, the Dow Jones Industrial Average posted its three largest one-day point losses of all time. Official unemployment shot up from 3.5 percent in February to 14.7 percent in April, and the pain persisted long after the figures recovered.

Hardest hit was the massive service sector, as the hospitality, tourism, food services, and retail trades took the full brunt of lockdown orders, quarantines, and social-distancing requirements. Having a traditional job with a large corporate employer (or a big government agency or, in my case, a university) was suddenly quite beneficial, as long as you were privileged enough to have a stable position and the ability to work from the safety of your home. Less fortunate people in precarious work situations, on the other hand, fared far worse. People of color, younger workers (twenty-five to thirty-four years old), people without college degrees, and mothers of school-age children were most affected in the early months of the pandemic and felt the recovery much more slowly.[1]

The twin crises—a deadly pandemic that pushed healthcare workers to the brink and extinguished millions of lives around the world, and the accompanying economic chaos—shone a harsh light on the way we work. The term "essential worker" burst into the popular lexicon, posing vital questions about whose work was socially indispensable and whose we could live without for a while. And in many cases, the sobering reality was that the most essential workers were less well paid and less socially valued than the so-called unessential workers. Agricultural and food-production workers, doctors, nurses, caregivers, public-safety officers, sanitation workers—nearly always employed by large organizations like corporations, hospitals, and municipal governments, kept on getting up and going out to work, despite the growing risks to their health and their loved ones.

Meanwhile, many of us who performed "unessential" work found ways to do it remotely from home, relying on communications technologies that simply had not existed until quite recently. Safely ensconced in houses and apartments, we cut out our commutes, ate lunch in our kitchens, and watched tremendous amounts of television. And still a lot of folks complained of going stir crazy, of spending too much time with spouses and children, of not being able to eat in a restaurant or take in a rock concert.

Sitting at home and staring into the abyss of Zoom, many people started to reconsider the nature of their work, and why it had to be done the way it always had been. The country was split—some people relished the work-from-home lifestyle, while others couldn't wait to get back to the office. Employers, too, were divided. Sending your workforce home with a laptop saved a lot on overhead. At the same time, some bosses fretted that their "unessential" workers were not productive enough without the rigid discipline of the office environment.

The years since the onset of the Covid-19 pandemic have brought renewed public attention to all aspects of modern work. In addition to debates about working from home, the American airwaves were soon overwhelmed with reports of the so-called Great Resignation, the phenomenon by which substantial numbers of people appeared to leave their jobs—at a variety of levels, but largely in the vast and underpaid service industries. Employers at large national chains, franchises, and small companies alike complained that they couldn't attract workers for the wages they were able, or willing, to pay. Disaffected workers and their political allies suggested that, perhaps, employers should find ways to make work more enticing— higher wages, greater flexibility, better benefits. Employers blamed worker demands for the sharp rise in inflation in 2021 and 2022. (Others attributed rising prices to other factors—post-Covid supply-chain disruptions, government stimulus spending, and the Federal Reserve's interest-rate policies.)

Covid-19 and the subsequent economic upheaval prompted optimists to hope that perhaps we were on the verge of forging a new relationship to work, employment, and opportunity. The phenomenon of "quiet quitting," which occupied the national press in 2022, described a workplace culture in which employees—especially younger ones—self-consciously committed to *not* going the extra mile, to *not* running themselves ragged to outperform and impress, to *not* becoming "intrapreneurs." Rather, they simply did what they were paid to do, and left it at that. Perhaps the spirit of constant hustle, of making your own way, could be tamped down, replaced by a more humane and progressive approach. Perhaps we could pay people well, provide for their needs, and reward them for both their skill *and* their humanity. Perhaps worker organizing would make strides, especially in the larger and more stable sectors where unions have traditionally been most successful (but also where anti-union lobbying has been strongest). Perhaps young people would demand more of their jobs rather than let their jobs demand more of them.

But perhaps not. How we respond to social crises is conditioned by our cultural values. And for fifty years or so, those values have privileged individual initiative and entrepreneurship, and they have eschewed collective action. For even as the aftermath of the Covid-19 pandemic has forced a reckoning with modern work life, it has also revealed the stubborn persistence of the very cultural assumptions that created our go-it-alone society in the first place. Our ability to think productively about how to respond to the problems that the pandemic exposed is hindered by the ideology of work that we have cultivated so powerfully over the last half century.

Think back to the immediate policy response to Covid, for example. The CARES (Coronavirus Aid, Relief, and Economic Security) Act authorized massive emergency spending aimed at stanching the economic bleeding, ignoring underlying frailties within the workforce in the name of immediate relief. The political clout of independent business owners, cultivated over decades, meant that the bulk of financial relief flowed from the government to employers rather than to households, in the hopes that shuttered stores, restaurants, bars, and offices might continue to make payroll. (This, in a callback to the 1980s, was the ultimate "supply side" approach.) In a scene that would be comic if it weren't so tragic, scandal erupted in the summer of 2020 amid reports that millions of dollars from the Paycheck Protection Program (PPP) had gone to large national chains, franchise networks, and entities owned by wealthy private equity firms (which typically employ fewer than five hundred people).[2]

Post-pandemic policy debates, moreover, still focus on how tax and regulatory policies can encourage start-ups and innovation, the same nostrums that have dominated national debate since the 1980s. Efforts to raise the minimum wage, although at times hopeful, face stiff headwinds. Legal efforts to stop exploitative independent contractor relationships run up against sophisticated lobbying campaigns from app-based companies. At the end of the day, Americans still love cheap stuff—groceries, clothes, gasoline, and rides around town. And particularly in the wake of the pandemic, we have learned to expect things to be delivered right to our doors, a day (or sometimes a few hours) after we order them, with little regard for who does the delivering. Improving pay and working conditions in a society with such expectations will not come easy.

And we are still in the grip of an ethos that exalts above all the people who take their economic livelihood into their own hands. Our national culture remains fixated on the emancipatory potential of the individual business owner, the risk-taker, the *Shark Tank* entrepreneur. In 2021, a survey of swing voters revealed that politicians whose previous job was "small-business owner" engendered more positive feelings than those who had been teachers, veterans, or construction workers (to say nothing of lawyers and Fortune 500 CEOs).[3] That affirmation of the virtue of business owners is reflected in the ubiquitous ads we find on TV, radio, and the Internet that broadcast services for business owners, from tax preparation and specialized software to loans and consultancies. Even though the vast majority of Americans *don't* own a business, these messages reinforce the idea that everyone *ought* to. According to a billboard I recently saw on the side of the highway: "Working for other people sucks and you should stop it."

The dream of working for yourself that conquered America in the last fifty years emerged from a contested cauldron of conflicting visions—a tradition of rugged individualism on the one hand, and a faith in modern production, organization, and shared prosperity on the other. During the tumultuous economic history that began in the 1970s and ran roughshod over American life in the decades that followed, the old individualist tradition pulled ahead. Amid rising inequality and weak long-term growth, the whispering voices of our culture created a new mantra for modern life: "One day I'll work for myself."

In the wake of the Covid-19 pandemic, we confront yet another in a long series of seismic economic disruptions. How we emerge from it will ultimately depend on whether we repeat the patterns of the past or whether we learn from them and try something new.

Acknowledgments

This book marinated for many years before I finally threw it on the grill and plated it for your consumption. Over that time, I have accumulated a vast number of personal and intellectual debts, and it is an honor to acknowledge the many people who played key roles in this project. Since 2009, I have found a professional home in the History Department at the University of North Carolina at Chapel Hill, where I benefit from a supportive community of colleagues and students. Most of all, I am grateful to the tremendous department staff who do the essential work that makes our teaching and scholarship possible. Thanks especially to Jennifer Parker, Sharon Anderson, David Culclasure, and the late Joyce Loftin, whom I miss dearly.

Many UNC students were involved in the evolution of the ideas in this book, even when they didn't know it. Back in 2015, a cadre of unsuspecting honors students wandered into my seminar on "The History of Small Business," where they trekked with me through a range of ideas and debates that shaped my early thinking. More recently, the 2022 cohort of History Department senior thesis writers allowed me to hitch myself to their schedule and churn out chapters alongside them, a process that proved vital to the end of the writing process. They read my drafts and gave critical feedback, and I am grateful they did. The intrepid grad students in my dissertation writers' group also did unheralded service as interlocutors, readers, and critics. Finally, I am grateful to several students—at UNC and beyond—who provided essential research and editorial assistance: Anna Taylor, Isaac Lee, Ian Boley, Nicole Harry, and most especially Melanie Sheehan.

This book would quite simply not exist without the faith, wisdom, and keen insight of my agent, Lucy Cleland, and my editor, Melanie Tortoroli. Lucy believed in this project from the beginning and steered it through, from the rough conceptual waters of the early drafts to the finishing touches. Melanie always knew what questions to ask to keep me on target, and suffered through several brunches with me in Greenwich Village as I talked her ear off. I am also grateful to the staff at W. W. Norton, especially Annabel Brazaitis, and to Rachelle Mandik for her exceptional copyediting.

Several academic institutions provided vital financial and intellectual support. I am grateful to UNC's Institute for the Arts and Humanities, the UNC History Department's Dickson Fund, the Hagley Museum and Library, and the Schlesinger Library at Harvard, which awarded me a research grant. Some of my early musings on these topics appeared in *Aeon.co* in 2017, and I thank Sam Haselby for shepherding that article into being. My thanks also go to the Johns Hopkins Seminar on the History of Capitalism, especially Christy Chapin, Angus Burgin, and Lou Galambos, as well as audiences at the Business History Conference, the Policy History Conference, and Duke University.

Many colleagues and friends read parts of the manuscript in various stages and engaged my ideas and arguments in formal and informal settings, providing invaluable comments and perspectives. I have learned from them all. Thanks to Matt Andrews, Fitz Brundage, Brian Callaci, Peter Coclanis, Jeff Cowie, Larry Glickman, Roger Horowitz, Richard John, Marc Levinson, Lisa Lindsay, Ken Lipartito, Christina Lubinski,

Nancy MacLean, Aaron Patillo Lunt, Kim Phillips-Fein, Andrew Popp, Erica Robles-Anderson, Laura Phillips Sawyer, Dan Wadhwani, and Joanne Yates. Colleagues at UNC's Institute for the Arts and Humanities, where I was a Faculty Fellow in fall 2022, provided interdisciplinary insights, reading suggestions, and encouragement as I finalized the manuscript. Thanks to Karen Auerbach, Florence Dore, Sam Gates, Alicia Monroe, Antonia Randolph, Vin Steponaitis, Brendan Thornton, Waleed Ziad, and our fearless seminar leader, Oswaldo Estrada.

Jake Ruddiman, who was present at the creation of my misadventures as a historian, read a full draft and provided insightful queries, witty asides, and boundless support. Thanks to William Thomas for always lending a wise and encouraging ear. As ever, I am grateful to Professor Walter Jean for his soapbox theory.

A special group of colleagues not only read a full draft but also gave up an entire day to participate in a manuscript workshop, hosted by UNC's Institute for the Arts and Humanities. My debt to them is far greater than I could express or repay, but I'll give both a shot. My eternal thanks and a giant IOU go to: Ed Balleisen, Jennifer Delton, Arne Kalleberg, and Katie Turk, as well as Kathleen DuVal, Erik Gellman, Evan Hepler-Smith, Ashton Merck, Melanie Sheehan, William Sturkey, Will Raby, Cristian Walk, and Molly Worthen.

Most of all, I am deeply grateful to Lee Vinsel. Over the course of many years, Lee has been this project's biggest public and private cheerleader, a most astute critic, and a very loyal friend. He not only schlepped down from the mountains of Blacksburg for my manuscript workshop but also read multiple full iterations of the book, had me up to Virginia Tech for a one-on-one tutorial, spent a weekend at a writing retreat plying me with coffee while I wrote an early version of chapter 2, organized multiple conference panels with me on these themes, talked and texted with me ad nauseam about business, technology, and American culture, and otherwise just proved himself to be a wonderful and generous man. Thank you, Lee.

For many years, my parents Bill and Claudia read every word I wrote. That sadly won't be the case with this book, but their influence and inspiration mark every page (and not just where they make cameo appearances). My children, Luna and Gabriel, passed through a large chunk of their childhoods during the time I've been working on this project, and I hope they read it someday. Being their father is the honor of my life, and I am so proud of the young adults they are becoming. Finally, I dedicate this work to Daniela Leite Waterhouse, who, for more than twenty years, has been the best partner—in all senses of the word—I could possibly have for all of life's adventures. She is my steady compass and the rock of my soul, and her wisdom guided every step of this process. *À la tienne, mon ange.*

A Note on Sources

Research for this book has taken me the better part of the last fifteen years. The earliest germs of the ideas here came about when I was still in graduate school, writing a dissertation on big-business corporate lobbyists in the 1970s and 1980s. That thesis became my first book, *Lobbying America*, which I published in 2014. Three years later, I published another book about the whole sweep of U.S. business history, *The Land of Enterprise*, where I tried to connect the main events of the corporate world with the broader tide of American history and life. Through all that time, though, I was still nurturing the idea of studying those businesspeople who didn't grab the headlines and run the giant corporations, but who seemed—collectively, at least—to have so much sway over how Americans understood their modern economic lives.

My task was figuring out how to find them. Since there are more than 30 million businesses in the United States today, I knew that trying to find a representative sampling wouldn't work. So I started looking around for their influence, those places in the historical record where individual business owners, as well as people speaking on their behalf, seemed to make a splash or contribute to an evolving understanding.

The investigations took me to a host of archival repositories. I spent time with the presidential archives of Ronald Reagan, George Bush (the first one), and Bill Clinton. I buried myself in the records of the Carter administration held by the National Archives in Maryland, as well as the papers of politicians like Gaylord Nelson of Wisconsin and business leaders like William Rosenberg, founder of Dunkin' Donuts. The Schlesinger Library at Harvard provided me a research grant that allowed me to dig into the papers of Joanne Henderson Pratt, the work-from-home consultant, as well as the archives of women's and mothers' home-based business groups. The Smith College Special Collections repository had a series of letters to the editor of *Working Woman* magazine that I plowed through. The Hagley Museum and Library in Wilmington, Delaware, has amazing sources on the U.S. Chamber of Commerce and the National Association of Manufacturers, both of which intensified their small business outreach and lobbying in the years I was studying. Finally, the National Federation of Independent Business very graciously sent me electronic copies of its publications, *The Mandate* and *How Congress Voted*, as well as its internal history.

In addition to archival research, I also spent a lot of time with a wide range of magazines and newspapers, from *Nation's Business* and *Black Enterprise* to *Inc., Fast Company, Fortune, The Wall Street Journal, The Washington Post, The New York Times,* and many others. I was fortunate that my employer, the University of North Carolina at Chapel Hill, has a robust library with a hardworking and helpful staff that helped me find a huge number of other published sources—from government reports and congressional testimony to long-forgotten how-to books and catalogs of franchise opportunities. And of course, my research depended heavily on the rich scholarly sources by historians, economists, sociologists, and political scientists whose works dot the notes and the bibliography that follow.

ARCHIVES

Bush Library
    George H. W. Bush Presidential Library, College Station, Texas
Clinton Library
    William J. Clinton Presidential Library, Little Rock, Arkansas
NARA
    National Archives and Records Administration, College
    Park, Maryland

Nelson Papers
    Gaylord Nelson Papers, 1954–2006, University of Wisconsin–Madison
Pratt Papers
    Papers of Joanne Henderson Pratt, 1942–2010, Schlesinger Library, Harvard
    Radcliffe Institute, Cambridge, Massachusetts
Reagan Library
    Ronald Reagan Presidential Library, Simi Valley, California
Rosenberg Papers
    William Rosenberg Papers, 1940–2002, Special Collections, University of
    New Hampshire
WEH Papers
    Papers of Women Entrepreneurs Homebased, Schlesinger Library, Harvard
    Radcliffe Institute, Cambridge, Massachusetts

PERIODICALS

The Afro-American

The Atlanta Constitution

The Balance: Small Business

Bizwomen

Black Enterprise

Bloomberg

Boston Globe

Business Insider

Chicago Tribune

CNN Business

Congressional Digest

Dallas Morning News

DBusiness

Detroit Free Press

Ebony

Economic Policy Institute

Fast Company

Fortune

The Guardian

Home Office Computing

Inc.

Los Angeles Times

The Milwaukee Journal

The Nation

Nation's Business

New Pittsburgh Courier

The New York Times

Philadelphia Tribune

Phoenix Gazette

ProPublica

Psychology Today

The Skanner (Portland, OR)

The Sun (Baltimore)

Sydney Morning Herald

Syracuse Herald Tribune

Time

Tri-State Defender

The Wall Street Journal

The Washington Post

Working Woman

BOOKS

Anglund, Sandra. *Small Business Policy and the American Creed.* Praeger, 2000.

Atkinson, Robert D., and Michael Lind. *Big Is Beautiful: Debunking the Myth of Small Business.* MIT Press, 2018.

Bean, Jonathan. *Beyond the Broker State: Federal Policies toward Small Business, 1936–1961.* University of North Carolina Press, 1996.

——. *Big Government and Affirmative Action: The Scandalous History of the Small Business Administration.* University Press of Kentucky, 2001.

Bell, Daniel. *The Coming of Post-Industrial Society: A Venture in Social Forecasting.* Basic Books, 1973.

Biggart, Nicole Woolsey. *Charismatic Capitalism: Direct Selling Organizations in America.* University of Chicago Press, 1989.

Birch, David. *Job Creation in America: How Our Smallest Companies Put the Most People to Work.* Free Press, 1987.

Blackford, Mansel. *A History of Small Business in America.* 2nd ed. University of North Carolina Press, 2003.

Blair, Roger D., and Francine Lafontaine, *The Economics of Franchising.* Cambridge University Press, 2005.

Boris, Eileen, and Cynthia Daniels, eds. *Homework: Historical and Contemporary Perspectives on Paid Labor at Home.* University of Illinois Press, 1989.

Chandler, Alfred. *The Visible Hand: The Managerial Revolution in American Business.* Harvard University Press, 1977.

Chapin, Christy. *Ensuring America's Health: The Public Creation of the Corporate Health Care System.* Cambridge University Press, 2015.

Chatelain, Marcia. *Franchise: The Golden Arches in Black America.* Liveright, 2020.

Cheffins, Brian R. *The Public Company Transformed.* Oxford University Press, 2019.

Christensen, Kathleen E. *The New Era of Home-Based Work: Directions and Policies.* Westview Press, 1988.

Clifford, Donald K., and Richard E. Cavanagh. *The Winning Performance: How America's High-Growth Midsize Companies Succeed.* Bantam, 1985.

Coopersmith, Jonathan. *Faxed: The Rise and Fall of the Fax Machine.* Johns Hopkins University Press, 2015.

Cortada, James W. *All the Facts: A History of Information in the United States Since 1870.* Oxford University Press, 2016.

Cowie, Jefferson. *Capital Moves: RCA's Seventy-Year Quest for Cheap Labor*. Cornell University Press, 1999.

———. *The Great Exception: The New Deal and the Limits of American Politics*. Princeton University Press, 2017.

———. *Stayin' Alive: The 1970s and the Last Days of the Working Class*. New Press, 2010.

Critchlow, Donald T. *Phyllis Schlafly and Grassroots Conservatism: A Woman's Crusade*. Princeton University Press, 2005.

Davis, Gerald E. *The Vanishing American Corporation: Navigating the Hazards of a New Economy*. Berrett-Koehler, 2016.

Davis, Joshua. *From Headshops to Whole Foods: The Rise and Fall of Activist Entrepreneurs*. Columbia University Press, 2017.

Dewhurst, J. Frederick. *America's Needs and Resources: A New Survey*. Twentieth Century Fund, 1955.

Dicke, Thomas D. *Franchising in America: The Development of a Business Method, 1840–1980*. University of North Carolina Press, 1992.

Drucker, Peter F. *Innovation and Entrepreneurship: Practice and Principles*. Harper and Row, 1985.

Edwards, Paul and Sarah. *Working from Home: Everything You Need to Know About Living and Working Under the Same Roof*. Jeremy P. Tarcher, Inc., 1985, 5th rev. edition, 1999.

Elias, Allison. *The Rise of Corporate Feminism: Women in the American Office, 1960–1990*. Columbia University Press, 2022.

Elmore, Bartow J. *Citizen Coke: The Making of Coca-Cola Capitalism*. W. W. Norton, 2014.

Evans, Sara. *Personal Politics: The Roots of Women's Liberation in the Civil Rights Movement and the New Left*. Vintage, 1979.

Formisano, Ronald P. *The Tea Party: A Brief History*. Johns Hopkins University Press, 2012.

Galbraith, John Kenneth. *American Capitalism: The Concept of Countervailing Power*. Houghton Mifflin, 1952.

———. *The Liberal Hour*. Houghton Mifflin, 1964.

Geismer, Lily. *Left Behind: The Democrats' Failed Attempt to Solve Inequality*. Public Affairs, 2022.

Goffee, Robert, and Richard Scase. *Entrepreneurship in Europe: The Social Processes*. Croom Helm, 1987.

Goldfarb, Brent, and David A. Kirsch. *Bubbles and Crashes: The Boom and Bust of Technological Innovation*. Stanford University Press, 2019.

Gordon, Robert. *The Rise and Fall of American Growth: The U.S. Standard of Living Since the Civil War*. Princeton University Press, 2016.

Greene, John Robert. *The Presidency of George H. W. Bush*. University of Kansas Press, 2000.

Hagan, Oliver, Carol Rivchun, and Donald Sexton. *Women-Owned Businesses*. Praeger, 1989.

Hamilton, Shane. *Supermarket USA: Food and Power in the Cold War Farms Race*. Yale University Press, 2018.

Harrison, Bennett. *Lean and Mean: The Changing Landscape of Corporate Power in the Age of Flexibility*. Basic Books, 1994.

Herman, Richard T., and Robert L. Smith. *Immigrant, Inc.: Why Immigrant Entrepreneurs Are Driving the New Economy (And How They Will Save the American Worker)*. Wiley, 2009.

Hill, Steven. *Raw Deal: How the "Uber Economy" and Runaway Capitalism are Screwing American Workers*. St. Martin's Press, 2015.

Hisrich, Robert D., and Candida G. Brush. *The Woman Entrepreneur: Starting, Financing, and Managing a Successful New Business*. Lexington Books, 1986.

Jacobs, Meg. *Panic at the Pump: The Energy Crisis and the Transformation of American Politics in the 1970s*. Hill and Wang, 2016.

John, Richard. *Network Nation: Inventing American Telecommunications*. Harvard University Press, 2015.

Kalleberg, Arne. *Good Jobs, Bad Jobs: The Rise of Polarized and Precarious Employment Systems in the United States, 1970s–2000s*. Russell Sage Foundation, 2011.

Kessler, Sarah. *Gigged: The End of the Job and the Future of Work*. St. Martin's Press, 2018.

Klein, Jennifer. *For All These Rights: Business, Labor, and the Shaping of America's Public-Private Welfare State*. Princeton University Press, 2003.

Kotz, David M. *The Rise and Fall of Neoliberal Capitalism*. Harvard University Press, 2015.

Kruse, Kevin, and Julian Zelizer. *Fault Lines: A History of the United States Since 1974*. W. W. Norton, 2019.

Kwolek-Folland, Angel. *Incorporating Women: A History of Women and Business in the United States.* Twayne, 1998.

Landstrom, Hans. *Pioneers in Entrepreneurship and Small Business Research.* Springer, 2005.

Levinson, Marc. *The Great A&P and the Struggle for Small Business in America.* Hill and Wang, 2012.

Lichtenstein, Nelson, and Judith Stein. *A Fabulous Failure: The Clinton Presidency and the Transformation of American Capitalism.* Princeton University Press, 2023.

Love, John F. *McDonald's: Behind the Arches.* Bantam, 1986.

MacLean, Nancy. *Freedom Is Not Enough: The Opening of the American Workforce.* Harvard University Press, 2006.

Mills, C. Wright. *White Collar: The American Middle Classes.* Oxford University Press, 1951.

Naisbitt, John. *Megatrends: Ten New Directions Transforming Our Lives.* Warner Books, 1982.

Negroponte, Nicholas. *Being Digital.* Alfred A. Knopf, 1995.

Nilles, Jack M., F. Roy Carlson Jr., Paul Gray, and Gerhard J. Hanneman. *The Telecommunications-Transportation Tradeoff: Options for Tomorrow.* Wiley, 1976.

O'Mara, Margaret. *The Code: Silicon Valley and the Remaking of America.* Penguin Press, 2019.

———. *Pivotal Tuesdays: Four Elections That Shaped the Twentieth Century.* University of Pennsylvania Press, 2015.

Pink, Daniel. *Free Agent Nation: How America's New Independent Workers Are Transforming the Way We Live.* Warner Books, 2001.

Plitt, Jane R. *Martha Matilda Harper and the American Dream: How One Woman Changed the Face of Modern Business.* Jade, 2019.

Purvin, Robert L. Jr. *The Franchise Fraud: How to Protect Yourself Before and After You Invest.* John Wiley and Sons, 1994.

Riesman, David, with Nathan Glazer and Reuel Denney. *The Lonely Crowd: A Study in Changing American Character.* Yale University Press, 1950.

Rivlin, Gary. *Saving Main Street: Small Business in the Time of Covid-19.* HarperCollins, 2022.

Rosenberg, William, with Jessica Brilliant Keener. *Time to Make the Donuts:*

The Founder of Dunkin' Donuts Shares an American Journey. Lebhar-Friedman, 2001.

Roszak, Theodore. *The Making of a Counter Culture: Reflections on the Technocratic Society and Its Youthful Opposition.* University of California Press, 1968.

Samuelson, Robert J. *The Great Inflation and Its Aftermath: The Past and Future of American Affluence.* Random House, 2008.

Sawyer, Laura Phillips. *American Fair Trade: Proprietary Capitalism, Corporatism, and the "New Competition," 1890–1940.* Cambridge University Press, 2018.

Schepp, Brad. *The Telecommuter's Handbook: How to Work for a Salary—Without Ever Leaving the House.* Pharos, 1990.

Schumpeter, Joseph A. *Capitalism, Socialism and Democracy.* Harper, 1942.

Scranton, Philip. *Endless Novelty: Specialty Production and American Industrialization, 1865–1925.* Princeton University Press, 1997.

Shook, Carrie, and Robert L. Shook. *Franchising: The Business Strategy That Changed the World.* Prentice Hall, 1993.

Skocpol, Theda, and Vanessa Williamson. *The Tea Party and the Remaking of the Republican Party.* Oxford University Press, 2012.

Solomon, Steven. *Small Business USA: The Role of Small Companies in Sparking America's Economic Transformation.* Crown, 1986.

Spellman, Susan. *Cornering the Market: Independent Grocers and Innovation in American Small Business.* Oxford University Press, 2016.

Stein, Judith. *Pivotal Decade: How the United States Traded Factories for Finance in the Seventies.* Yale University Press, 2010.

Strawser, Cornelia J. *Business Statistics of the United States: Patterns of Economic Change.* 19th edition, Bernan Press, 2014.

Terkel, Studs. *Working: People Talk About What They Do All Day and How They Feel About What They Do.* Pantheon, 1974.

Toffler, Alvin. *Future Shock.* Bantam, 1970.

——. *The Third Wave.* Bantam, 1980.

Turner, Fred. *From Counterculture to Cyber Culture: Stewart Brand, the Whole Earth Network, and the Rise of Digital Utopianism.* Chicago University Press, 2006.

Vesper, K. H. *Entrepreneurship Education: 1993.* Entrepreneurial Studies Center, 1993.

Waltman, Jerold. *The Politics of the Minimum Wage*. University of Illinois Press, 2000.

Wartzman, Rick. *The End of Loyalty: The Rise and Fall of Good Jobs in America*. PublicAffairs, 2017.

Weil, David. *The Fissured Workplace: Why Work Became So Bad for So Many and What Can Be Done to Improve It*. Harvard University Press, 2014.

Whitfield, John H. *"A Friend to All Mankind": Mrs. Annie Turnbo Malone and Poro College*. Createspace Independent Publishing Platform, 2015.

Whyte, William H. *The Organization Man*. Simon & Schuster, 1956.

Woodward, Bob. *The Agenda: Inside the Clinton White House*. Simon & Schuster, 1994.

Zelizer, Julian E. *Burning Down the House: Newt Gingrich and the Rise of the New Republican Party*. Penguin, 2020.

BOOK CHAPTERS, ARTICLES, AND DISSERTATIONS

Barns-Bryant, Terrian. "Franchisors Promote Minority Business Development." *Franchising World* 12, no. 6 (November/December 1992): 13.

Bidwell, Matthew J. "Who Contracts? Determinants of the Decision to Work As an Independent Contractor Among Information Technology Workers." *Academy of Management Journal* 52, no. 6 (2009): 1148–1168.

Brush, Candida, and Robert D. Hisrich. "Women-Owned Businesses: Why Do They Matter?" In *Are Small Firms Important? Their Role and Impact*, edited by Zoltan J. Acs. Kluwer Academic Publishers, 1999.

Boris, Eileen. "Homework in the Past, Its Meaning for the Future." In *The New Era of Home-Based Work*, edited by Kathleen E. Christensen. Westview Press, 1988.

Boulay, Jacques, Barbara Caemmerer, Heiner Evanschitzsky, and Krista Duniach. "Growth, Uniformity, Local Responsiveness and System-Wide Adaptation in Multiunit Franchising." *Journal of Business Management* 54, no. 4 (2016): 1193–1205.

Brettell, Caroline B., and Kristoffer E. Alstatt. "The Agency of Immigrant Entrepreneurs: Biographies of the Self-Employed in Ethnic and Occupational Niches of the Urban Labor Market." *Journal of Anthropological Research* 63, no. 3 (Fall 2007): 383–397.

Burgin, Angus. "The Reinvention of Entrepreneurship." In *American Laby-rinth: Intellectual History for Complicated Times*, edited by Raymond Haber-ski Jr. and Andrew Hartman. Cornell University Press, 2018.

Callaci, Brian. "Control Without Responsibility: The Legal Creation of Franchising, 1960–1980." *Enterprise and Society* 22, no. 1 (March 2021): 156–182.

———. *Vertical Power and the Creation of a Fissured Workplace: The Case of Fran-chising.* PhD Dissertation, University of Massachusetts, Amherst, 2018.

Capowski, Genevieve Soter. "Be Your Own Boss? Millions of Women Get Down to Business." *Management Review* (March 1, 1992): 24–31.

Carlson, Richard R. "Why the Law Still Can't Tell an Employee When It Sees One and How It Ought to Stop Trying." *Berkeley Journal of Employment and Labor Law* 22, no. 2 (2001): 295–368.

Christensen, Kathleen E. "Introduction." In *The New Era of Home-Based Work*, edited by Kathleen E. Christensen. Westview Press, 1988.

Clark, J. M. "Relations of History and Theory." *Journal of Economic History* 2, no. 1 (1942): 132–142.

Dana, Leo Paul, Calin Gurau, Ivan Light, and Nabeel Muhammed. "Fam-ily, Community, and Ethnic Capital as Entrepreneurial Resources: Toward an Integrated Model." *Journal of Small Business Management* (2019): 1–21.

Dourado, Elli, and Christopher Koopman. "Evaluating the Growth of the 1099 Workforce." *Mercatus Policy Series*, Mercatus Center, George Mason University, December 10, 2015.

Glover, Gere W., Chief Council for Advocacy, Small Business Administra-tion. "Preface." In *Are Small Firms Important? Their Role and Impact*, edited by Zoltan J. Acs. Kluwer Academic Publishers, 1999.

Goldin, Claudia. "A Grand Gender Convergence: Its Last Chapter." *American Economic Review* 104, no. 4 (April 2014): 1091–1119.

Hipple, Steven. "Self-Employment in the United States: An Update." *Monthly Labor Review* (July 2004): 13–23.

———. "Self-Employment in the United States: An Update." *Monthly Labor Review* (September 2010): 17–32.

Hisrich, Robert D. "Women Entrepreneurs: Problems and Prescriptions

for Success of the Future." In *Women-Owned Businesses*, edited by Oliver
   Hagan, Carol Rivchun, and Donald Sexton. Praeger, 1989.

Hoehn, Daryl. "Ethical Issues Connected with Multi-Level Marketing
   Schemes." *Journal of Business Ethics* 29 (2001): 153–160.

Hofstadter, Richard. "What Happened to the Antitrust Movement?" In *The
   Business Establishment*, edited by Earl F. Cheit. John Wiley and Sons, 1964.

Horvath, Francis W. "Work at Home: New Findings from the Current Population Survey." *Monthly Labor Review* (September 1986): 31–35.

Hyman, Louis. "Ending Discrimination, Legitimizing Debt: The Political
   Economy of Race, Gender, and Credit Access in the 1960s and 1970s."
   Enterprise and Society 12, no. 1 (March 2011): 200–232.

Jones, Geoffrey, and R. Daniel Wadhwani. "Entrepreneurship and Business
   History: Renewing the Research Agenda." Harvard Business School
   Working Paper 07–007 (2006).

Katz, Jerome. "The Chronology and Intellectual Trajectory of American
   Entrepreneurship Education, 1876–1999." *Journal of Business Venturing* 18
   (2003): 283–300.

Katz, Lawrence, and Alan Krueger. "Understanding Trends in Alternative
   Work Arrangements in the United States." *RSF: The Russell Sage Foundation Journal of the Social Sciences* 5, no. 5 (December 2019): 132–146.

Lafontaine, Francine, and Roger D. Blair. "The Evolution of Franchising and
   Franchise Contracts: Evidence from the United States." *Entrepreneurial
   Business Law Journal* 3, no. 2 (2009): 381–434.

Lofstrom, Magnus. "Labor Market Assimilation and the Self-Employment
   Decision of Immigrant Entrepreneurs." *Journal of Population Economics*
   15 (2002): 83–114.

Mayer, Arno J. "The Lower Middle Class as Historical Problem." *The Journal
   of Modern History* 47, no. 3 (September 1975): 409–436.

Muncy, James A. "Ethical Issues in Multilevel Marketing: Is It a Legitimate
   Business or Just Another Pyramid Scheme?" *Marketing Education Review*
   14, no. 3 (Fall 2004): 47–53.

Olson, Margrethe H. "Overview of Work-at-Home Trends in the United
   States." Working Paper Series, Stern IS-18 (August 1983): 83–97.

Plotnik, Robert D., Eugene Smolensky, Eirik Evenhouse, and Siobhan Reilly.
   "The Twentieth Century Record of Inequality and Poverty in the United

States." Institute for Research and Poverty Discussion Paper no. 1166–98 (July 1998).

Qvortrup, Lars. "From Teleworking to Networking: Definitions and Trends." In *Teleworking: International Perspectives: From Telecommuting to the Virtual Organization,* edited by Paul F. Jackson and Jos M. van der Wielen. Routledge, 1998.

Raijman, Rebeca, and Marta Tienda. "Immigrants' Pathways to Business Ownership: A Comparative Ethnic Perspective." *The International Migration Review* 34, no. 3 (Autumn 2000): 682–706.

Rivers, Dawn R. *Real Work: Self Employment, Labor Markets, and Economic Identities in a Mature Capitalist Economy.* PhD Dissertation, University of North Carolina at Chapel Hill, 2022.

Robinson, H. C. *Making a Digital Working Class: Uber Drivers in Boston, 2016–2017.* PhD Dissertation, Massachusetts Institute of Technology, 2017.

Schumpeter, Joseph A. "The Creative Response in Economic History." *The Journal of Economic History* 7, no. 2 (November 1947): 149–159.

Sedlacek, Petr, and Vincent Sterk. "Reviving American Entrepreneurship? Tax Reform and Business Dynamism." *Journal of Monetary Economics* 105 (2019): 94–108.

Sepper, Elizabeth, and Deborah Dinner. "Sex in Public." *Yale Law Journal* 129, no. 1 (October 2019): 78–147.

Simmons, Solon, and James Simmons. "The Politics of a Bittersweet Economy." In *Ross for Boss: The Perot Phenomenon and Beyond,* edited by Ted G. Jelen. State University of New York Press, 2001.

Stafford, Blake E. "Riding the Line Between Employee and Independent Contractor in the Modern Sharing Economy." *Wake Forest Law Review* 50, no. 5 (2016): 1223–1254.

Steinmetz, George, and Erik Olin Wright. "The Fall and Rise of the Petty Bourgeoisie: Changing Patterns of Self-Employment in the Postwar United States." *American Journal of Sociology* 94, no. 5 (March 1989): 973–1018.

Vander Nat, Peter J., and William W. Keep. "Marketing Fraud: An Approach for Differentiating Multilevel Marketing from Pyramid Schemes." *Journal of Public Policy and Marketing* 21 no. 1 (Spring 2002): 139–151.

Wadhwani, R. Daniel, and Christoph Viebig. "Social Imaginaries of Entrepreneurship Education: The United States and Germany, 1800–2020." *Academy of Management Learning and Education* 20, no. 3 (2021): 342–360.

Wharton, Jody. "The White House Conferences on Small Business: 1980–1995." Small Business Administration (2004).

Young, McGee. "The Political Roots of Small Business Identity." *Polity* 40, no. 4 (October 2008): 436–463.

Notes

CHAPTER 1: THE WAY WE WORKED

1. *Network*, directed by Sydney Lumet (Metro-Goldwyn-Mayer/United Artists, 1976), 2 hrs., 1 min.

2. Thomas Cochran and William Miller, *The Age of Enterprise: A Social History of Industrial America* (Macmillan, 1942), cited in Angus Burgin, "The Reinvention of Entrepreneurship," in *American Labyrinth: Intellectual History for Complicated Times*, ed. Raymond Haberski Jr. and Andrew Hartman (Cornell University Press, 2018), 167.

3. Richard Hofstadter, "What Happened to the Antitrust Movement?" in Earl F. Cheit, ed., *The Business Establishment* (John Wiley and Sons, 1964), 113–152.

4. Curt Gerling, *Smugtown U.S.A.* (Plaza, 1957, cited in Rick Wartzman, *The End of Loyalty: The Rise and Fall of Good Jobs in America* (PublicAffairs, 2017), 109.

5. Nancy MacLean, *Freedom Is Not Enough: The Opening of the American Workforce* (Harvard University Press, 2006).

6. National Organization for Women, "Statement of Purpose," in *Feminism in Our Time: The Essential Writings, World War II to the Present*, ed. Miriam Schneir (Vintage, 1994). On the history of NOW, see Katherine Turk, *The Women of NOW: How Feminists Built an Organization That Transformed America* (Farrar,

Straus and Giroux, 2023). On the slow legal implementation of the "sex" provision of Title VII, see Turk, *Equality on Trial: Gender and Rights in Modern America* (University of Pennsylvania Press, 2016).

7.   "What's the Wage Gap in the States?" National Partnership for Women &
Families, 2023, https://www.nationalpartnership.org/our-work/economic
-justice/wage-gap/; "Women in the Workforce: The Gender Pay Gap is Greater
for Certain Racial and Ethnic Groups and Varies by Education Level," U.S.
Government Accountability Office, December 15, 2022.

8.   Robert D. Plotnick, Eugene Smolensky, Eirik Evenhouse, and Siobhan Reilly,
"The Twentieth Century Record of Inequality and Poverty in the United
States," Institute for Research on Poverty, Discussion Paper no. 1166-98, July
1998. See also Jefferson Cowie, *The Great Exception: The New Deal and the Limits
of American Politics* (Princeton University Press, 2017).

9.   For recent scholarly treatments of managerial capitalism, see Brian R. Cheffins, *The Public Company Transformed* (Oxford, 2019) and Nicholas Lemann,
Transaction Man: The Rise of the Deal and the Decline of the American Dream (Farrar, Straus and Giroux, 2019), 23–70.

10. Milton Lehman, "Wizards of the Basement Workshop," *Nation's Business*, February 1950, 38–40, 64–66.

11. John Kenneth Galbraith, *American Capitalism: The Concept of Countervailing
Power* (Houghton Mifflin, 1952; Routledge, 2017 edition, p. 128); John Kenneth Galbraith, *The Liberal Hour* (Houghton Mifflin, 1964), 110.

12. For a detailed account of how this social contract operated at four major U.S.
employers—Kodak, Coca-Cola, General Motors, and General Electric—as
well as an explanation for how and why those arrangements collapsed, see
Wartzman, *The End of Loyalty*.

13. J. Frederick Dewhurst, *America's Needs and Resources: A New Survey* (Twentieth
Century Fund, 1955). For a breakdown of changing patterns in the length of
the average workweek, see Robert Waples, "Hours of Work in U.S. History,"
EH.Net Encyclopedia, August 14, 2001, http://eh.net/encyclopedia/hours-of
-work-in-u-s-history/.

14. George Steinmetz and Erik Olin Wright, "The Fall and Rise of the Petty
Bourgeoisie: Changing Patterns of Self-Employment in the Postwar United
States," *American Journal of Sociology* 94, no. 5 (March 1989), 973–1018.

15. Robert D. Atkinson and Michael Lind, *Big Is Beautiful: Debunking the Myth of
Small Business* (MIT Press, 2018).

16. Steven Hipple, "Self-Employment in the United States: An Update," *Monthly
Labor Review*, July 2004, 14.

17. Thomas Jefferson, *Notes on the State of Virginia*, Query XIX, 1784.

18. Abraham Lincoln, "First Annual Message," December 3, 1861, online by Gerhard Peters and John T. Woolley, *The American Presidency Project*, https://www.presidency.ucsb.edu/node/202175. Quoted in Steinmetz and Wright, "The Fall and Rise of the Petty Bourgeoisie."

19. David Riesman with Nathan Glazer and Reuel Denney, *The Lonely Crowd: A Study in the Changing American Character* (Yale University Press, 1950); C. Wright Mills, *White Collar: The American Middle Classes* (Oxford University Press, 1951).

20. William H. Whyte, *The Organization Man* (Simon & Schuster, 1956), 63–68.

21. Mario Savio, "Sit-In Address on the Steps of Sproul Hall," December 2, 1964, University of California at Berkeley.

22. "Tacky into the Wind," *Time*, February 28, 1964, 76.

23. Theodore Roszak, *The Making of a Counter Culture: Reflections on the Technocratic Society and Its Youthful Opposition* (University of California Press, 1968), 18.

24. Jefferson Cowie, *Stayin' Alive: The 1970s and the Last Days of the Working Class* (New Press, 2010).

25. Steve Wishnia, "The Lordstown Strike of '72: Dream of Factory Liberation Deferred," *Labor Press*, March 18, 2019, https://www.laborpress.org/the-lordstown-strike-of-72-dreams-of-factory-liberation-deferred/.

26. Studs Terkel, *Working: People Talk About What They Do All Day and How They Feel About What They Do* (Pantheon, 1974), 451–452.

27. "Unemployment Rate," U.S. Bureau of Labor Statistics, https://fred.stlouisfed.org/series/UNRATE.

28. Meg Jacobs, *Panic at the Pump: The Energy Crisis and the Transformation of American Politics in the 1970s* (Hill and Wang, 2016); Robert J. Samuelson, *The Great Inflation and Its Aftermath: The Past and Future of American Affluence* (Random House, 2008).

CHAPTER 2: AMERICA REDISCOVERS SMALL BUSINESS

1. Jimmy Carter, "White House Conference on Small Business Remarks at the Opening Session of the Conference," January 13, 1980. Online by Gerhard Peters and John T. Woolley, *The American Presidency Project*, https://www.presidency.ucsb.edu/node/249391.

2. Jane Seegal, "Businessmen Join Forces," *Syracuse Herald Tribune*, January 16, 1980, NARA, White House Conference on Small Business, Press Clippings,

1978–1980, Container 1, Press Clips July–October 1978 THRU December 1979, Box A1 39042-F.

3. Irving Kristol, "The New Forgotten Man," *Wall Street Journal*, November 13, 1975, 20. On the expression "forgotten man," see Lawrence Glickman, *Free Enterprise: An American History* (Yale University Press, 2018), 34–35.

4. "Gaylord Nelson: A Record of Achievement for Small Business," n.d.; Nelson Legislation—Small Business—1975–1980," n.d.; Progress Report, Gaylord Nelson, Chairman, Select Committee on Small Business, U.S. Senate," Nelson Papers, Box 67, Folder 19.

5. Hubert Humphrey, "Will the Decline of Small Business Continue?" letter to the editor, *Washington Post*, October 6, 1976, A14.

6. In 1972, the U.S. Census counted a total of 5,026,743 firms, of which 5,021,247 (99.89 percent) employed between 0 and 499 people. In 1982, after a bruising decade, the Census counted a total of 4,256,243, of which 4,249,213 (99.83 percent) employed between 0 and 499 people. The United States Bureau of the Census, *1972 Enterprise Statistics* (1976), Table 5, p. 142; United States Department of Commerce, Bureau of the Census, *1982 Enterprise Statistics* (1986), Table 3, p. 91. See also "Frequently Asked Questions," U.S. Small Business Administration Office of Advocacy (revised December 2021), https://cdn.advocacy.sba.gov/wp-content/uploads/2021/12/06095731/Small-Business-FAQ-Revised-December-2021.pdf.

7. Alfred Chandler, *The Visible Hand: The Managerial Revolution in American Business* (Harvard University Press, 1977). For a recent appraisal of Chandler's categorization of pre-Civil War American companies and their relative degrees of sophistication in the age before "big business," see especially Caitlyn Rosenthal, *Accounting for Capital: Masters and Management* (Harvard University Press, 2018).

8. Laura Phillips Sawyer, *American Fair Trade: Proprietary Capitalism, Corporatism, and the "New Competition," 1890–1940* (Cambridge University Press, 2018), 86–90.

9. Mansel Blackford, *A History of Small Business in America*, 2nd ed. (University of North Carolina Press, 2003), 49–50.

10. Philip Scranton, *Endless Novelty: Specialty Production and American Industrialization, 1865–1925* (Princeton University Press, 1997).

11. McGee Young, "The Political Roots of Small Business Identity," *Polity* 40, no. 4, October 2008, 436–463. See also Arno J. Mayer, "The Lower Middle Class as Historical Problem," *The Journal of Modern History* 47, no. 3 (September 1975), 409–436.

12. Jonathan Bean, *Beyond the Broker State: Federal Policies Toward Small Business, 1936–1961* (University of North Carolina Press, 1996), 21–26.

13. "Does the Chain Store System Threaten the Nation's Welfare?" *Congressional Digest*, August–September 1930. See also Susan Spellman, *Cornering the Market: Independent Grocers and Innovation in American Small Business* (Oxford University Press, 2016).

14. Marc Levinson, *The Great A&P and the Struggle for Small Business in America* (Hill and Wang, 2012), 151–152. On Patman's legislative career and for an elaboration on his belief that white supremacy was not central to his politics, see Matt Stoller, *Goliath: The 100 Year War Between Monopoly Power and Democracy* (Simon & Schuster, 2019).

15. Levinson, *The Great A&P*, 162.

16. Senator Marvel Logan (KY), *Congressional Record 80: 6* (April 28, 1936), S6283. Cited and analyzed in Spellman, *Cornering the Market*, 170.

17. Levinson, *The Great A&P*, 163–165.

18. Shane Hamilton, *Supermarket USA: Food and Power in the Cold War Farms Race* (Yale University Press, 2018), 10.

19. On the relationship between big business and the U.S. war effort, see Mark Wilson, *Destructive Creation: American Business and the Winning of World War II* (University of Pennsylvania Press, 2016). On the importance of consumer culture to postwar society, see Lizabeth Cohen, *A Consumers' Republic: The Politics of Mass Consumption in Postwar America* (Vintage, 2003).

20. On advertising and public relations, see Roland Marchand, *Creating the Corporate Soul: The Rise of Public Relations and Corporate Imagery in American Big Business* (University of California Press, 2001). On consulting, see Christopher McKenna, *The World's Newest Profession: Management Consulting in the Twentieth Century* (Cambridge University Press, 2010) and Louis Hyman, *Temp: How American Work, American Business, and the American Dream Became Temporary* (Viking, 2018). On lobbying, see Benjamin C. Waterhouse, *Lobbying America: The Politics of Business from Nixon to NAFTA* (Princeton University Press, 2014).

21. This story was told by Wilson Johnson, who claimed to have witnessed the exchange, in "NFIB: A History, 1943–1985," internal organization history in possession of the author, page 9. Johnson would go on to lead the National Federation of Independent Business, about which we'll see more in chapter 3.

22. Bean, *Beyond the Broker State*, 135–139; Blackford, *A History of Small Business*, 134–135; Young, "The Political Roots of Small Business Identity," 400; Bean

dra Anglund, *Small Business Policy and the American Creed* (Praeger, 2000), 43–46.

23. "An Act to Dissolve the Reconstruction Finance Corporation, to Establish the Small Business Administration, and for Other Purposes," Public Law 163, 67 Stat., July 30, 1953.

24. Jonathan Bean, *Big Government and Affirmative Action: The Scandalous History of the Small Business Administration* (University Press of Kentucky, 2001), 58.

25. For a full history of the politics of Black capitalism, and, more recently, the #BlackLivesMatter movement, see Marcia Chatelain, *Franchise: The Golden Arches in Black America* (Liveright, 2020). For the Nixon quote, see page 73.

26. "Taking Care of Business," *Ebony*, September 1978, 146–150.

27. Jere W. Glover, Chief Counsel for Advocacy, Small Business Administration, "Preface," in *Are Small Firms Important? Their Role and Impact*, ed. Zoltan J. Acs (Kluwer Academic Publishers, 1999).

28. Robert T. Gray, "Problems Persist, But . . . Small Business Shows Big Clout," *Nation's Business*, September 1978.

29. Colman McCarthy, "Workers and Their Satisfactions," *Washington Post*, September 6, 1976.

30. On legal theory and intellectual debates surrounding antitrust, see Tim Wu, *The Curse of Bigness: Antitrust in the New Gilded Age* (Columbia Global Reports, 2018).

31. Hans Landstrom, *Pioneers in Entrepreneurship and Small Business Research* (Springer, 2005), 159–161.

32. Bennett Harrison, *Lean and Mean: The Changing Landscape of Corporate Power in the Age of Flexibility* (Basic Books, 1994), 41.

33. Anglund, *Small Business Policy and the American Creed*, 123.

34. David Birch, *Job Creation in America: How Our Smallest Companies Put the Most People to Work* (Free Press, 1987).

35. Harrison, *Lean and Mean*, 42.

36. Harrison, *Lean and Mean*, 41.

37. Robert D. Atkinson and Michael Lind, *Big Is Beautiful: Debunking the Myth of Small Business* (MIT Press, 2018), 83.

38. According to some estimates, the share of firms with fewer than five hundred employees declined from 55.5 percent in 1958 to 52.5 percent in 1977. See Zoltan J. Acs, "The New American Evolution," in *Are Small Firms Important?* 5. Another estimate puts the percentage at 51 percent in 1976 and a slightly

higher 52.9 percent in 1984. See Mansel Blackford, "Small Business in America: A Historiographic Survey," *The Business History Review* 65, no. 1, 6–7.

39. David Wessel and Buck Brown, "The Hyping of Small-Firm Job Growth," *Wall Street Journal*, November 8, 1988, B1.

40. Wessel and Brown, "The Hyping of Small-Firm Job Growth."

41. Memorandum, Larry Yuspeh to Senator Nelson, October 8, 1976, Nelson Papers, Box 68, Folder 31; Memorandum Re: White House Conference on Small Business, from the Senate Select Committee on Small Business, December 5, 1976, Nelson Papers, Box 68, Folder 31.

42. Jody Wharton, "The White House Conferences on Small Business, 1980–1995," Small Business Administration (2004).

43. Lois J. Jenkins to Vernon Weaver, December 26, 1978, 2, NARA, White House Conference on Small Business, General Correspondence of the Executive Director, 1978–1980, Container 2, Box A1 39042-A.

44. Pat O'Brien, "Uncle Is Listening, but Will He Hear?" *Inc.*, January 1980.

45. James H. Wilkinson to Jimmy Carter, June 8, 1979, NARA, White House Conference on Small Business, General Correspondence of the Executive Director, 1978–1980, Container 2, Box A1 39042-A.

CHAPTER 3: BUSINESS OWNERS OF THE WORLD, UNITE

1. Arthur Levitt Jr., "In Praise of Small Business," *New York Times*, December 6, 1981.

2. On big-business lobbying, see Benjamin C. Waterhouse, *Lobbying America: The Politics of Business from Nixon to NAFTA* (Princeton University Press, 2014).

3. Joshua Davis, *From Headshops to Whole Foods: The Rise and Fall of Activist Entrepreneurs* (Columbia University Press, 2017).

4. Fred Turner, *From Counterculture to Cyber Culture: Stewart Brand, the Whole Earth Network, and the Rise of Digital Utopianism* (University of Chicago Press, 2006), 8.

5. This account of the origins of the NFIB comes from "NFIB: A History, 1943–1985," an internally published document written by the NFIB (no specific author is credited) that is in possession of the author. Where possible, I have tried to corroborate specific details and facts; direct quotes from the document should be taken with a grain of salt.

6. Jonathan Bean, *Big Government and Affirmative Action: The Scandalous History of the Small Business Administration* (University Press of Kentucky, 2001), 173, *n32*.

7. National Federation of Independent Business, *The Mandate*, n.d., Bulletin

112. Thanks to the NFIB for providing the author with digital copies of *The Mandate* from the 1940s through 2012, the earliest of which are undated.

8. On economic education, see Kim Phillips-Fein, *Invisible Hands: The Making of the Conservative Movement from the New Deal to Reagan* (W. W. Norton, 2009); Bethany Moreton, *To Serve God and Wal-Mart: The Making of Christian Free Enterprise* (Harvard University Press, 2009); and Waterhouse, *Lobbying America.* Lawrence Glickman's *Free Enterprise* uncovers the deep intellectual and tactical roots of the amorphous concept of "free enterprise" and shows its political deployment in attacks on social welfare, regulation, and economic justice issues from the New Deal period forward. See Glickman, *Free Enterprise: An American History* (Yale University Press, 2018).

9. On the history of political action committees, see Julian Zelizer, "Seeds of Cynicism: The Struggle over Campaign Finance, 1956-1974," *Journal of Policy History* 14, no. 1 (2002), 73-111, and Waterhouse, *Lobbying America,* 27-29.

10. "NFIB: A History, 1943-1985," 18.

11. National Federation of Independent Business, *The Mandate,* no. 420, July 1979.

12. "NFIB: A History, 1943-1985," 20-21.

13. Albert Crenshaw, "Small Business Shows Its Clout with Big Victories on Capitol Hill," *Washington Post,* October 2, 1989.

14. The story of NAWBO's founding comes from: Hilary Burns, "NAWBO turns 40: A Look Back at the Organization That Changed the Game for Women in Business in the U.S.," *Bizwomen,* March 3, 2015.

15. "Jaycees Vote to Admit Women to Membership," August 17, 1984.

16. Elizabeth Sepper and Deborah Dinner, "Sex in Public," *Yale Law Journal* 129, no. 1 (October 2019), 78-147.

17. Burns, "NAWBO Turns 40."

18. Louis Hyman, "Ending Discrimination, Legitimating Debt: The Political Economy of Race, Gender, and Credit Access in the 1960s and 1970s," *Enterprise and Society* 12, no. 1 (March 2011), 200-232.

19. Davis, *From Headshops to Whole Foods,* 171; Robert D. Hisrich, "Women Entrepreneurs: Problems and Prescriptions for Success in the Future," in *Women-Owned Businesses,* ed. Oliver Hagan, Carol Rivchun, and Donald Sexton (Praeger, 1989), 5-8; Ying Lowrey, "U.S. Sole Proprietorships: A Gender Comparison, 1985-2000," SBA Office of Advocacy, February 2008.

20. Margaret Bengs, "Women Entrepreneurs: Making It the Hard Way," *Boston Globe,* June 24, 1979.

21. The quotation from Hager is found on NAWBO's webpage: https://www .nawbo.org/about/history-timeline.

22. Sandy Banisky, "Compiling a Directory of Women-Owned Businesses," *The Sun* (Baltimore), December 7, 1976.

23. NAWBO History & Timeline, https://www.nawbo.org/about/history-timeline.

24. See Davis, *From Headshops to Whole Foods*, 130.

25. Marianne M. Doctor, "They Should Compete," *The Sun* (Baltimore), December 11, 1979.

26. Jody R. Johns, "Women in Business," *The Sun* (Baltimore), December 16, 1976.

27. Sara Evans, *Personal Politics: The Roots of Women's Liberation in the Civil Rights Movement and the New Left* (Vintage, 1979).

28. Mary King, *Freedom Song: A Personal Story of the 1960s Civil Rights Movement* (William Morrow, 1987), 541.

29. Jurate Kazickas, "She's Carter's Frustrated Advisor," *Detroit Free Press*, June 12, 1977.

30. Burns, "NAWBO Turns 40."

31. Jimmy Carter, "Memorandum for the Heads of Certain Departments and Agencies on Task Force on Women Business Owners," August 4, 1977. Online by Gerhard Peters and John T. Woolley, *The American Presidency Project*, https:// www.presidency.ucsb.edu/node/243744.

32. Burns, "NAWBO Turns 40." On the history of the office, see "Office of Women's Business Ownership," Small Business Administration, https://www.sba .gov/about-sba/sba-locations/headquarters-offices/office-womens-business -ownership.

33. Philip Bump, "The Story of Jimmy Carter's Peanut Farm Is a Bit More Complicated Than You May Have Heard," *Washington Post*, September 18, 2019; George Lardner, "Probe Leaders Want President as Witness," *Washington Post*, July 26, 1980.

34. David Cooper, "Congress Has Never Let the Federal Minimum Wage Erode for This Long," *Economic Policy Institute*, June 17, 2019, https://www.epi.org/ publication/congress-has-never-let-the-federal-minimum-wage-erode-for -this-long.

35. "Billy Carter: Frustrations of a Small Businessman," *Nation's Business*, May 1977, 28–42.

36. *NFIB Legislative Priorities, 97th Congress*, page 4.

37. Davis, *From Headshops to Whole Foods*, 67.

38. "Concerns of Minority Women Business Owners Not Addressed by President," *The Skanner* (Portland, OR), May 18, 1978.

39. Congressional Research Service, "SBA's '8(a) Program': Overview, History, and Current Issues," Updated June 15, 2021, https://fas.org/sgp/crs/misc/R44844.pdf.

40. Audrey Weaver, "Women's Group Has Femmes Bucking Blacks," *Tri-State Defender* (Memphis), September 9, 1978.

41. Jane Seaberry, "Small Business Becomes a Force to Contend With: The Wooing of Small Business," *Washington Post*, December 16, 1979, F1.

42. Jeanne Saddler, "Small Firms Are Buttonholing Members of Congress," *Wall Street Journal*, May 1, 1990.

43. Candida Brush and Robert D. Hisrich, "Women-Owned Businesses: Why Do They Matter?" in *Are Small Firms Important? Their Role and Impact*, ed. Zoltan J. Acs (Kluwer Academic Publishers, 1999), 111–127.

44. Peter Reich, "SBA Chief Hails Dynamic Role of Women in Business," *Phoenix Gazette*, November 2, 1989.

45. Crenshaw, "Small Business Shows Its Clout."

CHAPTER 4: WHITE-COLLAR GROWTH MACHINE

1. Roberta Graham, "Small Business: Fighting to Stay Alive," *Nation's Business* (July 1980), 33–36.

2. "US Inflation Rate, 1960–2022," Macrotrends, https://www.macrotrends.net/countries/USA/united-states/inflation-rate-cpi.

3. "Hearing before the Committee on Small Business, United States Senate, 97th Congress, Second Session on The State of Small Business: A Report of the President, March 31, 1982," Government Printing Office, 1982, pages 1 and 18.

4. On the shift in factory production first to lower-wage states and eventually to lower-wage countries, see especially Jefferson Cowie, *Capital Moves: RCA's Seventy-Year Quest for Cheap Labor* (Cornell University Press, 1999).

5. J. M. Clark, "Relations of History and Theory," *Journal of Economic History* 2, S1 (1942), cited in Angus Burgin, "The Reinvention of Entrepreneurship," in *American Labyrinth: Intellectual History for Complicated Times*, eds. Raymond Haberski Jr. and Andrew Hartman (Cornell University Press, 2018), 163–180.

6. Burgin, "Reinvention of Entrepreneurship," 175.

7. Robert Goffee and Richard Scase, *Entrepreneurship in Europe: The Social Processes* (Croom Helm, 1987), 1.

8. See Burgin, "Reinvention of Entrepreneurship," 178, *n*16.

9. Albert Shapero, "The Displaced, Uncomfortable Entrepreneur," *Psychology Today,* November 1975, 83–88; 133.

10. Louis Uchitelle, "Heeding the Call to Do Your Own Thing," *New York Times,* September 23, 1998, G1.

11. Don Daszkowski, "The History of Dunkin' Donuts," *The Balance: Small Business,* September 24, 2018, https://www.thebalancesmb.com/the-history-of -dunkin-donuts-3973232; *Looking Back, Looking Ahead: An IFA 25th Anniversary Retrospective* (International Franchise Association, 1985), 3.

12. "Business Group Likes Reagan Plan," *Boston Globe,* February 12, 1981.

13. Donald K. Clifford Jr. and Richard E. Cavanagh, *The Winning Performance: How America's High-Growth Midsize Companies Succeed* (Bantam, 1985), xiv.

14. Clifford and Cavanagh, *Winning Performance,* xii–xiv.

15. Suzanne Garment, "Hope and Hoopla: Levitt's Lobbyists Go to Washington," *Wall Street Journal,* February 13, 1981.

16. David Treadwell, "New Lobbying Group Quickly Gains Influence," *Los Angeles Times,* September 19, 1983; Ronald Reagan, "Appointment of John M. Albertine as a Member of the Aviation Safety Commission, and Designation as Chairman," May 6, 1987, *The American Presidency Project,* online by Gerhard Peters and John T. Woolley, https://www.presidency.ucsb.edu/documents/ appointment-john-m-albertine-member-the-aviation-safety-commission -and-designation.

17. On the effect of the conglomerate wave on corporate management style, see Louis Hyman, *Temp: How American Work, American Business, and the American Dream Became Temporary* (Viking, 2018), chapter 8.

18. Arthur Levitt and John M. Albertine, "Preface," in Clifford and Cavanagh, *Winning Performance,* x.

19. Arthur Levitt and Jack Albertine, "The Successful Entrepreneur: A Personality Profile," *Wall Street Journal,* August 29, 1983.

20. Levitt and Albertine, "Successful Entrepreneur."

21. Alfred Chandler, *The Visible Hand: The Managerial Revolution in American Business* (Harvard University Press, 1977).

22. Clifford and Cavanagh, *Winning Performance,* 12.

23. *Boston Globe,* "Business Group Likes Reagan Plan."

24. Nick Poulos, "Business Group Making Points with Congress," *The Atlanta Constitution,* July 20, 1982; Jonathan Fuerbringer, "Business Chiefs Ask Budget Cut: Military, Social Spending Cited," *New York Times,* November 15, 1982.

25. "The Impresario of Corporate Rate Cuts," *Fortune*, June 13, 1983, 32.

26. David Treadwell, "New Lobbying Group Quickly Gains Influence," *Los Angeles Times*, September 19, 1983.

27. Joel Kotkin and Don Gervirtz, "Why Entrepreneurs Trust No Politician," *Washington Post*, January 16, 1983.

28. K. H. Vesper, *Entrepreneurship Education: 1993* (Entrepreneurial Studies Center, 1993), cited in Burgin, "Reinvention of Entrepreneurship."

29. Jerome Katz, "The Chronology and Intellectual Trajectory of American Entrepreneurship Education, 1876-1999," *Journal of Business Venturing* 18 (2003), 283–300.

30. R. Daniel Wadhwani and Christoph Viebig, "Social Imaginaries of Entrepreneurship Education: The United States and Germany, 1800-2020," *Academy of Management Learning and Education* 20, no. 3 (2021), 342–360.

31. On Schumpeter's career, ideas, influence, and personal life, see Thomas K. McCraw, *Prophet of Innovation: Joseph Schumpeter and Creative Destruction* (Belknap Press, 2007).

32. Joseph A. Schumpeter, "The Creative Response in Economic History," *The Journal of Economic History* 7, no. 2 (November 1947), 149–159.

33. Joseph A. Schumpeter, *Capitalism, Socialism and Democracy* (Harper, 1942).

34. Geoffrey Jones and R. Daniel Wadhwani, "Entrepreneurship and Business History: Renewing the Research Agenda," *Harvard Business School Working Paper* 07-007, 2006.

35. I am grateful to Angus Burgin for this analysis of the evolution of Drucker's thinking. See Burgin, "Reinvention of Entrepreneurship."

36. Peter F. Drucker, *Innovation and Entrepreneurship: Practice and Principles* (Harper and Row, 1985).

37. Wadhwani and Viebig, "Social Imaginaries of Entrepreneurship Education," 351.

38. For a critique of the unquestioned faith in newness, which the authors describe as "innovation-speak," and an elaboration on Zuckerberg's famous dictum, see Lee Vinsel and Andrew Russell, *The Innovation Delusion: How Our Obsession with the New Has Disrupted the Work That Matters Most* (Currency, 2020).

39. Katz, "Chronology and Intellectual Trajectory," 295.

40. Donald Kuratko, "Entrepreneurship Education: Emerging Trends and Challenges for the 21st Century," 2003 Coleman Foundation White Paper Series for the U.S. Association of Small Business & Entrepreneurship.

41. Kotkin and Gervitz, "Why Entrepreneurs Trust No Politician."

42. Treadwell, "New Lobbying Group Quickly Gains Influence."

43. Elizabeth H. Dole, "Memorandum for the Vice President: Consolidating Our Small Business Constituency," October 28, 1981, Reagan Library, Dole, Elizabeth, Series I: Subject 81-83, Box 16.

44. Red Cavaney to Ed Rollins and Ed Harper, February 16, 1983, Reagan Library, WHORM Subject Files BE, Box 102.

45. Treadwell, "New Lobbying Group Quickly Gains Influence."

46. Lily Geismer, *Left Behind: The Democrats' Failed Attempt to Solve Inequality* (PublicAffairs, 2022), 17–18.

47. Margaret O'Mara, *The Code: Silicon Valley and the Remaking of America* (Penguin Press, 2019), 192–194.

48. Kotkin and Gervitz, "Why Entrepreneurs Trust No Politician."

49. Cavaney to Rollins and Harper, February 16, 1983.

50. Ronald Reagan, "Remarks at a White House Briefing for Minority Business Owners," July 15, 1987, *The American Presidency Project*, online by Gerhard Peters and John T. Wooley, https://www.presidency.ucsb.edu/node/253445.

51. For a first-person account of this dynamic, see David Stockman, *The Triumph of Politics: Why the Reagan Revolution Failed* (Harper and Row, 1986).

52. Jonathan Bean, *Big Government and Affirmative Action: The Scandalous History of the Small Business Administration* (University of Kentucky Press, 2001), 108–111.

53. Bean, *Big Government and Affirmative Action*, 121–123; Nathaniel C. Nash, "Campaign to Kill S.B.A. Is Scrapped," *New York Times*, August 28, 1986.

54. Wharton, "White House Conferences on Small Business."

55. Sanford L. Jacobs, "Lukewarm Support from Reagan Leaves Atmosphere of Discontent," *Wall Street Journal*, August 18, 1986.

56. "Statement of Vice President George Bush on Womens [*sic*] Business Ownership, October 26, 1988," Bush Library, White House Office of Records Management, Box FG252, Folder 060289 to 099229.

57. Susan Engeleiter, "Cut in Capital Gains Rate Would Help Small Business," *The Milwaukee Journal*, November 5, 1989.

58. Statista, "Real and Nominal Value of the Federal Minimum Wage in the United States from 1938 to 2020," https://www.statista.com/statistics/1065466/real-nominal-value-minimum-wage-us/.

59. *NFIB Legislative Priorities*, 98th Congress, page 11.

60. T. Peter Ruane, Chairman, Small Business Legislative Council, to George Bush, March 23, 1989, Bush Library, White House Office of Records Management, Box FG 252, File 010614 to 058940SS.

61. John Robert Greene, *The Presidency of George H. W. Bush* (University Press of Kansas, 2000), 73.

62. Jerold Waltman, *The Politics of the Minimum Wage* (University of Illinois Press, 2000), 44–47, 97–99.

63. Brian R. Cheffins, *The Public Company Transformed* (Oxford University Press, 2019), 155–156.

64. Gerald E. Davis, *The Vanishing American Corporation: Navigating the Hazards of a New Economy* (Berrett-Koehler, 2016), 59.

65. T. Boone Pickens, "Two Titans Square Off: How Big Business Stacks the Deck," *New York Times,* March 1, 1987.

66. *Wall Street*, dir. Oliver Stone (American Entertainment Partners/Amercent Films, 1987), 2 hrs., 6 min.

67. David M. Kotz, *The Rise and Fall of Neoliberal Capitalism* (Harvard University Press, 2015), 35.

68. Bennett Harrison, *Lean and Mean: The Changing Landscape of Corporate Power in the Age of Flexibility* (Basic Books, 1994), 38–39.

69. The National Commission on Jobs and Small Business, *Making America Work Again: Jobs, Small Business, and the International Challenge* (Library of Congress, 1987).

70. Petr Sedlacek and Vincent Sterk, "Reviving American Entrepreneurship? Tax Reform and Business Dynamism," *Journal of Monetary Economics* 105 (2019), 94–108.

71. Economic Innovation Group, "Dynamism in Retreat: Consequences for Regions, Markets, and Workers," February 2017.

CHAPTER 5: BRING THE WORK HOME

1. Edwards told the story about her health scare in her book *Working from Home.* Other details about her life and work are available on her webpage. See Paul Edwards and Sarah Edwards, *Working from Home: Everything You Need to Know About Living and Working Under the Same Roof* (Jeremy P. Tarcher, Inc., 1985, 5th rev. edition, 1999), xi–xii. See also: Dr. Sarah Edwards, PhD, LSCW, https://www.drsarahedwards.com/about-me/.

2. "About Paul Robert Edwards," Local Marketing Center, https://localmarketing.center/about-us/.

3. Edwards and Edwards, *Working from Home*, 7.

4. Nick Sullivan, "Home and Office Worlds Merge," *Home Office Computing* 6, no. 1, September 1988.

5. David E. Sumner and Shirrel Rhoades, *Magazines: A Complete Guide to the Industry* (P. Lang, 2006).

6. Margrethe H. Olson, "Overview of Work-at-Home Trends in the United States," *Working Paper Series* Sterne IS-18-83-87; Andrew Pollack, "Rising Trend of Computer Age: Employees Who Work at Home," *New York Times*, May 12, 1981.

7. Francis W. Horvath, "Work at Home: New Findings from the Current Population Survey," *Monthly Labor Review*, September 1986.

8. Sullivan, "Home and Office Worlds Merge"; "Table 10-1A, Summary Labor Force, Employment, and Unemployment: Recent Data," in *Business Statistics of the United States: Patterns of Economic Change*, 19th edition, ed. Cornelia J. Strawser (Bernan Press, 2014), 342.

9. Joanne Pratt, *Myths and Realities of Working at Home: Characteristics of Homebased Business Owners and Telecommuters* (Small Business Administration Office of Advocacy, 1993).

10. "Alvin Toffler, Author of *Future Shock*, Dies Aged 87," *The Guardian*, June 29, 2016.

11. Alvin Toffler, *Future Shock* (Bantam, 1970).

12. Alvin Toffler, *The Third Wave* (Bantam, 1980).

13. Daniel Bell, *The Coming of Post-Industrial Society: A Venture in Social Forecasting* (Basic Books, 1973), 381n. On the "future schlock" epithet, see Jasper Verschoor, *"More Than Planners, Less Than Utopians": 1960s Futurism and Post-Industrial Theory* (PhD dissertation, Ohio University, 2017), 12.

14. Edwards and Edwards, *Working from Home*.

15. For an overview of the rise of the factory system and the end of the "autonomy of the family working together at home," see Joyce Appleby, *The Relentless Revolution: A History of Capitalism* (W. W. Norton, 2010).

16. On "separate spheres" ideology, see, for example, Jeanne Boydston, *Home and Work: Housework, Wages, and the Ideology of Labor in the Early Republic* (Oxford, 1990).

17. Toffler, *Third Wave*, 194.

18. See Lizabeth Cohen, *A Consumers' Republic: The Politics of Mass Consumption in Postwar America* (Vintage, 2003).

19. Alvin Toffler, Interview with *Home Office Computing* (September 1988).

20. Brad Schepp, *The Telecommuter's Handbook: How to Work for a Salary—Without Ever Leaving the House* (Pharos, 1990).

21. Schepp, *Telecommuter's Handbook*, 1.

22. Jack M. Nilles, F. Roy Carlson Jr., Paul Gray, and Gerhard J. Hanneman, *The*

Telecommunications-Transportation Tradeoff: Options for Tomorrow (Wiley, 1976); Vicky Gan, "The Invention of Telecommuting," *Bloomberg*, December 1, 2015.

23. George Bush, "Remarks at the National Transportation Policy Meeting," March 8, 1990, *The American Presidency Project*, online by Gerhard Peters and John T. Woolley, https://www.presidency.ucsb.edu/documents/remarks-the -national-transportation-policy-meeting.

24. Olson, "Overview of Work-at-Home Trends."

25. Jonathan Coopersmith, *Faxed: The Rise and Fall of the Fax Machine* (Johns Hopkins University Press, 2015).

26. James W. Cortada, *All the Facts: A History of Information in the United States Since 1870* (Oxford University Press, 2016), 382–385.

27. John Naisbitt, *Megatrends: Ten New Directions Transforming Our Lives* (Warner Books, 1982), 25.

28. Margaret O'Mara, *The Code: Silicon Valley and the Remaking of America* (Penguin, 2019), 192.

29. Gil E. Gordon, "Putting Your PC to Work at Home," 1988, Pratt Papers, Box 16, Folder 5.

30. Kathleen E. Christensen, ed., *The New Era of Home-Based Work: Directions and Policies* (Westview Press, 1988), 7–8.

31. *Popular Science*, June 1990, 64; "Home Office Resources," Pratt Papers, Box 9, Folder 5. The real story of how and where Bell and others invented telephony is, naturally, far more complicated. See Richard John, *Network Nation: Inventing American Telecommunications* (Harvard University Press, 2015).

32. "As it turned out the brains were essential, but I didn't need the calculator . . . I needed a Macintosh," Apple ad copy, n.d., c. 1988, Pratt Papers, Box 9, Folder 6.

33. "Current Hypotheses Concerning the Peculiar Characteristics and Behavior of Home-Based Businesses Compared to Other Businesses," Pratt Papers, Box 65, Folder 2. See also Joanne H. Pratt, *Measurement and Evaluation of the Populations of Family-Owned and Home-Based Businesses* (U.S. Small Business Administration, Office of Advocacy, 1987).

34. "Joanne H. Pratt Associates," personal biography, Pratt Papers, Box 65, Folder 8. "Joanne H. Pratt, Résumé," Box 5, Folder 6. For a summary of Pratt's career, see also Pratt Papers Finding Aid.

35. Joanne H. Pratt to Jim Bowden, Ministry of Regional Development, Victoria, British Columbia, February 24, 1989, Pratt Papers, Box 9, Folder 5.

36. "Proceedings of the Symposium, Working at Home: Challenge for Federal Policy and Statistics, Washington, D.C., October 28, 1986," Pratt Papers, Box 66, Folder 8.

37. Joanne Pratt, "Shop Talk: Planning a Mail-Order Business," *Home Office Computing*, May 1990.

38. Joanne Pratt, "Shop Talk: Deciphering Zoning Codes," *Home Office Computing*, January 1990.

39. Joanne Pratt, "Shop Talk: How to Play the Bidding Game," *Home Office Computing*, February 1990.

40. Irving Mardes to Joanne Pratt, December 13, 1988, Pratt Papers, Box 57, Folder 5.

41. "Home-Based Business: Trends," SBA Advisory Panel, 1984–1986, Pratt Papers, Box 65, Folder 2.

42. Lars Qvortrup, "From Teleworking to Networking: Definitions and Trends," in *Teleworking: International Perspectives: From Telecommuting to the Virtual Organization*, eds. Paul F. Jackson and Jos M. van der Wielen (Routledge, 1998), 21–39.

43. Kathleen E. Christensen, "Introduction," in Christensen, *New Era of Home-Based Work.*

44. Horvath, "Work at Home."

45. Joanne H. Pratt, "Home-Based Businesses: Opportunity or Trap," April 21, 1987, Pratt Papers, Box 28, Folder 5.

46. Georganne Fiumara and Constance Hallian Lagan, *Mothers' M$ney Making Manual: Your At-Home Career Guide*, self-published pamphlet, Pratt Papers, Box 16, Folder 5.

47. Donata Glassmeyer, "Momma's Time to Work," and Carol Kotsher Marden, "kids&career: New Ideas and Options for Mothers," Volume 1, Number 1, 1988, Pratt Papers, Box 16, Folder 5.

48. "Homeworking Mothers Really Can Have It All," Mothers' Home Business Network Membership Application, n.d., Pratt Papers, Box 5, Folder 16.

49. Donald T. Critchlow, *Phyllis Schlafly and Grassroots Conservatism: A Woman's Crusade* (Princeton University Press, 2005).

50. Colleen Parro to Joanne H. Pratt, November 6, 1987, Pratt Papers, Box 16, Folder 5.

51. Eileen Boris, "Homework in the Past, Its Meaning for the Future," in Christensen, *New Era of Home-Based Work.*

52. Eileen Boris to Joanne Pratt, June 24, 1986, Pratt Papers, Box 25, Folder 6.

53. Eileen Boris and Cynthia Daniels, eds., *Homework: Historical and Contemporary Perspectives on Paid Labor at Home* (University of Illinois Press, 1989).

54. "Home-Based Business: Trends," SBA Advisory Panel draft, Pratt Papers, Box 65, Folder 2.

55. Pratt, *Myths and Realities*, 3.

56. Amy Lyman, "The HUB Program for Women's Enterprise: A Survey of Philadelphia Women Business Owners" (Philadelphia: Warton Center for Applied Research, University of Pennsylvania, 1987), in Pratt Papers, Box 16, Folder 5.

57. United States Census Bureau, "The Number of People Primarily Working from Home Tripled Between 2019 and 2021," September 15, 2022, https://www.census.gov/newsroom/press-releases/2022/people-working-from-home.html.

58. David Streitfeld, "The Long, Unhappy History of Working from Home," *New York Times*, June 29, 2020; Ben Grubb, "Do As We Say, Not As We Do: Googlers Don't Telecommute," *Sydney Morning Herald*, February 19, 2013.

59. U.S. Career Institute advertisement in private possession of the author. Hat-tip to Isaac's mom for this source.

CHAPTER 6: LAND OF FRANCHISE

1. Angela Flagg, "A Different World," *Black Enterprise* (September 1991), 71–72.

2. "Company History—Signs Now Signage and Graphics," https://www.signsnow.com/company-history.

3. Roger D. Blair and Francine Lafontaine, *The Economics of Franchising* (Cambridge University Press, 2005).

4. Thomas Petzinger Jr., "So You Want to Get Rich?" *Wall Street Journal*, May 15, 1987, 67.

5. International Franchise Association, *Franchise Opportunities Guide*, 1995 edition. See also Blair and Lafontaine, *Economics of Franchising*, 23.

6. More about Norm Gobert's career can be found in Ann Givens, "Norm's Charm Offensive," *The Bitter Southerner*, April 23, 2020, https://bittersoutherner.com/southern-perspective/2020/norms-charm-offensive. On Michelle Gobert's business, see Image360 Meet the Team, https://centralneworleansla.image360.com/meet-the-team.

7. Kevin D. Thompson, "Franchising Grows Up," *Black Enterprise*, September 1991.

8. Carrie Shook and Robert L. Shook, *Franchising: The Business Strategy That Changed the World* (Prentice Hall, 1993), ix.

9. Blair and Lafontaine, *Economics of Franchising*, 3.

10. Francine Lafontaine and Roger D. Blair, "The Evolution of Franchising and Franchise Contracts: Evidence from the United States," *Entrepreneurial Business Law Journal* 3, no. 2 (2009), 381–434.

11. Blair and Lafontaine, *Economics of Franchising*, 5; Thomas D. Dicke, *Franchising in America: The Development of a Business Method, 1840–1980* (University of North Carolina Press, 1992), 12–47.

12. Ronald Ahrens, "Cadillac Man," *DBusiness*, December 20, 2010; "Milestones," *Time*, April 24, 1933.

13. Dicke, *Franchising in America*, 83.

14. Dicke, *Franchising in America*, 86.

15. Bartow J. Elmore, *Citizen Coke: The Making of Coca-Cola Capitalism* (W. W. Norton, 2014).

16. Jane R. Plitt, *Martha Matilda Harper and the American Dream: How One Woman Changed the Face of Modern Business* (Jade, 2019).

17. John H. Whitfield, *"A Friend to All Mankind": Mrs. Annie Turnbo Malone and Poro College* (CreateSpace Independent Publishing Platform, 2015).

18. Blair and Lafontaine, *Economics of Franchising*, 7.

19. Dicke, *Franchising in America*, 10.

20. Robert Gordon, *The Rise and Fall of American Growth: The U.S. Standard of Living Since the Civil War* (Princeton University Press, 2016), 76.

21. John F. Love, *McDonald's: Behind the Arches* (Bantam, 1986), 20.

22. "Lessons of Leadership: Appealing to a Mass Market," *Nation's Business* (July 1968), 72.

23. Marcia Chatelain, *Franchise: The Golden Arches in Black America* (Liveright, 2020), 36–37.

24. "Lessons of Leadership," *Nation's Business*, July 1968, 73.

25. The 1995 Edition of the *Franchise Opportunity Guide*, compiled by the International Franchise Association, listed 70 categories of franchise "opportunities," of which only seven involved food or beverage sales. See also Robert L. Purvin Jr., *The Franchise Fraud: How to Protect Yourself Before and After You Invest* (John Wiley and Sons, 1994), 49.

26. Blair and Lafontaine, *Economics of Franchising*, 24–25. On the failure rate of franchise establishments in the 1980s, see Scott A. Shane, "Hybrid Organizational Arrangements and Their Implications for Firm Growth and Survival: A Study of New Franchisors," *Academy of Management Journal* 39, no. 1 (1996).

27. Bárbara Zamora-Appel and Nidaal Jurbran, "Franchising Is More Than Just Fast Food: Nearly 300 Industries Offer Franchise Opportunities," *United*

States Census Bureau, December 1, 2021, census.gov/library/stories/2021/12/
franchising-is-more-than-just-fast-food.html.

28. For a clear discussion of the principal-agent problem in modern business
     theory, with particular attention to the work of business theorist Michael
     Jensen, see Nicholas Lemann, *Transaction Man: The Rise of the Deal and the
     Decline of the American Dream* (Farrar, Straus and Giroux, 2019).

29. Brian Callaci, "Control Without Responsibility: The Legal Creation of
     Franchising, 1960–1980," *Enterprise and Society* 22, no. 1 (March 2021),
     156–182.

30. Brian Callaci, *Vertical Power and the Creation of a Fissured Workplace: The Case of
     Franchising* (PhD dissertation, University of Massachusetts, Amherst, 2018),
     13.

31. William Rosenberg with Jessica Brilliant Keener, *Time to Make the Donuts:
     The Founder of Dunkin' Donuts Shares an American Journey* (Lebhar-Friedman,
     2001).

32. "Guide to the William Rosenberg Papers, 1940–2002," Rosenberg Papers.

33. James J. Nagle, "Big Gains Shown for Franchising: New Types of Operations
     Are Entering the Field," *New York Times,* November 1, 1964, F27.

34. "By-Laws International Franchise Association, Inc.," January 28, 1960,
     Rosenberg Papers, Series III, Subseries A, Box 2, Folder 5.

35. Callaci, *Vertical Power,* 10.

36. Joe Koach, "Opening Remarks," in *Management and Law: A Play in Three Acts,*
     Produced by the Legal-Legislative and Program Committees, Official Tran-
     script of Proceedings, Thirteenth Annual Legal and Government Affairs
     Symposium, Capital Hilton Hotel, Washington, D.C., May 6–7, 1980 (Inter-
     national Franchise Association).

37. "SBA Conference for Franchises," *Philadelphia Tribune,* November 12, 1985,
     10A.

38. For a full history of the relationship of McDonald's with Black Amer-
     ica, including the Black Freedom Struggle, the politics of Black capital-
     ism, and, more recently, the #BlackLivesMatter movement, see Chatelain,
     Franchise.

39. U.S. Department of Commerce, *Franchise Opportunity Handbook* (U.S. Gov-
     ernment Printing Office, 1976); "Franchise Information Available," *Afro-
     American,* August 14, 1976.

40. Terrian Barnes-Bryant, "Franchisors Promote Minority Business Develop-
     ment," *Franchising World* 24, no. 6, (November/December 1992), 13.

41. Carolyn M. Brown, "More Than Just Window Dressing?" *Black Enterprise,* September 1994, 103.

42. International Franchise Association, *IFA's Franchise Opportunities Guide, 1995,* "The Success Story of the 1990s," 14.

43. International Franchise Association, *IFA's Franchise Opportunities Guide, 1995.*

44. "Franchising May Be the Perfect Opportunity But, Is It For You?" *New Pittsburgh Courier,* December 12, 1987, 9.

45. Stanley Penn, "Franchisees Form Militant Trade Groups to Meet Fears About Power of Licensers," *Wall Street Journal,* August 8, 1979.

46. Purvin, *Franchise Fraud,* 7.

47. Mary Rowland, "Buying Your Own Franchise," *New York Times,* March 10, 1991.

48. Jacques Boulay, Barbara Caemmerer, Heiner Evanschitzsky, and Krista Duniach, "Growth, Uniformity, Local Responsiveness, and System-Wide Adaptation in Multiunit Franchising," *Journal of Business Management* 54, no. 4 (2016), 1193–1205.

49. Nicole Woolsey Biggart, *Charismatic Capitalism: Direct Selling Organizations in America* (University of Chicago Press, 1989).

50. See Walter Friedman, *The Birth of a Salesman: The Transformation of Selling in America* (Harvard University Press, 2005).

51. On the history and gendered dynamics of Multi-Level Marketing, see especially Tiffany Lamoreaux, *Home Is Where the Work Is: Women, Direct Sales, and Technologies of Gender* (PhD dissertation, Arizona State University, 2013). See also Mary Wrenn and William Waller, "Boss Babes and Predatory Optimism: Neoliberalism, Multi-Level Marketing Schemes, and Gender," *Journal of Economic Issues* 55, no. 2 (June 2021).

52. James A. Muncy, "Ethical Issues in Multilevel Marketing: Is It a Legitimate Business or Just Another Pyramid Scheme?" *Marketing Education Review* 14:3 (Fall 2004).

53. Jon M. Taylor, "The Case (for and) Against Multi-Level Marketing," Consumer Awareness Institute, 2011: 8–63.

54. Bill Clinton, "Video Message to Direct Sellers Association," September 23, 1996, Chris Janssen, "Former President Clinton's remarks to Direct Selling Association," YouTube video, 2:34, https://www.youtube.com/watch?v=bSh6BjxApq4. See also "Direct Selling Association—Collection Finding Aid," Clinton Digital Library, https://clinton.presidentiallibraries.us/items/show/36003

CHAPTER 7: BE YOUR OWN BOSS

1. Roger Ricklefs, "Making the Transition to Small Business," *Wall Street Journal*, February 28, 1989, B1.

2. David Wessel, "Do as I Do: More Consultants Quit Profession to Start New Businesses," *Wall Street Journal*, October 15, 1986, 1.

3. That figure includes people who incorporate through C-Corps and S-Corps, as well as those who do not. The share of self-employed people who incorporate appears to have risen gradually since the 1970s, although reliable numbers are not available until the late 1980s. In non-agricultural industries, "incorporated self-employment" increased from 2.9 percent (compared to 7.5 percent unincorporated) in 1990 to 3.9 percent (compared to 6.5 percent unincorporated) in 2009. Within a few tenths of a percent, those numbers have remained roughly the same ever since. See Steven Hipple, "Self-Employment in the United States: An Update," *Monthly Labor Review*, September 2010. See also Steven F. Hipple and Laurel A. Hammond, "Self-Employment in the United States," Spotlight on Statistics: U.S. Bureau of Labor Statistics, https://www.bls.gov/spotlight/2016/self-employment-in -the-united-states/home.htm.

4. Hipple, "Self-Employment in the United States," 2010, Tables 5 and 6.

5. Caroline B. Brettell and Kristoffer E. Alstatt, "The Agency of Immigrant Entrepreneurs: Biographies of the Self-Employed in Ethnic and Occupational Niches of the Urban Labor Market," *Journal of Anthropological Research* 63:3 (Fall 2007), 383–397.

6. Leo-Paul Dana, Calin Gurau, Ivan Light, and Nabeel Muhammed, "Family, Community, and Ethnic Capital as Entrepreneurial Resources: Toward an Integrated Model," *Journal of Small Business Management* (2019), 1–21.

7. For a recent economic analysis of that long history that deploys data analysis to break through both nativist and sentimental myths, see Ran Abramitzky and Leah Boustan, *Streets of Gold: America's Untold Story of Immigrant Success* (Public Affairs, 2022).

8. For a comprehensive count of immigration by decade, see Mae Ngai, *Impossible Subjects: Illegal Aliens and the Making of Modern America* (Princeton University Press, 2004), Table A1, p. 272. On the rise in self-employment among immigrants starting in the 1970s, see George J. Borjas, "The Self-Employment Experience of Immigrants," Working Paper No. 1942, National Bureau of Economic Research, June 1986.

9. Magnus Lofstrom, "Labor Market Assimilation and the Self-Employment

Decision of Immigrant Entrepreneurs," *Journal of Population Economics* 15 (2002), 83–114.

10. Steven Hipple, "Self-Employment in the United States: An Update," *Monthly Labor Review*, July 2004, Table 3; Abby Budiman, Christine Tamir, Lauren Mora, and Luis Noe-Bustamante, "Facts on U.S. Immigrants, 2018," *Pew Research Center*, August 20, 2020.

11. *The Problem with Apu*, dir. Michael Melamedoff (Avalon Television, 2017), 49 min.

12. Steven Solomon, *Small Business USA: The Role of Small Companies in Sparking America's Economic Transformation* (Crown, 1986), 202–203.

13. Richard T. Herman and Robert L. Smith, *Immigrant, Inc.: Why Immigrant Entrepreneurs Are Driving the New Economy (And How They Will Save the American Worker)*, (Wiley, 2009), xxiv–xxv.

14. The stories of Hei and Tae-Jon Kim and of Antiono Perez come from: Rebeca Raijman and Marta Tienda, "Immigrants' Pathways to Business Ownership: A Comparative Ethnic Perspective," *The International Migration Review* 34, no. 3 (Autumn 2000), 682–706.

15. "Women's Work '94: A Conference for You," conference program, n.d., Pratt Papers, Box 17, Folder 1.

16. Genevieve Soter Capowski, "Be Your Own Boss? Millions of Women Get Down to Business," *Management Review* (March 1, 1992).

17. Oliver Hagan, Carol Rivchun, and Donald Sexton, eds., *Women-Owned Businesses* (Praeger, 1989), xiii.

18. Ying Lowrey, "U.S. Sole Proprietorships: A Gender Comparison, 1985–2000," SBA Office of Advocacy, February 2008.

19. Candida Brush and Robert D. Hisrich, "Women-Owned Businesses: Why Do They Matter?" in *Are Small Firms Important? Their Role and Impact,* ed. Zoltan J. Acs (Kluwer Academic Publishers, 1999), 111–127. For current estimates of the total number of women-owned businesses, see NAWBO, "Women Business Owner Statistics," nawbo.org/resources/women-business-owner-statistics.

20. "Frequently Asked Questions," U.S. Small Business Administration Office of Advocacy (revised March 2023), https://cdn.advocacy.sba.gov/wp-content/uploads/2023/03/07121547/Frequently-Asked-Questions-About-Small-Business-March-2023-508c.pdf.

21. Nora Esposito, "Small Business Facts: Spotlight on Women-Owned Employer Businesses," U.S. Small Business Administration Office of Advocacy, March 2019, https://advocacy.sba.gov/2019/03/25/small-business-facts-spotlight-on-women-owned-employer-businesses/.

22. Claudia Goldin, "A Grand Gender Convergence: Its Last Chapter," *American Economic Review* 104, no. 4 (April 2014), 1091–1119.

23. Robert D. Hisrich and Candida G. Brush, *The Woman Entrepreneur: Starting, Financing, and Managing a Successful New Business* (Lexington Books, 1986), 8.

24. Angel Kwolek-Folland, *Incorporating Women: A History of Women and Business in the United States* (Twayne, 1998), 192.

25. Kwolek-Folland, *Incorporating Women*, 172.

26. Suzanne Gordon, "The New Corporate Feminism," *The Nation*, February 5, 1983.

27. On the history of corporate feminism, see Allison Elias, *The Rise of Corporate Feminism: Women in the American Office, 1960–1990* (Columbia University Press, 2022).

28. Jeanette R. Scollard, "Earning Her Stripes," *Entrepreneurial Woman*, in WEH Papers, Box 1, Folder MC 517 WEH #12, Official Records 1993.

29. "Testimony of Jeanette Reddish Scollard, President, SCS Communications, New York, NY," *New Economic Realities: The Role of Women Entrepreneurs, Hearings before the Committee on Small Business*, House of Representatives, One Hundredth Congress, Second Session (U.S. Government Printing Office: April 26–27; May 10, 11, 17, and 19, 1988). The Stock Exchange had installed a single women's bathroom the previous year, in 1987.

30. Scollard, "Earning Her Stripes."

31. Scollard, "Earning Her Stripes."

32. Description of An Income of Her Own board game from "Game Teaches Teens How to Be 'Job Makers,'" *Women's Business Exclusive*, Clinton Library, Presidential Personnel, McNay, Susan, White House Conference on Small Business [Program on Entrepreneurship for Young Women] [OA/ID 5316]. Question descriptions from https://boardgamegeek.com/image/817838/income-her-own.

33. Penelope Rowlands, "Rebel with a Cause," *Working Woman*, March 1993, 52–55; 89.

34. Jeanie M. Barnett, "From the Editor," *Women's Business Exclusive*, Clinton Library, Presidential Personnel, McNay, Susan, White House Conference on Small Business [Program on Entrepreneurship for Young Women] [OA/ID 5316].

35. *Women's Business Exclusive*, "Game Teaches Teens."

36. Joline Godfrey, *Our Wildest Dreams: Women Entrepreneurs Making Money, Having Fun, Doing Good* (HarperBusiness, 1992), xii.

37. "Going It Alone in Nonprofits," *Fortune*, February 20, 1995; Melinda B. Con-

rad and Nancy Kamprath, "Joline Godfrey and Polaroid Corp. (A)," Harvard Business School Case Study #492037-PDF-ENG.

38. Rowlands, "Rebel with a Cause."

39. Joline Godfrey to Members (of An Income of Her Own), memo, April 1995, Clinton Library, Presidential Personnel, McNay, Susan, White House Conference on Small Business [Program on Entrepreneurship for Young Women] [OA/ID 5316].

CHAPTER 8: THE BACKBONE

1. KNOWwhoUvote4, "Meet Joe Plumber/ Obama talks to Joe Plumber (FULL VIDEO)," YouTube video, 5:36, October 16, 2008, https://www.youtube.com/watch?v=BRPbCSSXyp0.

2. Amanda Noss, "Household Income for States: 2008 and 2009," *U.S. Department of the Census*, September 2010. On Wurzelbacher's actual professional and financial situation, see Larry Vellequette and Tom Troy, "'Joe the Plumber' Isn't Licensed," *Toledo Blade*, October 16, 2008.

3. "'Joe the Plumber' Happy to Help Candidates Make Point," CNN ElectionCenter 2008, October 16, 2008, cnn.com/2008/POLITICS/10/16/joe.plumber/index.html.

4. Jose Pagliery, "Obama's 18 Small Business Tax Cuts—Explained," *CNN Business*, September 24, 2012.

5. John Robert Greene, *The Presidency of George H. W. Bush*, 2nd edition (University of Kansas Press, 2015), 207; Kevin Kruse and Julian Zelizer, *Fault Lines: A History of the United States Since 1974* (W. W. Norton, 2019), 189; Gerald Davis, *The Vanishing American Corporation: Navigating the Hazards of a New Economy* (Berrett-Koehler, 2016), 91.

6. Daniel Yankelovich, "Foreign Affairs After the Election," *Foreign Affairs* 71 (1992), 1–12, cited in Solon Simmons and James Simmons, "The Politics of a Bittersweet Economy," in *Ross for Boss: The Perot Phenomenon and Beyond*, ed. Ted G. Jelen (State University of New York Press, 2001), 87–117.

7. David Rosenbaum, "Clinton Leads Experts in Discussion on Economy," *New York Times*, December 15, 1992, A1; "A Valuable Economics Seminar," *New York Times*, December 16, 1992, A30. Solow quote cited in Nelson Lichtenstein and Judith Stein, *A Fabulous Failure: The Clinton Presidency and the Transformation of American Capitalism* (Princeton University Press, 2023).

8. Margaret O'Mara, *Pivotal Tuesdays: Four Elections That Shaped the Twentieth Century* (University of Pennsylvania Press, 2015).

9.   Judith Stein, *Pivotal Decade: How the United States Traded Factories for Finance in the Seventies* (Yale University Press, 2010), 269.

10. Pat Widder, "Survey Shows Small-Business Tilt Toward Perot," *Chicago Tribune*, June 15, 1992.

11. Simmons and Simmons, "Politics of a Bittersweet Economy."

12. Commission on Presidential Debates, October 15, 1992, "First Half Debate Transcript," https://www.debates.org/voter-education/debate-transcripts/october-15-1992-first-half-debate-transcript/.

13. A brief video made by John Watkin and Eamon Harrington for FiveThirtyEight and ESPN Films summarizes the argument that Perot did not cost Bush re-election, based on exit polls that show that Perot voters would have split evenly between Bush and Clinton had Perot not run. What effect Perot had on damaging Bush's popularity leading up to the election, of course, cannot be determined precisely. See "The Ross Perot Myth," https://fivethirtyeight.com/videos/the-ross-perot-myth/.

14. "IBM Prepares Job Cuts Far Exceeding 25,000 Already Announced," *The Sun* (Baltimore), February 11, 1993.

15. Bob Woodward, *The Agenda: Inside the Clinton White House* (Simon & Schuster, 1994); Lily Geismer, *Left Behind: The Democrats' Failed Attempt to Solve Inequality* (Public Affairs, 2022); Lichtenstein and Stein, *A Fabulous Failure*, 21

16. Bill Clinton, *The State of Small Business: A Report of the President* (Government Printing Office, 1993).

17. Jennifer Klein, *For All These Rights: Business, Labor, and the Shaping of America's Public-Private Welfare State* (Princeton University Press, 2003).

18. Christy Chapin, *Ensuring America's Health: The Public Creation of the Corporate Health Care System* (Cambridge University Press, 2015).

19. Nisha Kurani, Jared Ortaliza, Emma Wager, Lucas Fox, and Krutika Amin, "How Has U.S. Spending on Healthcare Changed over Time?" Peterson-KFF Health System Tracker, February 25, 2022, https://www.healthsystemtracker.org/chart-collection/u-s-spending-healthcare-changed-time/#item-start.

20. Arthur Andersen Enterprise Group, "Survey of Small and Mid-Sized Businesses: Trends for 1993," Clinton Library, First Lady's Office, Cicetti, Pam, Health Care Materials 1993–1994, National Small Business United presents "Health Care Reform: The Small Business Perspective," July 1993, OA/ID 12500.

21. "Testimony of Alan Peres, Manager, Benefits Planning, Ameritech Corporation, on Behalf of the National Association of Manufacturers on the Impact of Health Costs on Employers Before the Subcommittee on Health Care,

House Ways and Means Committee, March 2, 1993," Clinton Library, Health Care Task Force, Magaziner, Ira, National Association of Manufacturers, OA/ID 3304.

22. William J. Clinton, "Address to a Joint Session of the Congress on Health Care Reform," September 22, 1993, *The American Presidency Project*, online by Gerhard Peters and John T. Woolley, https://www.presidency.ucsb.edu/node/217830.

23. Hilary Stout and Rick Wartzman, "Administration Is Trying to Woo Small Business in Bid to Overhaul Nation's Health-Care System," *Wall Street Journal*, March 29, 1993.

24. "Will an Employer Mandate Sink Small Business?" *Medicine & Health Perspectives*, April 12, 1993, Clinton Library, First Lady's Office, Cicetti, Pam, Health Care Materials, 1993–1994, National Small Business United presents Health Care Reform: The Small Business Perspective, July 1993, OA/ID 12500.

25. Stout and Wartzman, "Administration Is Trying to Woo Small Business in Bid to Overhaul Nation's Health-Care System."

26. John Motley to Ira Magaziner, May 25, 1993, Clinton Library, Health Care Task Force, Magaziner, Ira, National Federation of Independent Business Study, OA/ID 3304. Enclosed with letter: "The Employment Impact of Proposed Health Care Reform on Small Business," prepared for the NFIB Foundation by Consad Research Corporation, May 20, 1993.

27. Garry Wills, "The Clinton Principle," *New York Times*, January 19, 1997.

28. See Julian Zelizer, *Burning Down the House: Newt Gingrich, the Fall of a Speaker, and the Rise of the New Republican Party* (Penguin, 2020).

29. Helene Cooper, "Big Business and Clinton May Be Forced to Ally to Protect Commerce Department from GOP Ax," *Wall Street Journal*, December 28, 1994, A14.

30. Joline Godfrey to Jim Johnson, April 12, 1995, Clinton Presidential Records, Presidential Personnel, McNay, Susan, White House Conference on Small Business [Program on Entrepreneurship for Young Women] [OA/ID 5316].

31. Alan J. Patricof to Erskine Bowles, December 29, 1994; Erskine Bowles to Harold Ickes, December 30, 1994; Harold Ickes to Erskine Bowles, March 6, 1995, in Clinton Library, Chief of Staff files, Ickes, Harold, Small Business Conference, White House [OA/ID9298].

32. William J. Clinton, "Remarks to the White House Conference on Small Business," *The American Presidency Project*, online by Gerhard Peters and John T. Woolley, https://www.presidency.ucsb.edu/node/221083

33. Our World in Data, "Share of the Population Using the Internet," https://ourworldindata.org/internet.

34. Cheryl Hall, "Elenor's Secret: Former Manicurist's Part-Time Project Evolved into a Life-Saver for Many Plus-Sized Women," *Dallas Morning News*, February 18, 2001, 1H.

35. Nicholas Negroponte, *Being Digital* (Alfred A. Knopf, 1995), 4.

36. Joanne H. Pratt, "E-Biz.com: Strategies for Small Business Success," *Small Business Research Summary (Small Business Administration Office of Advocacy)*, no. 220, October 2002.

37. Laurence Zuckerman, "With Internet Cachet, Not Profit, a New Stock Is Wall St.'s Darling," *New York Times*, August 10, 1995; The 1995 Blog, "Memorable Moment in an Exceptional Year: The Netscape IPO of 1995," https://1995blog .com/2020/08/07/memorable-moment-in-an-exceptional-year-the-netscape -ipo-of-1995/.

38. Brent Goldfarb and David A. Kirsch, *Bubbles and Crashes: The Boom and Bust of Technological Innovation* (Stanford University Press, 2019).

39. Madeleine Vallieres to workingops@aarp.org, November 22, 1999; Lindy Doty to workingops@aarp.org, May 24, 1999; Louise Francke to workingopps@aarp.org, August 26, 2000. All emails in Pratt Files, Box 10, Folder 1, "JHPA: AARP: Survey of Home-based businesses, 2000–2001." Email addresses omitted.

40. Paul Edwards and Sarah Edwards, *Working from Home: Everything You Need to Know About Living and Working Under the Same Roof*, 5th edition (Putnam, 1999), 102–103.

41. On the history of fraud, deception, and American capitalism, see Stephen Mihm, *A Nation of Counterfeiters: Capitalists, Con-Men and the Making of the United States* (Harvard University Press, 2007) and Edward Balleisen, *Fraud: An American History from Barnum to Madoff* (Princeton University Press, 2017).

42. Daryl Koehn, "Ethical Issues Connected with Multi-Level Marketing Schemes," *Journal of Business Ethics* 29 (2001), 153–160.

43. Peter J. Vander Nat and William W. Keep, "Marketing Fraud: An Approach for Differentiating Multilevel Marketing from Pyramid Schemes," *Journal of Public Policy & Marketing* 21:1 (Spring 2002), 139–151.

44. *Last Week Tonight*, "Corporate Consolidation: Last Week Tonight with John Oliver (HBO)," YouTube video, 15:09, September 25, 2017, https://www .youtube.com/watch?v=00wQYmvfhn4.

45. On the Great Society, see, for example, Julian Zelizer, *The Fierce Urgency of*

Now: Lyndon Johnson, Congress, and the Battle for the Great Society (Penguin, 2015).

46. Naomi Klein, "Disowned by the Ownership Society," January 31, 2008, https://naomiklein.org/disowned-ownership-society/.

47. Ronald P. Formisano, *The Tea Party: A Brief History* (Johns Hopkins University Press, 2012).

48. Theda Skocpol and Vanessa Williamson, *The Tea Party and the Remaking of the Republican Party* (Oxford University Press, 2012), 23.

CHAPTER 9: THE NEW GIGS ARISE

1. Sarah Kessler, *Gigged: The End of the Job and the Future of Work* (St. Martin's Press, 2018), 12.

2. Steven Melendez, "How Uber Conquered the World in 2013," *Fast Company,* January 3, 2014.

3. Steven Hill, *Raw Deal: How the "Uber Economy" and Runaway Capitalism Are Screwing American Workers* (St. Martin's Press, 2015), 2.

4. Daniel Pink, *Free Agent Nation: How America's New Independent Workers Are Transforming the Way We Live* (Warner Books, 2001), 1–4.

5. Daniel Pink, "Free Agent Nation," *Fast Company,* December 31, 1997.

6. Pink, *Free Agent Nation,* 14.

7. Kemba J. Dunham, "Free-Lancers of the World 'Unite' for Work and Benefits," *Wall Street Journal,* June 3, 2003.

8. Pink, "Free Agent Nation"; Pink, *Free Agent Nation,* 225–226.

9. Steven Hipple, "Self-Employment in the United States," *Monthly Labor Review,* September 2010.

10. Arne Kalleberg, *Good Jobs, Bad Jobs: The Rise of Polarized and Precarious Employment Systems in the United States, 1970s–2000s* (Russell Sage Foundation, 2011), 90–91; Karen Kosanovich, "Workers in Alternative Employment Arrangements," U.S. Bureau of Labor Statistics, November 2018.

11. Kim Clark, "The Myth of the 'Free-Agent Nation,'" *Fortune,* June 8, 1998, 40–44.

12. "Frequently Asked Questions," U.S. Small Business Administration Office of Advocacy (revised March 2023), https://cdn.advocacy.sba.gov/wp-content/uploads/2023/03/07121547/Frequently-Asked-Questions-About-Small-Business-March-2023-508c.pdf.

13. Dawn R. Rivers, *Real Work: Self-Employment, Labor Markets, and Economic Identi-*

ties in a Mature Capitalist Economy (PhD dissertation, University of North Carolina at Chapel Hill, 2022).

14. *Solis v. Cascom Inc. et al.*, Civil Action No. 3:09-cv-00257, U.S. District Court, Southern District of Ohio, August 27, 2013. See also Richard Reibstein, "Cable Company's Installers Were Misclassified as Independent Contractors: Another Business That Failed to Properly Structure and Document Its Independent Contractor Relationship," Independent Contractor Misclassification & Compliance Blog, October 7, 2011, https://www.independentcontractor compliance.com/2011/10/07/cable-companys-installers-were-misclassified -as-independent-contractors-yet-another-company-that-failed-to-properly -structure-and-document-its-independent-contractor-relationship/.

15. Bill Porkony, "Court: Cable Installers Employees, Not Independent Contractors," *Wage & Hours Insights: Guidance Solutions for Employers*, October 10, 2011, https://www.jdsupra.com/legalnews/court-cable-installers-employees -not-i-23215/; David Weil, *The Fissured Workplace: Why Work Became So Bad for So Many and What Can Be Done to Improve It* (Harvard University Press, 2014), 118–120. Weil, a labor economist who served as administrator of the Department of Labor's Wage and Price Division between 2014 and 2017, cited the Cascom case as one of many examples of the broader trend toward subcontracting and other forms of "fissuring" in the modern workplace.

16. "Court Orders Cascom to Pay $1.5 Million to 250 Misclassified Cable Installers in Ohio," *Bloomberg Law*, August 30, 2013, https://news.bloomberglaw .com/daily-labor-report/court-orders-cascom-to-pay-15-million-to-250 -misclassified-cable-installers-in-ohio.

17. Weil, *Fissured Workplace*, 205.

18. Richard R. Carlson, "Why the Law Still Can't Tell an Employee When It Sees One and How It Ought to Stop Trying," *Berkeley Journal of Employment and Labor Law* 22, no. 2 (2001), 295–368.

19. Fair Labor Standards Act of 1938, 29 U.S.C. § 203.

20. *NLRB v. Hearst Publications, Inc.*, 322 U.S. 111 (1944).

21. Blake E. Stafford, "Riding the Line Between Employee and Independent Contractor in the Modern Sharing Economy," *Wake Forest Law Review* 51:5 (2016), 1223–1254. See also Weil, *The Fissured Workplace*, 21.

22. Stafford, "Riding the Line."

23. See, for example, National Academies of Sciences, Engineering, and Medicine, *Alternative Work Arrangements for Research and Policy* (The National Academies Press, 2020).

24. Kalleberg, *Good Jobs, Bad Jobs*, 90–91; Matthew J. Bidwell, "Who Contracts?

Determinants of the Decision to Work as an Independent Contractor Among Information Technology Workers," *Academy of Management Journal* 52:6 (2009), 1148–1168.

25. Eli Dourado and Christopher Koopman, "Evaluating the Growth of the 1099 Workforce," *Mercatus Policy Series*, Mercatus Center, George Mason University, December 10, 2015.

26. Lawrence Katz and Alan Krueger, "Understanding Trends in Alternative Work Arrangements in the United States," *RSF: The Russell Sage Foundation Journal of the Social Sciences* 5:5 (December 2019), 132–146.

27. Dourado and Koopman, "Evaluating the Growth of the 1099 Workforce."

28. Monica Anderson, Colleen McClain, Michelle Faverio, and Risa Gelles-Watnick, "The State of Gig Work in 2021," *Pew Research Center*, December 8, 2021, https://www.pewresearch.org/internet/2021/12/08/the-state-of-gig-work -in-2021/.

29. Avery Hartmans and Paige Leskin, "The History of How Uber Went from the Most Feared Startup in the World to Its Massive IPO," *Business Insider*, May 18, 2019; Melendez, "How Uber Conquered the World in 2013."

30. Kessler, *Gigged*, 8.

31. Hartmans and Leskin, "The History of How Uber Went."

32. H. C. Robinson, *Making a Digital Working Class: Uber Drivers in Boston, 2016–2017* (PhD dissertation, Massachusetts Institute of Technology, 2017), 178.

33. *Dynamex Operations W. v. Superior Court*—4 Cal. 5th 903 (Cal. 2018) 232 Cal. Rptr. 3d 1, 416 P.3d 1.

34. Brian Chen and Laura Padin, "Prop 22 Was a Failure for California's App-Based Workers. Now It's Also Unconstitutional," National Employment Law Project, September 16, 2021, https://www.nelp.org/blog/prop-22 -unconstitutional/.

35. Weil, *Fissured Workplace*, 134–135. Journalist Krissy Clark's podcast "The Uncertain Hour," in affiliation with National Public Radio's *Marketplace*, dedicated its fifth season to the proliferation of franchises like Jan-Pro and other examples of exploitative work. https://www.marketplace.org/shows/ the-uncertain-hour/.

36. Arise, "Our BPO Call Center Heritage," arise.com/about.

37. Ken Armstrong, Justin Elliott, and Ariana Tobin, "Meet the Customer Service Reps for Disney and Airbnb Who Have to Pay to Talk to You," *ProPublica*, October 2, 2020. Special thanks to Dr. Jessica Auer for alerting me to this article.

38. Quoted in Armstrong, Elliott, and Tobin, "Meet the Customer Service Reps."

39. Quoted in Kessler, *Gigged*, 79.

40. Quoted in Armstrong, Elliott, and Tobin, "Meet the Customer Service Reps."

41. "AG Racine Announces Lawsuit Against Arise Virtual Solutions & Comcast Cable Communications Management for Failing to Pay Legally Due Wages to Customer Service Agents," *Office of the Attorney General for the District of Columbia*, January 19, 2022, https://oag.dc.gov/release/ag-racine-announces -lawsuit-against-arise-virtual.

42. Armstrong, Elliott, and Tobin, "Meet the Customer Service Reps."

43. "Millennials and the Gig Economy," Hearing before the Committee on Small Business, United States House of Representatives, One Hundred Fifteenth Congress, Second Session (U.S. Government Publishing Office, June 6, 2018).

EPILOGUE: THE WAY WE WORK

1. Heather Long, Andrew Van Dam, Alyssa Fowers, and Leslie Shapiro, "The Covid-19 Recession Is the Most Unequal in Modern U.S. History," *Washington Post*, September 30, 2020.

2. Jonathan O'Connell, Aaron Gregg, Steven Rich, and Anu Narayanswamy, "Treasury, SBA Data Show Small-Business Loans Went to Private-Equity Backed Chains, Members of Congress," *Washington Post*, July 6, 2020.

3. David Leonhardt, "What Moves Swing Voters," *New York Times*, November 9, 2021.

Production Credits

With tremendous gratitude, I wish to acknowledge the vital work of the outstanding editorial and production team at W. W. Norton.

Editor Melanie Tortoroli
Editorial Assistant Annabel Brazaitis
Copyeditor Rachelle Mandik
Proofreader Laura Starrett
Publicist Will Scarlett
Marketer Steve Colca
Production Manager Louise Mattarelliano
Project Editor Robert Byrne
Indexer Julie Shawvan

Index

Note: Page numbers in *italics* refer to graphs or their captions.